Rescuing
Regulation

Rescuing
Regulation

REZA R. DIBADJ

State University of New York Press

Published by
State University of New York Press, Albany

© 2006 State University of New York

For information, address State University of New York Press,
194 Washington Avenue, Suite 305, Albany, NY 12210-2384

Production by Judith Block
Marketing by Michael Campochiaro

Library of Congress Cataloging-in-Publication Data

Dibadj, Reza R.
    Rescuing regulation / Reza R. Dibadj.
        p. cm.
    Includes bibiographical references and index.
    ISBN-10: 0-7914-6883-6 (hardcover : alk. paper)
    ISBN-13: 978-0-7914-6883-8 (hardcover : alk. paper)
    ISBN-13: 978-0-7914-6884-5 (pbk. : alk. paper)
    1. Police power—Philosophy. 2. Industrial laws and legislation.
3. Industrial laws and legislation—Social aspects. 4. Trade regulation.
5. Trade regulation—Social aspects. I. Title.

K3840.D53 2006
343'.07—dc22   2005036227

10 9 8 7 6 5 4 3 2 1

CONTENTS

Preface

The traditional debate on government regulation has run its course. On the one hand, so-called economically minded analysts point to regulation's inefficiency, and hence futility, advocating instead for a society organized via private contract. On the other hand, those focused on "justice" often purposefully avoid the economic paradigm to focus on regulation's role as a protector of consumers, employees, and society's disadvantaged. I challenge both camps by telling a different story about why we need to regulate. To those readers who view government regulation as a waste of time and money, I try to build a case for regulation that squarely addresses the shortcomings of their conventional "economic" critique. To those who view the law and economics paradigm as an apology for laissez-faire public policy, I attempt to show that there is a different way to do law and economics—a path that can address social inequities and abusive market behavior.

This may be an ambitious agenda, but a simple structure guides the argument. The book is organized into three principal sections, which attempt to guide the reader through a process of discovery: from (part 1) recognizing the staleness of the current pro- vs. antiregulation debate, to (part 2) the belief that there is a different way to do law and economics, to (part 3) a variety of specific ideas for logical regulatory reform. Within these sections, a series of questions—designed to build upon one another—are addressed:

1. What were the original justifications for regulation?

2. How were these justifications trashed and why?

3. Where does the regulatory status quo leave us as a society?

4. Were conventional economists correct in trashing regulation?

5. What is the new economic research telling us?

6. How can we create better regulatory law that accords with logic and with technological and economic reality?

7. How should we reform our regulatory institutions?

One chapter is devoted to each question. The book's central ambition is to tell a new, untold story of why regulation must be an essential public policy tool. Whether and how regulation should be implemented in a particular instance will depend on contextual specifics. But its fundamental principles must be understood and improved upon, rather than simply dismissed.

One overarching purpose has attracted me to this project: the urgent need to reassess the justifications for regulation, and in doing so, fill significant gaps in existing treatments. On the heels of a burst economic bubble that destroyed jobs and pensions—often highlighting market failures and shattering faith in "the system"—public debate has emerged across the political spectrum around how to define a proper role for regulatory agencies. Hardly a day passes without some regulatory agency making national headlines. Recent writings in the business press have even begun to suggest that not enough regulation, or poor deregulation, has led to the current economic crisis.[1] Meanwhile, in the academy the law and economics paradigm, so powerful in the 1960s and 1970s, is today often met with skepticism. There is a need to argue for a new type of law and economics that can inform public debate on regulation.

While there are a number of excellent books on regulation, none of them address the problem in the way I hope to. The most thought-provoking and trailblazing works, notably Alfred Kahn's *The Economics of Regulation* and Stephen Breyer's *Regulation and Its Reform*, were written in the 1970s and 1980s. There is a need to build on their seminal contributions by writing a book that treats regulation holistically while at the same time incorporating new ideas and research findings. Other successful efforts, such as W. Kip Viscusi et al.'s, *Economics of Regulation and Antitrust* and Jean Tirole's *The Theory of Industrial Organization*, are intended primarily as university economics textbooks and are not designed to tell the story of regulation to a broader audience. Still other works on regulation delve into fascinating, but narrower, aspects of the regulatory state—for instance, how the judiciary should interpret regulatory statutes, whether natural monopolies should be regulated, or how to manage environmental and health care risks. For their part, the vast majority of books on law and economics deals with the subject according to the strictures of neoclassical price theory. Those efforts which begin challenging the neoclassical orthodoxy do not seek to offer normative proposals in the regulatory context.

In sum, even though there exist several impressive books on both regulation and law and economics, I have not found one that purports to tackle the problems I propose using the methods outlined. Beyond books, there are a number of important articles in the legal and economics literature, but these are not easily digestible unless one has spent years specializing in the field. Part of my enthusiasm for writing *Rescuing Regulation* thus stems from the desire to begin filling a big hole in the existing literature.

Academic lawyers and economists who work within the law and economics paradigm will hopefully see a new, different treatment that takes issue with the conventional wisdom of neoclassicism. Those lawyers and economists who do not work at the intersection of law and economics— often because of their mistrust of the other discipline's supposed normative bent or inelegant analytic tools—should be interested in a new thesis on why and how economics should inform law. Economics, or at least a different kind of economics than has traditionally been associated with the law and economics movement, must fruitfully shape regulatory policy.

On a more philosophical level, the book should appeal to those who are interested in how the social sciences can affect normative legal discourse and public policy. Indeed, the narrative of the misunderstood story of regulation unfolds in a manner that should be easily understandable to social science scholars outside economics and law. No advanced mathematical or legal background is necessary, with many of the more quantitative economic and specialized legal references appearing in endnotes, making them available to the interested researcher without impeding the development of the overall story. Beyond its scholarly audience, *Rescuing Regulation* can also serve as supplemental reading in law and business schools, as well as undergraduate and graduate economics classes. The book should also be of use to government public policy analysts.

Above all, my fervent hope is that it will also have an appeal to a larger group of informed citizens interested in some of the most pressing administrative issues: like it or not, regulatory agencies such as the Federal Communications Commission (FCC), Securities and Exchange Commission

(SEC), and Food and Drug Administration (FDA) impact all Americans'
lives every day. My desire is to contribute to awareness and discourse
about how to improve our public agencies, something that an educated
reader interested in public policy will hopefully find both rewarding and
useful. The ultimate goal is for a greater number of thoughtful citizens
to join the debate.

ACKNOWLEDGMENTS

The inspiration for writing this book emerged in Cambridge, Massachusetts, during a series of conversations with a number of distinguished scholars, including Gerald Frug, Jon Hanson, Jerry Hausman, Howell Jackson, David L. Shapiro, Steven Shavell, and Detlev Vagts. Its ideas were further developed during the two years I spent at the University of Miami, where I am particularly grateful for my discussions with Professors David Afshartous, Anita Cava, Michael Connolly, Ann Morales Olazábal, and especially René Sacasas.

Work hit full stride in San Francisco, where the manuscript was written. I am grateful to my colleagues at the University of San Francisco School of Law for creating a supportive environment in which to write. In particular, I thank Dean Jeffrey Brand, and Professors John Denvir, Peter Jan Honigsberg, and Joshua Rosenberg, who read and provided valuable comments on the text. I am also indebted to the anonymous referees who studied the manuscript in great detail and provided very insightful suggestions for improvement.

During the final stages of preparation, the work was fortunate to benefit from the encouragement and insights of three extraordinary scholars and public intellectuals: Amitai Etzioni, Alfred E. Kahn and Peter H. Schuck.

Finally, I would like to express my appreciation to the entire team at SUNY Press, including Judith Block, Michael Campochiaro, Wyatt Benner, and Llewelyn Somers. I am especially grateful to Michael Rinella for his superb advice and extraordinary leadership of the project.

PART I

CONVENTIONAL POLARITIES

Chapter 1

———

Traditional Perspectives

Definitions and History

Before trying to reframe debates that have consumed regulatory theory, it is important to outline some fundamentals of regulation. The discussion will center on what regulation is and how it has evolved over time, as well as what its traditional justifications have been. Since many readers will likely have encountered these themes scattered in a variety of other treatments, the discussion will be as brief as possible.

Brilliant commentators have wisely sidestepped the question of specifying the precise meaning of the murky word "regulation." For example, in Stephen Breyer's *Regulation and Its Reform*, "no serious effort is made to define 'regulation.' "[1] As merely a starting point for discussion, however, I do hazard a simple definition: regulation consists of direct public intervention in private contractual arrangements.[2] What often makes regulation so controversial is that government is the only social institution capable of legitimately coercing people into action. Regulation is thus "the use of this [coercive] power for the purpose of restricting the decisions of economic agents."[3] Typically, commentators have divided regulations somewhat loosely into "economic" regulations, and "social" or "health, safety and environmental" regulations. The former consists of regulating the practices of an entire industry—historically, this has involved "government-imposed restrictions on firm decisions over price, quantity, and entry and exit."[4] Canonical examples involve the regulation of railroads, utilities, air transportation, or telecommunications. The latter type of regulation consists of rules designed to minimize the risks to citizens, employees, and consumers. Rather than regulating the behavior of an industry in toto, social regulations are developed with regard to specific products or activities—whether it be food preparation, pharmaceutical development, workplace safety, environmental pollution, or municipal building codes.

But what about other forms of government intervention? The most obvious, of course, is public finance, where government uses fiscal policy to set social priorities. The difference is that taxes affect behavior only indirectly by creating incentives and disincentives to certain activities, while economic and social regulation consists of direct public intervention.[5]

Whether antitrust policy belongs in a discussion of regulatory policy, however, is a far more complex and controversial subject. Historically, antitrust and regulation have been bifurcated, and remain so in the minds of prominent observers. Stephen Breyer, for example, draws a contrast between "private anticompetitive behavior,"[6] the domain of antitrust, and "market failures"[7] that call for regulation:

> The antitrust laws seek to create or maintain the *conditions* of a competitive marketplace rather than replicate the *results* of competition or correct for the defects of competitive markets. In doing so, they act negatively, through a few highly general provisions *prohibiting* certain forms of private conduct. They do not affirmatively order firms to behave in specified ways; for the most part, they tell private firms what not to do.[8]

Herbert Hovenkamp notes that as markets "pass out of the realm of strict agency control and into the realm of private, market-based decision making, *antitrust picks up where the regulatory regime leaves off.*"[9] Paul Joskow warns how "[e]fforts to mix antitrust policies designed to promote competition with regulatory policies that restrict it can cause numerous difficulties."[10] A new and different, albeit controversial, perspective is to recognize that "antitrust is nothing if not economic regulation,"[11] and that the "attempt to draw a sharp demarcation between antitrust and regulatory objectives is a mistake."[12] As Thomas Moore points out, "The Sherman Act [is] the most encompassing regulatory statute and the second oldest federal regulatory law. . . . Only recently have economists begun to recognize that antitrust laws are regulatory statutes."[13] After an extensive discussion of antitrust issues in the health care sector, Peter Hammer and William Sage conclude that the "most important lesson is that competition can and should meet regulation at an interface, not a boundary."[14]

The advantage of bucking the conventional wisdom should hopefully be apparent—a new bridge between these two traditionally distinct areas of policy allows the development of common analytical tools. As William Baumol and Gregory Sidak observe,

> This harmony between regulation and antitrust has three important implications. First, the same basic tools of microeconomic analysis can be employed in one as in the other. . . . Second, changes in technology or other circumstances that permit natural monopoly to give way to competition impart continuity to the relationship between economic regulation and antitrust. Third, many of the thorniest problems in antitrust law . . . are fundamentally regulatory in nature, involving issues such as entry or the pricing of intermediate goods sold to competitors. Thus, the economic scholarship on regulation can in many instances enrich antitrust jurisprudence.[15]

Put more starkly, "antitrust and regulation strike at the same rocks"[16]—one of the central messages in subsequent chapters is to urge policymakers to treat regulation and antitrust holistically.[17] Once the scope of regulation has been framed as economic and social regulation (including antitrust), a brief historical perspective on developments in these areas might be helpful in gaining some sense of the development of American regulatory policy.

The late nineteenth and early twentieth centuries saw the birth of the first regulatory mandates. In the realm of economic regulation, the most notable examples are the mandate of the Interstate Commerce Commission, founded in 1887 to regulate the railroads,[18] and the mandate for the regulation of civil aviation beginning with the Air Commerce Act of 1926.[19] The most prominent illustration with respect to social regulation was the formation of the Bureau of Chemistry in 1908 in response to scandals surrounding adulterated food and drugs.[20] The year 1890 saw the passage of the Sherman Act—the foundational statute in antitrust law that seeks to prevent collusion and monopoly; the Clayton and Federal Trade Commission Acts followed in 1914.[21]

Despite these early forays into regulation, the contours of the modern regulatory state were defined only as a reaction to the excesses of the 1920s and the ensuing Great Depression. As Alfred Kahn chronicles, "[The] Great Depression seemed to justify a thorough reexamination of the microorganization of our economy and a widespread skepticism about unregulated markets. . . . And it was this attitude, as well as the depth of the depression, that led to the cartelization of the entire economy under the National Recovery Act."[22] Roosevelt's New Deal saw the creation of a number of prominent regulatory agencies, mostly in the realm of economic regulation. Examples fall into two categories. The first consists of those designed to make markets work better, such as the Federal Deposit Insurance Corporation (1933) to protect consumers from unscrupulous banks, and the Securities and Exchange Commission (1935) to rein in Wall Street's excesses. The second category of interventions sought effectively to manage industrywide cartels—for example, the Federal Communications Commission (1934) to manage the nation's telephones and airwaves, and the Civil Aeronautics Authority (1938) to set airline rates. The 1930s were a significant decade in American regulatory policy not only due to the sheer volume of agencies created, but also because of the virtually unlimited faith progressive ideology placed in the expertise of these administrative bureaucracies.[23] Stephen Breyer points out this marked shift:

> When administrative agencies began to grow in power at the beginning of the twentieth century, the source of their authority was seen to be Congress, and the role of administrative law was to ensure that the agency faithfully carried out its congressional mandate. The agency was a "transmission belt," applying a congressional statute to changing factual circumstances. . . . *This procedural model broke down with the New Deal.* As congressional delegations were made in broader and broader language, the traditional model could not adequately check the agency's power.[24]

Chapter 7 will return to this observation, since avoiding the institutional errors of the New Deal will be central to crafting better regulatory institutions.

With World War II, the Korean War, and the economic expansion of the 1950s and early 1960s, few new regulatory mandates emerged. Antitrust enforcement, for its part, became increasingly strong, especially with respect to merger reviews—even prompting some commentators to speak of the emergence of a newly reinvigorated Sherman Act.[25]

The cultural revolution and Lyndon Johnson's plans for a "Great Society" brought the expansion of social regulation in the mid-1960s. Ironically, the pace of new social regulation reached a feverish pitch during the otherwise conservative Nixon administration in the early 1970s. Kip Viscusi writes:

> The decade of the 1970s marked the emergence of almost every major risk or environmental regulation agency. The U.S. Environmental Protection Agency [1970], the National Highway Traffic Safety Administration [1970], the Consumer Product Safety Commission [1973], the Occupational Safety and Health Administration [1972], and the Nuclear Regulatory Commission [1975] all began operation in that decade.[26]

Much of this social regulation still stands, at least in form; however, as chapter 6 will explore, it has been cut back in practice primarily through misapplication of the principles of economic cost/benefit analysis. As the macroeconomic dislocations of the late 1970s set in, however, much of economic regulation began unraveling.[27] Many formerly regulated industries—notably in the transportation and telecommunications sectors—began to undergo dramatic change.

As Alfred Kahn notes, "[B]y 1981 the federal government would have deregulated or substantially deregulated trucking, the airlines, the railroads, and financial markets, and made some progress toward deregulating communications."[28] Two points cannot be overemphasized in this regard. The first is that this movement was, at least as practiced by its leaders, focused primarily on undoing the "cartelization" of the economy wrought by certain aspects of the New Deal. The central idea was to foster competition by "subjecting protectionist regulations that suppress competition to much more critical scrutiny."[29] The second—no doubt due to the sheer force of public intellectuals such as Kahn—is that the deregulation movement benefited from widespread support across the political spectrum for a fight against industry "cartels." In the context of airline deregulation, for instance, the stunning scope of collaboration produced

> an immensely diversified and ultimately irresistible coalition of politicians and private and public interest groups across the country— Senators Edward Kennedy and Howard Cannon, Presidents Ford and Carter, the Consumer Federation of America, Common Cause, Ralph Nader and his various followers, the National Association of Manufacturers, along with such established airlines as United and Frontier, and aggressive would-be entrants like Southwest.[30]

As industries were being subjected to the vagaries of competition, antitrust enforcement waned during the 1970s and receded even more dramatically during the 1980s,[31] with the Reagan administration's appointment of William Baxter to be head of the Department of Justice's Antitrust Division.[32]

How to summarize these twists and turns? While ascendant in the early part of the twentieth century, regulation has suffered a gradual decline in respectability over the past thirty years. As Paul Joskow and Nancy Rose remark:

> The massive economic disruptions of the 1930s gave rise to a vast array of federal regulations, most of which persisted through the next forty years. The recent wave of federal regulatory reforms arose from the substantial supply shocks and macroeconomic disturbances of the 1970s, which have been characterized as the most severe disruptions since the 1930s. These reforms have dismantled or refigured much of the 1930s federal regulatory apparatus.[33]

The wisdom of recent deregulatory fervor is left to future chapters. For now, it is important to understand the justifications for regulation that historically have been used to defend its existence. These arguments serve as one pole of the conventional regulatory debate—the other pole being the neoclassical economic critique of regulation discussed in chapter 2.

JUSTIFICATIONS FOR REGULATION

From an often bewildering array of arguments that permeate the literature, a taxonomy of five classical justifications for regulation emerges—three are economic (natural monopoly, externality, informational imperfection),[34] and two are traditionally considered noneconomic (redistribution and paternalism). As defined above, regulation is government intervention into private contractual arrangements: economic justifications of regulation, then, must necessarily show "why markets may fail, i.e. why mutual gains are not necessarily fully exploited by decentralized decision-makers."[35]

The existence of a natural monopoly has, historically, provided the quintessential economic justification for regulation.[36] In these markets, cost per unit decreases as output level increases,[37] making it most efficient for a single large firm to provide service.[38] Such a situation typically evolves in industries where "there is a large fixed-cost component to cost"[39]—prototypical examples are energy or telecommunications utilities. The reason why an unregulated natural monopoly is economically wasteful is that the monopolist "will restrict output to attain a higher price and higher profits than is possible under free competition between many small sellers."[40] This economic logic is the reason why basic infrastructure industries were the first to be regulated in the late nineteenth century. As Roger Noll points out,

> In the United States, the first examples of regulatory programs were justified on the basis of natural monopoly: a specific good or service (in this case, grain elevators, water supply, and railroads) could be produced at lowest cost only if supplied by a single firm, but this would give rise to monopolistic abuse and dead-weight loss in an unregulated market.[41]

Regulators controlled entry and exit into an industry to prevent abuse of scale economies, set rates to protect consumers, and even dictated what products and services the monopolist could offer.[42] In many ways, natural monopolies provided the temptation to overreach and engage in "command and control" regulation in the belief that regulators could manage all aspects of an industry. This temptation will be revisited in chapter 7.

The second economic justification for regulation is that of "externality." Simply put, externalities arise "when economic agents impose costs on, or deliver benefits to, others who are not parties to their transaction."[43] In other words, economic actors are affecting the welfare of society, yet are not made to internalize this effect: these differences "between true social costs and unregulated price are 'spillover' costs (or benefits)."[44] The result is a mismatch between private and social welfare.[45] Most prominently, externalities have provided justification for environmental regulation;[46] after all, as one book on welfare economics warns, "polluters do not have to pay for the losses they inflict on others. This means that the resource allocation provided by the market may not be efficient."[47]

Positive externalities, for their part, are intricately related to the frequently confused notion of "public goods." The link is to recognize that private market transactions typically do not have the incentive to produce goods that have positive externalities—these public goods include parks, national defense, roads and highways, and even broadband infrastructure.[48] After all, "since consumers cannot be excluded from consuming a pure public good it is very difficult to provide such goods via the market. *Who is willing to pay not only for their consumption, but also for everyone else's consumption?*[49] The result is a need for government intervention, as James Q. Wilson notes:

> [G]overnment (that is, an institution wielding coercive powers) must compel us to pay for national defense or clean air because the market will not supply these things. The reason is simple: Since everybody will benefit from national defense or clean air if anyone in particular benefits, no one has any incentive to pay for these things voluntarily. We all would be free riders because none of us feasibly could be excluded from these benefits if he or she refused to pay.[50]

The third economic rationale for regulation is to remedy informational imperfections among buyers and sellers, the consumers and producers, in private markets. As Stephen Breyer argues:

> Markets for information may on occasion not function well for several reasons. First, the incentives to produce and to disseminate information may be skewed. . . . Thus, those in the best position to produce the information may not do so, or they may hesitate to disseminate it, for fear that the benefits will go not to themselves but only to others. . . . Second, one of the parties to a transaction may seek deliberately to mislead the other, by conveying false information or by omitting key facts. . . . Third, even after locating potentially competing sellers, the buyer may not be able to evaluate the characteristics of the products or services they offer.[51]

The presence of these informational imperfections, or asymmetries, has been invoked to justify much social regulation that tries to protect consumers and workers against health, safety, and environmental risks. Roger Noll notes that imperfect information

> has been the rationale for regulating consumer products and workplaces, beginning with the Pure Food and Drug Act of 1906. Complex, costly information can lead to poorly informed and sometimes potentially hazardous decisions about goods, services, and jobs. It can also lead suppliers to provide either too much or too little quality, and industries to adopt inefficient technical compatibility standards. In principle, regulation can provide two types of efficiency gains. First, by increasing the supply of information, it can reduce

uncertainties about the consequences of market decisions, thereby causing the market to make a better match between suppliers and demanders. Second, by setting minimum standards, it can protect uninformed participants against bad outcomes, including a "market for lemons" equilibrium in which quality is supplied at inefficiently low levels.[52]

Needless to say, the economic justifications for regulation are not mutually exclusive. In particular, the externality and informational arguments have frequently been combined in the context of social regulation. As Kip Viscusi cogently argues,

> The chief impetus for the health, safety, and environmental regulations is twofold. First, substantial externalities often result from economic behavior. The operation of businesses often generates air pollution, water pollution, and toxic waste. Individual consumption decisions are also the source of externalities, as the fuel we burn in our cars gives rise to air pollution. Informational issues also play a salient role. Because of the peculiar nature of information as an economic commodity, it is more efficient for the government to be the producer of much information and to disseminate the information broadly. Individual firms, for example, will not have the same kind of incentives to do scientific research unless they can reap the benefits of the information. As a result, it is largely through the efforts of government agencies that society has funded research into the implications of various kinds of hazards so that we can form an assessment of their consequences and determine the degree to which they should be regulated.[53]

Beyond the three interwoven economic justifications for regulation, there are, as mentioned, two often-overlooked traditionally noneconomic justifications that have little to do with price or output per se: redistribution and paternalism. Here, moral and political rather than economic argument often reigns. As one commentator notes, "[F]rom a political view, perhaps the most significant feature of regulation is that it redistributes income."[54] Thus, arguments for regulation that revolve around controlling the "rents" or "excess profits" producers enjoy are not efficiency based; rather, the "justification rests upon the desirability of transferring income—from producers to consumers."[55] Much to the chagrin of many neoclassical economists, distributional goals are especially stark in economic regulation. Examples include "universal service" in telecommunications, which funds telephone services to low-income consumers,[56] the "duty to serve" of electrical utilities,[57] and "diversity" and "localism" in media.[58] Rationales behind these mandates "argue for regulation for reasons related not to more efficient use of the world's resources, but to a fairer income distribution."[59] In a closely analogous manner, congressional intent behind the antitrust laws reveals a concern for consumers and small businesses, not for overall economic efficiency.[60]

A related rationale for regulation is paternalism—that government can help shape preferences when individuals act in self-destructive ways:

> It is sometimes argued that individuals don't necessarily behave in ways that are consistent with what is in their own best interest. Not all of us voluntarily use seat belts or complete elementary education, although we should. This argument for government intervention is called *paternalism*. It expresses a particular view concerning the extent to which one should respect consumer preferences, and has nothing to do per se with the presence or absence of market failures.[61]

It is important to dwell on the traditionally noneconomic rationales for regulation, precisely because they are either ignored or disparaged in the mainstream law and economics literature. As Gregory Sidak and Daniel Spulber observe, "Economists may posture as purists and assert that regulators are misguided to pursue any goal other than economic efficiency. However correct that position may be as a matter of theory, it does not take the institutional setting of regulation as it really is."[62]

Is there a common framework for these five seemingly disparate justifications for regulation? All of the arguments made in this section can be combined under one rubric: government regulation is designed to protect the "public interest." More precisely, economists have labeled the "public interest" view of regulation as "normative analysis as a positive theory" (NPT).[63] NPT combines a positive description of inefficient or inequitable markets with the normative goal of rectifying these problems through government intervention.[64] As Viscusi points out, NPT

> uses normative analysis to generate a positive theory by saying that regulation is supplied in response to the public's demand for the correction of a market failure or for the correction of highly inequi-

table practices (for example, price discrimination, or firms' receiving windfall profits as a result of some change in industry conditions).[65]

The blending of positive and normative arguments is part of a long intellectual tradition, dating back at least as far as David Hume's observation that "is" and "ought" often blend in moral reasoning.[66] As one prominent legal scholar observes, "We have no methodology to move directly from the discourses we perceive as descriptive, such as natural or social science, to decisions about the way to organize our society and the kinds of laws we should establish to effect that organization."[67] NPT at least reflects this intellectual realism. Yet its underlying premises have suffered a massive, perhaps even fatal, attack from a group of intellectuals cleverly portraying themselves as the "law and economics" vanguard.[68]

Chapter 2

Lambasting Regulation

Chapter 1 has tried to paint a picture of the traditional justifications for regulation: natural monopoly, externality, information asymmetry, redistribution, and even paternalism. Beginning in the 1950s, however, many of the most brilliant economists began lambasting these reasons as part of a broader attempt to undo NPT.[1] As we shall see, their criticisms come in different flavors. Yet at their core, they are premised on one straightforward thesis: the belief that progressive regulatory agencies misalign incentives and are economically wasteful. Since this so-called economic assault began fifty years ago, those who believe in a need for regulation—typically lawyers and public policy analysts—have consistently dismissed these critiques, and in so doing scorned the law and economics movement. While this frustration is understandable, I will propose a different path to help narrow the chasm between scholarship in the "economic" and "social justice" traditions. Before mounting an economic argument to show that regulation does have its place, however, we must come to terms with the most biting condemnations of the regulatory state. If we can point out why there is an economic case to be made for the regulatory state, then we will have addressed these scholars on their own terms to show that law and economics is compatible with regulation.

FOUNDATIONS OF THE CRITIQUE

In analyzing the traditional law and economics movement, the importance of three seminal articles cannot be underestimated: Ronald Coase's *The Problem of Social Cost*,[2] Harvey Averch and Leland Johnson's *Behavior of the Firm Under Regulatory Constraint*,[3] and George Stigler's *The Theory*

15

of Economic Regulation.[4] Each has been interpreted as a scathing critique of regulation using the tools of law and economics.

In 1960, Ronald Coase wrote what is still to this day perhaps the most important article in the law and economics literature. Coase imagined a world of zero transaction costs, a magical land where "the pricing system is assumed to work without cost."[5] Coase argued that in such a world, if private parties are given property rights, they will negotiate to strike a bargain via the price mechanism that puts the resources to their most efficient use:

> Land, labor, and capital are all scarce, but this, of itself, does not call for government regulation. It is true that some mechanism has to be employed to decide who, out of the many claimants, should be allowed to use the scarce resource. But the way this is usually done in the American economic system is to employ the *price mechanism*, and this allocates resources to users without the need for government regulation.[6]

An important corollary to this hypothesis is that in such a perfect world, an efficient outcome will attain regardless of who is given the initial entitlement. As Coase points out, "It is always possible to modify by transactions on the market the initial legal delimitation of rights. And, of course, if such market transactions are costless, such a rearrangement of rights will always take place if it would lead to an increase in the value of production."[7] The bottom line is thus that "the allocation of resources should be determined by the forces of the market rather than as a result of government decisions."[8] As one might imagine, this perspective seems to extol the virtues of private law at the expense of public regulation.

Two years later, in 1962, Harvey Averch and Leland Johnson published another landmark piece. Though somewhat technical and mathematical in its methodology, their article postulated that rate-of-return regulation creates a misallocation of resources, leading telephone carriers to overinvest in their plant and equipment.[9] This analysis, of course, placed a giant cloud on the economic viability of retail rate regulation, a principal tool of economic regulation.[10]

Nearly a decade later, in 1971, George Stigler wrote *The Theory of Economic Regulation*. Unlike Averch and Johnson, Stigler's mathematics are remarkably simple—he develops his arguments using basic regression analyses. Stigler's essential contribution was to perform an empirical study of various regulations and to suggest on this basis that the more powerful the interests being regulated were, the more advantageous the regulations turned out to be for them. For instance, he studied interstate trucking and concluded that the "regulations on [truck] weight were less onerous; the larger the truck population in farming, the less competitive the trucks were to railroads (i.e., the longer the rail hauls), and the better the highway system."[11] He also came to similar conclusions in the context of occupational licensing.[12] His hypothesis, devastating to those who believe in NPT, is that "regulation is acquired for the industry and designed and operated primarily for its benefit."[13] Thus, Stigler's work is the root of so-called capture theory, which postulates that regulators are captured by the interests they regulate.

Coase, Averch and Johnson, and Stigler's masterful contributions must be assessed on two levels. On one level, it would not be an exaggeration to suggest that they have written the foundational texts of the law and economics movement. In particular, Coase and Stigler's straightforward and mathematically simple, yet brilliant, expositions have helped their work achieve widespread prominence. Their efforts were eventually rewarded on a grand scale: Stigler won a Nobel Prize in Economic Sciences in 1982, and Coase followed in 1991.

On another level, and more directly relevant for our study, each article has been widely interpreted to be avowedly antiregulation. Whether or not this is an accurate assessment is left to later chapters. For now, it is crucial to understand that the most influential movements at the intersection of law and economics and regulation—the Chicago school, contestability theory, and public choice—can be properly assessed only by first understanding that their core ideas are based on these seminal works.

PROGENY

1. Chicago school

Perhaps the most famous and well-studied of the law and economics movements is the Chicago school, so named since many of its leaders trained under the tutelage of Aaron Director at the University of Chicago. Director himself wrote very little, but he was able to surround himself with successful scholars who did. Well-known economists associated with this movement include Harold Demsetz and Director's brother-in-law, the Nobel laureate Milton Friedman. On the legal side, much of Chicago's influence can be traced to the appointment of several of its intellectual leaders to the federal judiciary—notably Richard Posner, Robert Bork, Frank Easterbrook, and Antonin Scalia. Chicago's principal allure is its simplicity. Based on neoclassical price theory, it envisions a world of simple downward sloping demand schedules neatly intersecting supply curves at equilibrium.[14] The goal is efficiency—more specifically, maximizing "allocative efficiency," which seeks to increase the aggregate welfare of society by rearranging resources so that they occupy their most valued use.[15]

If this seemingly innocuous proposition is the bedrock of their methodology, then one might reasonably ask why the Chicago school is so closely associated with laissez-faire economics? The linkage is both intuitive and straightforward: in the world of neoclassical economics, markets are assumed to function well—much like they do in Coase's world of zero transaction costs.[16] In the land of perfectly functioning markets, then, the normative bias is naturally away from government regulation. After all, why should bureaucrats interfere with the beauty of the free market? Why introduce messy concepts that have nothing to do with efficiency—concepts like redistribution, justice, and other social values?

Indeed, Chicago's normative agenda is fundamentally about the failure of government intervention and the efficiency of the common law.[17] Its scholars have tried to apply their approach not only to substantive law, but to the administration of the judicial system itself.[18] Despite this breadth, to this day Chicago's greatest inroads remain in antitrust law, the first doctrinal area the movement sought to reform. Its proponents successfully argued that much corporate activity, formerly thought to be anticompetitive, is actually somehow efficient.[19] An early example is Ward Bowman's argument that attempts to control adjacent products, such as tying,[20] do not present real anticompetitive danger, since a company attempting to tie will lose profits in the market for the tied product.[21] Perhaps the best example of this laissez-faire ethos is Robert Bork's influential book *The Antitrust Paradox*,[22] where he lucidly lays out his vision of an antitrust that protects only against explicit collusion, large horizontal mergers, and extreme forms of predation.[23] A passage from Bork's book sums up the Chicago school ethos particularly well:

The law should permit agreements on prices, territories, refusals to deal, and other suppressions of rivalry that are ancillary, in the sense discussed, to an integration of productive economic activity. It should abandon its concern with such beneficial practices as small horizontal mergers, all vertical and conglomerate mergers, vertical price maintenance and market division, tying arrangements, exclusive dealing and requirements contracts, "predatory" price cutting, price "discrimination," and the like.[24]

In an analogous vein, and most directly relevant for our purposes, the Chicago school began questioning the value of regulation. In one classic piece, Harold Demsetz argued that the "theory of natural monopoly is deficient for it fails to reveal the logical steps that carry it from scale economies in production to monopoly price in the market place,"[25] concluding that "[i]n the case of utility industries, resort to the rivalry of the market place would relieve companies of the discomforts of commission regulation."[26]

Similarly, one of Richard Posner's important early pieces claimed that "even in markets where efficiency dictates monopoly we might do better to allow natural economic forces to determine business conduct and performance subject only to the constraints of antitrust policy,"[27] since "the benefits of regulation are dubious, not only because the evils of natural monopoly are exaggerated but also because the effectiveness of regulation in controlling them is highly questionable."[28] His policy prescriptions included advocating

(1) the deregulation of those industries that are not natural monopolies, such as natural-gas production, aviation, and trucking, and, (2) in the other regulated industries, (a) removal of restrictions on entry and of controls over specific rates and (b) substitution of an excess-profits tax for regulatory limitations of overall profits.[29]

Curiously, and without offering any proof, Posner argues that monopolies that evolve without regulation are not nearly as harmful: "[T]he costs of monopoly are quite probably much greater in the regulated than in the unregulated sector of the economy, despite the greater size of the latter sector."[30]

The merits of these arguments will be discussed in future chapters. For now, it is important to reflect on the Chicago school's larger-than-life personalities. In particular, it is worth pausing to note how Posner has served as Chicago's ambassador, given his exceptional scholarly productivity. As one writer puts it:

> As much as for his contentious opinions, Posner is famous for his freakish productivity. He publishes a book every half hour. Now sixty-two [in 2001], he has written thirty-one books, more than three hundred articles, and nearly nineteen hundred judicial opinions. He has written books about AIDS, law and literature and the Clinton impeachment trial, and articles about pornography, Hegel, and medieval Iceland.[31]

Posner's impact on the influence of the Chicago school cannot be overstated. As Laura Kalman has written, Posner is the scholar who "symbolized the [law and economics] movement and whose lucid prose and 'unstinting confidence' explained so much of its impact on law in the 1970s."[32] Robert Ellickson has even called Posner "not only the premier legal scholar of our time, but, indeed, one of the extraordinary intellectuals of the late Twentieth Century."[33] Now in its fifth edition, Posner's *Economic Analysis of Law*[34] remains a central law and economics text and seeks to apply the simple paradigms of neoclassical economics to a host of activities, including "drug addiction, thefts of art, sexual acts, surrogate motherhood, rescues at sea, flag desecration, and religious observances."[35] The book's ambition is vast.

I dwell on Posner's talents and influence because, strangely enough, his prominence provides a window into a number of questions that are central to my thesis that law and economics can be compatible with regulation. Is the Chicago school's regulation-unfriendly brand of law and economics most prevalent because its ideas are better, or rather because its missionaries are hardworking and charismatic—decades later still launching well-publicized offensives against the regulatory state?[36] Not to mention that the law and economics movement has been brilliantly funded by its conservative benefactors.[37] On the other hand, is the disdain many lawyers and public policy analysts have for the law and economics movement a function of the movement's inability to evolve in any meaningful way beyond its love affair with neoclassical economics that began in the 1960s and 1970s? If so, is it not time to overcome this intellectual stagnation and animosity by having a new generation of scholars come out from the shadows of giants like Posner?

2. Contestability theory

Initially separate from the Chicago school's efforts, William Baumol, Robert Willig, and Elizabeth Bailey developed the theory of contestability. Rather than focus on the intuitive notion that actual competition creates competitive equilibrium, they argued that the threat of competition is enough to discipline a market if firms are free to exit and enter:

> The key element of contestability is that a market is vulnerable to competitive forces even when it is currently occupied by an oligopoly or a monopoly. That is, if any incumbent is inefficient or charges excessive prices or exploits consumers in any other way, successful entry must be possible and profitable. Thus, in contestable markets, entry and exit must be free and easy.[38]

The essence of their argument was that in a market with no sunk costs,[39] even a monopolist is vulnerable to the threat of a potential entrant; in other words, the "equilibrium of a contestable market is often a better standard for public policy than the competitive model, particularly in the presence of economies of scale and scope."[40]

Contestability theory further shook the foundations of regulation. If free entry and exit are the key to a robust market, then barriers to entry and exit should be removed, since "[i]mpediments to entry and exit, or concentration or scale of operations, may be the primary source of interference with the workings of the invisible hand."[41] Contestability theorists argue that "any proposed regulatory barrier to entry must start off with a heavy *presumption* against its adoption."[42] Interestingly, some influential Chicago school leaders such as Harold Demsetz implicitly added contestability theory to their arsenal by broadly assuming markets are contestable, and then using this assumption to argue against government intervention.[43] Since government is the one imposing such barriers, then what role for regulation? The result was yet another clever attack on regulation.

3. Public choice

Public choice's attack on the regulatory state is more systemic than that of either the Chicago school or contestability theory. It postulates that government is captive to private interests. As Daniel Farber and Philip Frickey succinctly point out, "In public choice, government is merely a mechanism for combining private preferences into a social decision."[44] The theory is especially leery of regulation, since it postulates that government intervention is simply a product of special interest politics.

Public choice is at heart a contractarian movement that has its roots in the pioneering work of yet another Nobel laureate, James Buchanan.[45] Since Buchanan developed his ideas while at the University of Virginia and the Virginia Polytechnic Institute, public choice is sometimes called the "Virginia school." Conceptually, Buchanan successfully took Stigler's pro-producer (or "capture") theory of regulation and combined it with primacy of private law, reminiscent of the oft-cited portions of *Problem of Social Cost*, to derive what is often misleadingly called the "economic theory" of regulation, which posits that regulation is merely a response to various interest groups. To address this supposed perversity, Buchanan argues that economics must come "closer to being a 'science of contract' than a 'science of choice,' "[46] where the "unifying principle becomes gains-from-trade, not [social] maximization."[47]

There is, of course, much truth to Buchanan's insight.[48] His ideas can even be traced back to Madison's account of how "factions" can organize to push their own agendas to the detriment of society at large.[49] During the 1960s, Mancur Olson's research on group dynamics added a critical organizational dimension, giving public choice ideas further credence:

> The smaller groups—the privileged and intermediate groups—can often defeat the large groups—the latent groups—which are normally supposed to prevail in democracy. The privileged and intermediate groups often triumph over the numerically superior forces in the latent or large groups because the *former are generally organized and active while the latter are normally unorganized and inactive*.[50]

But what is public choice's prescription against the lobbyists representing these special interest groups? Rather than seek ways to make government better, public choice theorists devolve to a greater reliance on private law. In particular, these commentators propose that social ordering be reduced to a world of private contract: get government out of the way and let private parties bargain.[51]

Thanks to public choice, terms like "government failure" have entered the lexicon to describe regulation.[52] This is in marked contrast to the benign view of regulation, or "normative analysis as a positive theory"

(NPT), discussed in chapter 1.[53] The Virginia school has had such an impact that numerous scholars not themselves associated with it have perhaps unwittingly internalized its perspective. For instance, finance theorists such as Michael Jensen and William Meckling, when turning to public policy issues, lament that "*government is destroying the system of contract rights, which has been the wellspring of our economic growth.*"[54] After all, they argue, "[r]evocation and abrogation of rights is the currency in which politicians and bureaucrats deal."[55] Other observers even use constitutional language to argue that if government takes back benefits already bestowed to a regulated firm, it has somehow engaged in a "taking."[56] For his part, Thomas Hazlett, one of the leading telecommunications commentators, represents the public choice ethos well when he argues that in "a world where regulators have consistently proven themselves to favor monopoly over competition, producers over consumers, and government over the market, the institution of law offers an eminently reasonable remedy."[57]

Public choice is in some sense the most cynical of the law and economics movements, and envisions an even smaller role for government than Chicago does. Perhaps the best example of conflict with Chicago is in the area of antitrust. While Chicago school scholars such as Bork,[58] Posner,[59] and Friedman[60] at least countenance some role for competition law, Virginia does not—arguing plainly that "antitrust enforcement agencies are shaped by politics"[61] and that antitrust should essentially be abolished, since "there is widespread acknowledgement that antitrust has repeatedly failed to protect the interests of consumers."[62] Indeed, the public choice school criticizes the fact that Chicago sees any room for antitrust at all.[63]

The convergence of these masterful, economically minded, attacks on regulation—whether they be from the Chicago or Virginia schools, or their allies—have cast a pall on regulation. They have furnished intellectual legitimacy for the deregulatory trends of the past two decades—in trucking, railways, airlines, telecommunications, and electricity. They have also provided academic respectability for lax enforcement of our antitrust laws and cast serious doubt on the efficiency of health, safety, and environmental regulations. More broadly, these attitudes illustrate a massive shift in democratic discourse, "a sharp turn from the essentially republican vision of government that dominated Progressive legal thought, to a more classical liberal view emphasizing the uniqueness and centrality of individual preference, the efficiency and robustness of private markets, and the many imperfections of public processes."[64] Have the outcomes been positive? Chapter 3 is devoted to an understanding of the results of all this deregulatory fervor.

Chapter 3

Where Is Society Left?

The brilliantly crafted attacks by conventional law and economics scholars have given intellectual legitimacy to two decades of loosening public oversight on the U.S. economy. Unfortunately, indiscriminate and inconsistent deregulation has made for dubious public policy. Direct effects involve the increasing concentration of many industries and a litany of business scandals. Far more dangerous than even these realities, however, are the indirect effects of the laissez-faire ethos: fewer economic protections for citizens, and, most devastatingly of all, the exaltation of private gain above public welfare. Needless to say, the argument is not that deregulation is solely to blame for all the ills of modern society, but merely to say that its contribution cannot be ignored.

DIRECT EFFECTS: INDUSTRY CONSOLIDATION AND SCANDAL

The most immediate impact of deregulation has been to usher in a wave of mergers and acquisitions across a variety of industries—from banks to airlines to media interests.[1] Unfortunately, industry consolidation has been a disappointment; it is too often accompanied by higher prices, less choice, and inferior product quality. In fact, one is hard-pressed to find cases where industry consolidation has helped consumers. It is no coincidence that consumer advocates tend to oppose mergers. For instance, one detailed consumer report of various deregulated industries—airlines, banking, electricity, telephones, and cable TV—highlights the dramatic declines in service and quality:

> Broken promises, deceptive marketing, and dreadful service have become accepted business practices in an increasingly Wild West

marketplace, where incessant telemarketers interrupt your dinner but customer service won't answer the phone. . . . How did business practices get so shabby? One root cause is an economic experiment begun in the 1970s: deregulation.[2]

Perhaps most devastatingly, the report marshals data to debunk the common misperception that deregulation lowered consumer prices:

The oft-repeated claim that deregulation cut consumer prices while regulation kept prices artificially bloated is a myth. The inflation-adjusted cost of airfares, telephone service, and electricity were falling for decades before deregulation. Cable-television costs, which had decreased when the industry was regulated, rose sharply after deregulation. . . . Another myth is that discount tickets were an invention of deregulation.[3]

The airline industry, deregulated in 1978, is one instructive example. On the one hand, deregulation's defenders note the decline in fares[4] and greater availability of connections, given hub-and-spoke architectures;[5] on the other, they acknowledge "the general decline in the quality of the air travel experience."[6] Of course, deregulation is not the sole explanatory variable for these changes. Perhaps some blame lies with antitrust; after all, study after study, even some from contestability theorists, has confirmed that postderegulation, mergers "led to higher fares, creating wealth transfers from consumers."[7] Alfred Kahn, the great intellectual force behind airline deregulation, has questioned the attractiveness of further consolidation.[8] He is also careful to note that while today's airline industry offers lower fares on certain routes, travelers unable to benefit from these routes have been inconvenienced.[9] Consolidation in other industries, notably telecommunications and media,[10] has dangers that transcend consumers' pocketbooks and satisfaction—namely, homogenization of information sources becomes plainly harmful to diversity in democratic discourse.[11]

Corporate management's self-interest has combined with the legitimating effects of laissez-faire economics to condone industry consolidation. Executives often brag that mergers and acquisitions will unlock "synergies" and thus provide not only increased profits, but also greater value to consumers. The unfortunate reality is that such deals are consummated because of what managers believe will benefit them—even shareholder interests are frequently secondary. Walter Adams and James Brock's analysis of historical facts is sobering:

> Mergers, takeovers, and leveraged buyouts erupted in number, from some 1,500 in 1980 to more than 4,400 by 1986. Their annual value skyrocketed from an estimated $35 billion in 1980 to $236 billion in 1988. All told, some 31,000 corporate deals occurred over the decade, representing a cumulative value exceeding $1 trillion. Contrived upon a ramshackle base of excessive debt and "junk" bonds, the decade of the corporate deal collapsed in a record-breaking rate of defaults, the rate of bankruptcies soared 540% between 1986 and 1990, and assets of firms filing for bankruptcy in 1990 reached a level fifty times greater than that of a decade earlier.... [T]he vast sums wasted on corporate dealmaking were, at the same time, vast sums not invested directly in new plants, new research and development, new product commercialization, new jobs, or the development and implementation of state-of-the-art manufacturing techniques.[12]

The traditional bifurcation between economic regulation and antitrust has fueled the disaster. It is all too easy for those enamored of deregulation to argue that industry concentration is not a regulatory problem per se; after all, reining in big or powerful companies is antitrust's job. For example, the prominent economist Alfred Kahn correctly notes that "deregulation permits a fuller exploitation of monopoly power[,]"[13] adding that "[w]hile prepared to defend enthusiastically the deregulations with which I have been involved, I feel equally strongly that they have greatly accentuated the importance of antitrust enforcement."[14] As chapter 1 showed, however, antitrust is nothing but a branch of economic regulation. To boot, lax antitrust enforcement all too often accompanies deregulation. The result of this division is an environment where policy makers and pundits can conveniently avoid responsibility whenever deregulation goes awry simply by passing the buck to antitrust. As Alfred Kahn notes with great humility in his defense of deregulation,

> This kind of defense of the deregulation record—"It wasn't my fault, the trouble is you other people didn't do your job"—is a trifle glib. It contains more than a trace of justifying the abandonment of

direct regulation, because of its severe imperfections, in terms that implicitly demand perfection of performance by such agencies as the Department of Transportation, the Savings and Loan Bank Board and Congress—higher levels of prescience, conscientiousness, information, incorruptibility or simple effectiveness than can reasonably be expected.

To some extent, similarly, thrusting upon the antitrust authorities both blame for some of the monopolistic consequences of airline deregulation and responsibility for their future remedy implicitly expects more of competition-preserving policies than they can deliver.[15]

Only regulation and antitrust, acting together holistically, can stem the tide of pernicious mergers and other anticompetitive behavior.

Beyond consolidation, deregulation has perhaps unwittingly contributed to a spate of outrageous business fiascos. A few examples from different industries should drive home the point. The deregulation of the moving industry in 1995 has brought a skyrocketing number of instances where moving companies frequently hold goods hostage in exchange for exorbitant fees. To add insult to injury, shippers' complaints fall on deaf ears—the Department of Transportation's enforcement staff has all but disappeared.[16] Recurrent problems with food safety, engendered by an underfunded and haphazard inspection system,[17] can be traced to a loosening of regulations begun in the early 1980s. As one journalist sums it up:

> Back when we were falling for the theory of deregulation, we were forgetting about the reality of living in a complicated world filled with potentially dangerous foods and products. Parents don't want to find their children curled up sick on the bathroom floor just to help society weed out bad companies.[18]

The loosening of public oversight on electricity markets, begun in 1997, has not fared much better. Poorly designed deregulation of wholesale markets in California brought price gouging and rolling blackouts in 2002.[19] Lack of mandatory reliability standards caused a massive system failure in the Midwest and Northeast during the summer of 2003.[20] And emerging evidence suggests that electricity deregulation is hurting consumers and small businesses.[21] The energy industry itself suffers under a staggering debt load that "stems from a building-and-acquisition binge that began around 1997 . . . [when a] number of energy companies constructed and bought power plants around the country, aiming to sell electricity into a growing wholesale-power market prompted by deregulation."[22]

Moving scams, tainted food, and blackouts are one thing. The slew of scandals that has shaken corporate America since the late 1990s, however, belongs in an ignominious league of its own. For the past several years, a variety of once well-respected, even lionized, firms—Enron, MCI, Tyco, Adelphia, to name a few—have been embroiled in a variety of scandals, typically involving self-dealing and fraudulent financial reporting. As these fiascos came to light and stock prices tumbled, the life savings of many shareholders and employees were obliterated. One article begins to sum up the devastation at Enron alone:

> The breaking stories defied explanation—$30 million of self-dealing by the chief financial officer, $700 million of net earnings going up in smoke, $1.2 billion of shareholders' equity disappearing as if by erasure of a blackboard, more than $4 billion in hidden liabilities—and all in a company theretofore viewed as exemplar.[23]

Unfortunately, there has been precious little evidence of true corporate reform, and unsavory behavior persists.[24] No industry seems immune. Recently, in fall 2004, an investigation begun by New York Attorney General Eliot Spitzer, but eventually involving other states, probed the extent to which the nation's largest insurance companies have been rigging bids and colluding in kickback schemes.[25] The insurance scandal is but one example in a series of events that have violated institutional safeguards fundamental to capitalism itself. As one writer remarks:

> The scandals that have oozed out of corporate America with alarming regularity in recent months have repeatedly featured executives betraying the marketplace for their own short-term self-interest. From Enron to Global Crossing, Adelphia to WorldCom, the details differ but the stories boil down to the same theme: *the companies lied about their performance, and investors paid the price.* . . . [T]he corporate calamities of the new millennium are of a different ilk, one that challenges the credibility of the financial reporting system, and in turn the faith of investors in the capital markets—*the very engine that has driven capitalism to its success.*[26]

These debacles are, again quite unfortunately, linked to failures in regulatory policies. Sometimes, the connections are straightforward. For instance, for many years leading up to the scandals, the federal Securities and Exchange Commission (SEC) was seduced by free market arguments and the notion that abuses would somehow magically correct themselves. As a consequence, the SEC did not aggressively pursue transgressions perpetrated by corporations and their advisors.[27] Similarly, the weak, haphazard patchwork of state insurance regulators permitted the insurance scandal to grow.[28] Even seemingly esoteric decisions not to regulate can have dramatic repercussions down the line: as one financial journalist correctly observes, the "decision by policy makers in the 1990s not to regulate the arcane financial instruments known as over-the-counter derivatives made it tougher to uncover accounting tricks favored by Enron Corp."[29]

At other times, the road from deregulation to fiasco is less direct. Take, for instance, professional service providers to corporations—notably, accounting firms and investment banks—who were complicit in the cooked accounting statements and fictional investment research that helped perpetrate multiple instances of fraud.[30] In particular, the proliferation of shoddy investment banking research was a key instrument in misleading investors. Where do the root causes of this mischief lie? First, the deregulation of brokerage commissions in the 1960s led to an unraveling of the quality of investment banking research, by itself setting the stage for future scandals.[31] Next, to add fuel to the fire, the Glass-Steagall Act—which had placed a barrier between the lending activities of commercial banks and the underwriting and research activities of investment banks—was effectively abolished in the late 1980s and early 1990s.[32] The potential for conflicts of interest when a financial firm is vying for a corporation's lending and underwriting business and at the same time purporting to provide "objective" investment research is obvious.

One newspaper article marches through the seemingly endless deregulatory scandals in energy, and telecommunications and on Wall Street, and concludes:

> The much ballyhooed experiment in electricity deregulation spawned an unmitigated financial disaster for consumers, energy traders, utilities, and the state of California. The deregulation of the telecommunications industry led to a wave of overinvestment that left the industry with so much overcapacity and such low prices that even the strong companies are struggling to survive. Then there's the decision to lighten up on government supervision of Wall Street,

the banks and the investment banks, setting the stage for the recent corporate scandals.[33]

As one labor organizer laments, "Deregulation isn't directly responsible for every scandal in government and business, but it has created an atmosphere of 'anything goes,' which seems to have lowered standards of business behavior."[34]

INDIRECT EFFECTS: ECONOMIC INSECURITY AND THE RETREAT OF "PUBLICNESS"

As if industry consolidations and distasteful scandals were not enough, deregulation's indirect effects have been even more damaging. In particular, poor deregulation has been a major contribution to income disparity and economic insecurity, while at the same time fostering a social environment in which placing private gain ahead of public welfare becomes not only acceptable, but the desired norm.

Corporate scandals, where average citizens are left holding the bag, are only symptomatic of a broader trend: a shift in economic risk to the shoulders of middle-class and working Americans.[35] As one economics reporter has said,

> [D]eregulating industries, shrinking social programs and promoting a free-market ideal in which everyone must forge his or her own path, free to rise or fall on merit or luck . . . has come at a large and largely unnoticed price: a measurable increase in the risks that Americans must bear as they provide for their families, pay for their houses, save for their retirements and grab for the good life. A broad array of protections that families once depended on to shield them from economic turmoil—stable jobs, widely available health coverage, guaranteed pensions, short unemployment spells, long-lasting unemployment benefits and well-funded job training programs—have been scaled back or have vanished altogether. . . . *The bottom line: more risk for less reward.*[36]

In some cases the causality from unregulated markets to bad public policy is straightforward. For instance, 45 million Americans lack health care coverage, and even those with insurance are increasingly having trouble meeting rapidly escalating premiums.[37] Laissez-faire types who still cling to the delusions of private, for-profit-based medicine need simply look at some basic facts:

> Two decades ago, when Washington embraced the for-profit model to curb escalating charges, health care spending represented 10.5 percent of gross domestic product. Now it is approaching 16 percent. We spend more per capita on health care than any developed country. Yet on the important yardsticks, like life expectancy measured in healthy years, we don't even rank among the top 20 nations. . . . Unfortunately, it [the market] doesn't work in health care, where the goal should hardly be selling more heart bypass operations. Instead, the goal should be to prevent disease and illness. *But the money is in the treatment—not prevention—so the market and good health care are at odds.* Just how much at odds is seen in the current shortage of flu vaccine. . . . The reason for the shortage is this: Preventing a flu epidemic that could kill thousands is not nearly as profitable as making pills for something like erectile dysfunction, a decidedly non-fatal condition.[38]

Other times, the link between mismatched markets and public pain is less obvious, but still very present. One excellent example is Elizabeth Warren's demonstration that deregulation of the lending industry has encouraged financial institutions to prey on vulnerable consumers,[39] and how the emergence of "easy credit" has dramatically driven up the costs of a middle-class existence.[40] Unable to cope with escalating costs such as onerous monthly debt payments, even two-income middle-class families are declaring bankruptcy.[41]

Naturally, the story is radically different for those at the top of the socioeconomic food chain.[42] As one story in the *Economist* details,

> The highest profile cases of excessive pay, unfortunately, are not isolated exceptions. Bosses' pay has moved inexorably upwards, especially in America. In 1980, the average pay for the CEOs of America's biggest companies was about 40 times that of the average production worker. In 1990, it was about 85 times. Now this ratio is thought to be about 400. Profits of big firms fell last year [2002] and shares are still well down on their record high, but the average remuneration of the heads of America's companies rose by over 6%.[43]

Meanwhile, the losers in this game are middle-class and working Americans, many of whose fortunes are spiraling downward[44]—a disturbing phenomenon that has prompted national newspapers such as the *New York Times* and *Wall Street Journal* to devote major articles to class consciousness and the surprising lack of class mobility in America.[45] Even the prominent Chicago school economist Gary Becker says "it's still true if you come from a modest background it's easier to move ahead in the U.S. than elsewhere . . . *but the more data we get that doesn't show that, the more we have to accept the conclusions.*"[46] Again, while deregulation is not to blame for all these woes, it has been a key ingredient. One critic argues that:

> [i]n the absence of ground rules enforced by parties outside the market system—namely, government—opportunism abounds and capitalism goes haywire. . . . Labor deregulation—of pensions, bargaining rights, trade standards, health-and-safety protections—has also affected labor markets and left workers with fewer protections. This, in turn, weakens unions, allows companies to play off worker against worker, and contributes to a general widening of inequality in society. The promised general gains to the economy never quite materialize. Instead, executive pay just keeps soaring.[47]

Along with worsening income disparity comes an ethos of winner-take-all. Day-trading, so popular during the stock market boom of the 1990s, serves as a particularly telling symbol of how ordinary Americans, left to fare on their own without government protection against sophisticated market players, can be wiped out. One article in the *New Yorker* remarks,

> Like most amateur golfers, the vast majority of day traders did poorly. When the Massachusetts authorities investigated a day-trading firm in the state, they found that sixty-seven out of sixty-eight customers had lost money. Tales of disaster multiplied. A Chicago waiter with no trading experience blew a two-hundred-thousand-dollar inheritance. A Boston retiree went through two hundred and fifty thousand dollars of his wife's savings in a few hours. A California bank employee quit his job, borrowed forty thousand dollars on his credit cards to start trading, and promptly lost the lot. . . . *Behind the marketing hype about personal empowerment, day trading was a business that any Wall Street old hand could appreciate: the customers risked their capital; the brokers made the profits.*[48]

As if broad economic insecurity were not enough, perhaps the most tragic indirect repercussion of poor deregulation has been an ironic loss of "publicness" in civic life. This trend to privatization transcends even the trend to deregulation. One economic journalist, Peter Gosselin, has chronicled this reality through some simple, commonsense examples in a series of articles in the *Los Angeles Times*. Why, he asks, are there states like Nevada where, even during recent economic boom years, "more than half of public school students are housed in portable classrooms"?[49] Why do his interviewees, residents of an affluent Atlanta suburb, face situations where "manhole covers in their neighborhood keep blowing off, letting raw sewage spew across their lawns"?[50] Why does he find that "[a]t the great hospitals of the nation's major cities and ballooning suburbs, ambulances are being turned away and patients are being stacked in hallways like so much cordwood"?[51]

Gosselin's explanation has everything to do with the fact that the "prosperity of the last decade has been a peculiarly private affair":[52]

> While affluent Americans spent generously on themselves, the nation as a whole did not. On the contrary, it devoted a historically small fraction of its new economic bounty to the roads and airports, waterworks and sewer plants that have traditionally made up society's foundation. The result has been a broad deterioration that has left even the rich with their alignments wrecked by potholes, their travel trashed by flight delays and their health threatened by emergency care cutbacks. There has also been a crumbling of Americans' once-easy confidence that here at least the power was reliable, the water clean and the telephone service certain.[53]

The American Society of Civil Engineers corroborates such somber concerns: looking at twelve infrastructure categories, it recently issued a grade of D+ and signaled the need for an estimated 1.6 trillion dollar investment over a five-year period "to bring conditions to acceptable levels."[54] Simply put, basic public infrastructure desperately needs overhaul. As one observer notes, with some understatement, the "nation's commitment to public infrastructure and the taxes to pay for them have been shrinking for some time."[55] The well-known economist John Kenneth Galbraith has remarked, "It never ceases to amaze me how people complain about the undue burden of the public sector until forced to face reality by physical discomfort, inadequate income, bad health care or, if in California, stalled elevators."[56]

Yet despite these enormous concerns, not only is privatization in vogue, but its advocates are getting more brazen. For example, the seductive logic of selling off public assets such as electromagnetic spectrum to private parties has captured the public imagination.[57] As Eli Noam has pointed out, however, such ideas use a one-time cash inflow to fund ongoing annual expenditures: governments clearly should not be going around selling public assets to ease budgetary pressures—"[i]t's like New York City solving its budget problems by selling off Central Park to developers."[58] Transforming public airwaves into exclusionary private property is somehow assumed to be superior; other alternatives, such as a spectrum "commons" or licensed leases, are rarely given serious consideration.[59] Another example is the quasi privatization of public lands, including below-market grazing rights for ranchers[60] and concessionary stumpage fees for logging interests.[61] The result has been devastating to the general public, both environmentally[62] and economically.[63] As one observer notes, there have been generous private gains at the public's expense, since "[t]o date, such management has been nothing other than a nursery for industry harvest, all on the taxpayer's dime."[64]

Indeed, there is a stunning irony in all of this. The real emerging debate may not simply be between pro- and antiregulation camps; rather, it seems to be between those who would like to use public intervention in markets to help those who cannot fully participate in private contractual exchanges and those who want to use government merely to further private interests. This trend toward privatization is arguably more important than the trend toward deregulation. One should note, with some amusement, that in an era otherwise mesmerized by the putative evils of regulation, government suddenly becomes respectable when entrenching private interests. Zoning is a case in point. In his study of American suburbanization, Charles Haar laments the "invidious discrimination that can result from local community regulatory power"[65] and how such power is used to "exclude low-income groups."[66] For instance, by dictating that certain areas can only contain single-family homes, or particular lot sizes or setback requirements, a financial barrier is created that members of many socioeconomic groups cannot meet.[67] As Kenneth Jackson has pointed out, the result has been "to segregate the races, to concentrate the disadvantaged in inner cities, and to reinforce the image of suburbia as a place of refuge from the problems of race, crime, and poverty."[68]

Another poignant example is intellectual property, which, as Lawrence Sullivan notes, "is a comprehensive regulatory intervention."[69] Here, the growth of regulatory power to enrich private interests is unabashed. Patent law has grown increasingly expansive, allowing, for example, rights to ill-defined business processes.[70] Some corporations want to push trademark law to squelch free speech.[71] And there is a seemingly insatiable thirst to increase the length of copyright protection[72] while moving to limit fair use of digital information.[73] As Ruth Okediji has pointed out, increased copyright protection "favors those who create and own information, but fails tó consider the other vital component of the information revolution—public welfare."[74] The gradual extension of intellectual property is particularly troublesome, given that it chokes the very justification for this type of regulatory protection: the notion that rights will eventually revert to the public domain.[75] For some, this exaltation of the private over the public is not enough. To the extent that intellectual property still retains some concept of "publicness," even this remainder is threatened— for example, the Uniform Computer Information Transactions Act (UCITA) seeks to "replace the public law of copyright with the private law of contracts,"[76] making information exchanges increasingly difficult. The trend seems to have infected myriad policy areas—to take just one fairly esoteric example from the realm of ocean shipping, reform of the public Carriage of Goods by Sea Act has been hampered by the Ocean Shipping Reform Act, which allows private shippers to set terms by private contract, leaving small shippers to fend for themselves.[77]

There is one final, perverse twist to this mess. Many companies pushing to make government privatize the profit potential of public resources and regulatory regimes are, at the same time, the first to force the public to bear the costs when things go wrong. When the putative synergies of expensive acquisitions do not pan out, macroeconomic conditions deteriorate, or scandals grow out of control, taxpayers end up rescuing the deregulated marketplace. The most common and recurring example is the airline industry, which regularly flirts with bankruptcy and inevitably ends up in Washington looking for a handout, such as billions in cash and loan guarantees received in 2001.[78] But sometimes the techniques to privatize profit and externalize costs are much more subtle and ingenious. For instance, insurance companies in Florida have successfully convinced politicians to set up a public fund to pay a large share of claims, while at the same time using a private arbitration panel to strip regulators of power:

> After [Hurricane] Andrew in 1992, state officials agreed to set up a backstop fund called the Florida Hurricane Catastrophe Fund *guar-*

anteed *by the government that will pick up the bulk of the insurance companies' tabs* from Charley, Frances and other massive storms. Insurers also have been able to dramatically raise their premiums through an *unusual three-person private arbitration panel set up by the Florida legislature* in 1996 to settle price-increase disputes between insurance firms and the state insurance regulator. Previously, the state insurance commissioner held most of the power in approving rate increases.[79]

Needless to say, this maneuvering is part of a broad "legislative and regulatory effort to shift from insurance companies to consumers the burden for paying hundreds of millions of future storm-related losses."[80] One could be forgiven for thinking that it should be the insurance company collecting premiums, not the customer, who should bear the risk of loss.

Another clever technique to externalize cost takes us back to the consolidation issue: merged companies become so massive that they become "Too-Big-To-Fail" (TBTF). This danger is particularly vivid in the financial sector: recall the $300 billion savings and loan bailout in the 1980s,[81] and the intervention by the Federal Reserve in the late 1990s to bail out the gargantuan investment fund Long-Term Capital Management.[82] More recently, two Federal Reserve officials have argued that the TBTF scenario would apply to several banks: their collapse would so harm the overall economy that government would have no choice but to bail them out.[83] The legal critics Alan Freeman and Elizabeth Mensch point to the stunning inconsistency:

[C]onventional free-market ideology extols the virtues of private capital accumulation, entrepreneurial skill, and the harsh reality of risk. Yet tax breaks are granted to entice industries to invest or remain in localities. Cities compete for the opportunity to provide sports teams with ever more luxurious stadiums. Huge companies get government help when they face financial ruin. *Private companies rarely turn down the opportunity to feed greedily at the public trough.*[84]

The advent of unregulated markets has thus brought with it a peculiar absurdity: the public as benefactor of last resort.

We thus stand at a surreal juncture in the history of regulation. The prominent banker and diplomat Felix Rohatyn summarizes our sad state of affairs well:

I had always believed that this country's basic goals consisted of the primacy of freedom, the objective of fairness and the creation of wealth. This concept seemed to hold until the '80s, when greed overcame fairness and the creation of wealth became an individual fever that knew no limits. *Our present situation calls for a rethinking of many of our economic and social assumptions, especially the notion that there is but a minor role appropriate for the government in our economy. . . . I am also a capitalist and believe that market capitalism is the best economic system ever invented; but it must be fair, it must be regulated, and it must be ethical.* The last few years have shown that excesses can come about when finance capitalism and modern technology are abused in the service of naked greed. Only capitalists can kill capitalism but our system cannot stand much more abuse of the type we have witnessed recently, nor can it stand much more of the financial and social polarization we are seeing today.[85]

Hopefully, this chapter can provide a starting framework within which to begin addressing Rohatyn's plea for change. Notice that every problem surveyed in this chapter—aggressive industry consolidation, corporate scandal, economic insecurity, and the redefinition of "publicness"—is part of a disturbing overarching trend that transcends the pro- versus antiregulation debate: a desire by powerful economic actors to privatize benefits (profits) and socialize costs (losses). Perhaps the most socially conscious of the deregulators—those who espouse sensitivities different from the Chicago and Virginia schools—would wish things had turned out differently. Writing in 1981, Alfred Kahn powerfully warned that "the ideals of equality of opportunity, guaranteeing a social minimum, making creative use of government where an unregulated market manifestly does not work well, combating monopoly, protecting defenceless workers, consumers and the environment remain as valid and as pertinent to our social condition as ever."[86] He wrote eloquently of the need for "providing medical care to the 20m [now 45m] or so Americans who lack access to it, preserving and reviving our cities; absorbing minority youth into our productive labour force; improving the quality of our lives, as a society."[87] Twenty-five years later, these ideals remain unaddressed: a vastly more sophisticated message has gotten lost amid the buzzword "deregulation."

The remaining chapters will explore how to begin getting out of the contemporary morass. A first step might be to absorb a wonderfully simple example that the Nobel laureate George Akerlof provides:

If you let your toddler out of her playpen, you need to watch her more carefully. This wisdom is known by every American parent but has been systematically ignored in economic deregulation. For example, in the 1980's, savings and loans were given greatly expanded freedoms. But in misguided zeal for deregulation, regulatory budgets were cut, not raised. Enterprising individuals found ways to loot the savings and loans for their own gain. Taxpayers, as the ultimate guarantors of deposit insurance, were left holding the bag.... *Now is the time to remember the lessons of the playpen: increased scope for action must be accompanied by increased regulatory oversight.*[88]

Akerlof's unsupervised toddler can, of course, now not only injure others, but also herself. Before finding ways to watch her more carefully, however, we have to understand why the seductive assumptions that have left her free to wander around are wrong.

PART II

THE ECONOMIC CASE FOR REGULATION

Chapter 4

Beyond Flawed Assumptions . . .

The severe problems highlighted in chapter 3 should not come as a surprise. They have been caused, in part, by public policy that embraces the laissez-faire prescriptions of chapter 2 without questioning the assumptions that underlie such posturing. The goal of this chapter is to engage in a critique that challenges these deeply held notions of how economics should inform law. To do so, I will try to uncover and unpack the hidden assumptions behind the Chicago and Virginia schools, the two most powerful contributors to the demise of regulation's intellectual respectability.[1]

UNRAVELING THE CHICAGO SCHOOL

The Chicago school's influential ideas are based on four seductive assertions: that efficiency is a deity, that transaction costs are trivial, that behavioral biases are unimportant, and that initial entitlements do not matter. Unfortunately, none of these assumptions withstands critical inquiry.

1. Worshipping efficiency

Simply put, the Chicago school worships at the altar of efficiency. What its scholars mean by efficiency, however, is less precise. Efficiency, sometimes called "allocative efficiency," is loosely associated with the notion that the goal of law should be to put resources to their most valued use in order to maximize society's aggregate welfare. It is relatively common knowledge that the notion of Pareto optimality embodies efficiency: the law should create incentives for a transaction "that makes at least one

43

person better off and no one worse off."[2] So far, so good. What is less publicized, however, is that given third parties are often made worse off, traditional law and economics generally uses a less stringent form of efficiency, known as the Kaldor-Hicks standard. Under Kaldor-Hicks, a transaction is said to be efficient if those that are made better off "could compensate the losers, *whether or not they actually do*."[3] We are thus left with a standard that suggests that a transaction is efficient even though some members of society are left worse off. This represents a brazen disregard of any distributional considerations. As Herbert Hovenkamp has pointed out, "In the real world, efficiency and distributional effects generally cannot be separated from one another. It would probably be impossible to implement a policy that increased social wealth without affecting the way wealth is distributed."[4] In addition, Amartya Sen has made the profound point that notions of optimality are inconsistent with traditional liberalism.[5] After all, liberalism, the darling of neoclassical economics, extols the virtues of individual autonomy and free choice—so how to adhere to this when an individual's preferences run counter to maximizing aggregate social welfare, whether it be Pareto or Kaldor-Hicks optimality?[6]

To further complicate things for themselves, some distinguished Chicago school scholars—notably, Richard Posner himself—argue that wealth maximization, not utility, defines "efficiency."[7] For instance, even though Posner concedes that redistributing income might raise aggregate utility, he views such redistribution as indefensible based on wealth maximization grounds.[8] Joseph Singer has pointed out the inherent logical inconsistency: "Because wealth gives market power, a wealthy person may 'value' (in Posner's terms) an entitlement more than a poor person, even though everyone would agree that more utility would be created by giving the entitlement to the poor person than the rich person."[9]

Another inexplicable twist in Chicago's efficiency logic is the assumption that common law courts are somehow more efficient than legislatures and administrative agencies. Posner argues, for instance, that "the common law is best (not perfectly) explained as a system for maximizing the wealth of society. Statutory or constitutional as distinct from common law fields are less likely to promote efficiency. . . ."[10] Other commentators' attraction to the common law is even more pronounced and occasionally borders on mystical affection. Peter Huber, for instance, who believes that the common law "is the closest we will ever come to utopia,"[11] argues that "[f]rom markets and the common law . . . there emerges spontaneous order that is rational, efficient, and intelligent. . . . Small-scale and privately-centered common law is the only kind of law that sits comfortably with our traditions of individual freedom and private liberty."[12] Of course, no real proof is offered as to why the common law serves as an implicitly efficient allocative mechanism.[13] George Priest has insightfully observed the irony of adulation of traditional law and economics for judicial opinions, which are themselves by definition a far cry from a contestable market.[14] Herbert Hovenkamp notes the inconsistency where "[n]early all the world's other markets, including the common law, work quite well within the Chicago School paradigm. . . . However, for some reason one market that seems not to work is the political market."[15] Susan Rose-Ackerman has even explored how the focus of law and economics on the common law has hindered reform of public law.[16]

The bottom line is that efficiency has become a self-fulfilling, nonfalsifiable fetish. As Frederick Rowe argues, somewhat humorously:

> Per the truisms and axioms of circular logic, the market ensures efficiency and cures inefficiency if meddling governments keep out. Offering easy answers to . . . [the] law's hardest questions, the Efficiency Model tells what is efficient—but never when. *Over time's rainbow, in the radiance of revelation, what is efficient is what is.*[17]

Unfortunately, much of traditional law and economics is vulnerable to Rowe's critique. For instance, to argue for a limited role for government, Milton Friedman argues that the "preservation of freedom is the protective reason for limiting and decentralizing government power."[18] Note how this one elegant sentence contains a number of embedded assumptions that raise questions. For example: what proof is there that concentrated economic power in private hands is less dangerous than in public hands? What is "freedom"? Is it merely a negative right in a libertarian sense, or could it also be a positive right? One should never underestimate the power of good rhetoric to mask logical gaps.

2. Downplaying transaction costs

Even if one were somehow to get beyond the inherent flaws in the efficiency criterion, one is left with the thorny issue of transaction cost. Closely related to the concept of common law efficiency is the Chicago school's belief that private actors, left to their own devices, will achieve an optimal allocation of resources without need for administrative intervention. In Posner's words, "[R]esources tend to gravitate toward their most valuable uses if voluntary exchange—a market—is permitted."[19]

This tradition, of course, claims its intellectual roots in Coase's landmark article, *The Problem of Social Cost*, mentioned in chapter 2. However, neoclassicism's adherents conveniently limit their analysis to the first part of Coase's article, where he highlights a theoretical world of "perfect competition"[20] and zero transaction costs.[21] In the real world, of course, transaction costs matter and include "search and information costs, bargaining and decision costs, policing and enforcement costs."[22] There is a direct link between transaction costs and the externalities and informational imperfections discussed in chapter 1. For example, at the level of individual economic actors, products liability and securities laws are driven by information asymmetries between consumers and manufacturers, and between investors and corporate insiders. Decreasing asymmetries lowers transaction costs. At a more systemic level, transaction costs create externalities: typically, one group of actors with better information is able to externalize its costs onto another. For instance, Mancur Olson's work on the collective action problem suggests that large, diffuse groups such as consumers or environmentalists are unable to defend their interests against small, well-organized industry lobbies.[23] Proponents of an idealized zero-transaction-cost world would have to believe, for instance, that a group of private citizens could negotiate with a polluter to curb emissions under the auspices of private common law. Reality, including the historical emergence of an administrative state to curb abuses of private power,[24] flies in the face of this supposition.

Transaction costs are also a thorn in the side of scholars who disdain regulation and favor privatization. Imagine, for instance, the experiment in privatizing zoning rights that some writers have proposed.[25] For the right to be put to its most efficient use, market transactors must have information about precisely who owns which right. They then have to find each owner and negotiate to use the right—assuming, of course, that no owner will hold out for a better bargain. Then, even though the idea is to privatize, some authority figure needs to make sure the zoning right is being respected. At each step, the unfortunate reality of transaction costs challenges an elegant theory. Yochai Benkler has made an analogous argument to argue against the privatization of spectrum rights. He notes that:

[o]ur entire relationship with our physical surroundings would likely be altered fundamentally if, in order to leave our homes, we had to transact constantly with others, having a superior right to decide whether we could or could not take the route of our choice, at the time of our choice, using the vehicle of our choice.[26]

Enforcement is also problematic. The conventional reaction is simply to assume somehow that common law will protect rights, and antitrust law will curb monopoly.[27] Both assertions miss the mark. It is woefully unclear how a generalist judiciary has either the time or the expertise to serve as the surrogate for the administrative state. Similarly, as chapter 3 has chronicled, many industries have become concentrated despite antitrust law. In many network industries, competition is simply not possible without administrative oversight. Professors Jean-Jacques Laffont and Jean Tirole use the example of New Zealand—the telecommunications regulatory oversight there was abolished, then reinstated in response to market abuses by the incumbent—to demonstrate the "difficulty of ensuring competition in the absence of regulation."[28] The most sophisticated advocates of privatization, who concede that regulatory oversight would still be needed, gloss over the costs of such methods, or even whether deploying such "public" mechanisms eviscerates the core of their privatization argument.[29]

Transaction costs also help explain the emergence of group norms. Robert Ellickson's pathbreaking study of how farmers and ranchers settle disputes in rural Shasta County, California, indicates that people will resort to nonlegal dispute resolution norms precisely because the transaction costs of enforcing their legal rights is too high. He notes that "the presence of transaction costs is what leads people to ignore law in many situations. . . . In a world of costly information, however, one cannot assume that people will both know and honor law."[30] More broadly, human behavior is often shaped by a desire to avoid excessive transaction costs.

Perhaps the best illustration of why transaction costs are important is devastatingly simple: if we lived in a world of zero (or even low) transaction costs, then the modern firm would not even exist.[31] After all, if business could be transacted via the price mechanism, there would be no need for organizations to develop alongside markets. Indeed, an entire branch of economics, transaction cost economics (TCE)—building on Coase's early insights[32]—has developed to study this reality.[33] As Oliver

Williamson, one of TCE's leaders, succinctly points out, "[I]f transaction costs are negligible, the organization of economic activity is irrelevant, since any advantages one mode of organization appears to hold over another will simply be eliminated by costless contracting."[34] Anthony D'Amato even makes the provocative point that law and economics itself would not exist were it not for transaction costs:

> Or to restate the Coase theorem, it doesn't matter which party wins a lawsuit because the market will proceed to do its business as usual (if transaction costs are insignificant). Hence, at its birth, Lanec [law and economics] should have been stillborn. Whatever room there is in society for economics as a social science, it follows from Coase's theorem that there is little or no room in society for law based on economics.[35]

As Williamson sums up, the traditional

> "economic approach to law" is characteristically deficient in microanalytic respects. . . . [T]his tradition relies heavily on the fiction of frictionlessness and/or invokes transaction cost considerations selectively. However powerful and useful it is for classroom purposes and as a check against loose public policy prescriptions, it easily leads to extreme and untenable "solutions."[36]

Perhaps most painfully, the zero-transaction-cost assumption does not even do justice to Coase's *The Problem of Social Cost*. The typically overlooked second half of the article emphasizes the importance of transaction costs, with Coase stating plainly that the "argument has proceeded up to this point on the assumption . . . that there were no costs involved in carrying out market transactions. This is, of course, *a very unrealistic assumption.*"[37] Importantly, for the purposes of regulatory analysis, he postulates that

> there is no reason why, on occasion, such governmental administrative regulation should not lead to an improvement in economic efficiency. This would seem particularly likely when . . . a large number of people are involved and in which therefore the costs of handling the problem through the market or the firm may be high.[38]

In fact, the difficult problems—those we entrust to regulatory agencies—are precisely those that are messy and involve multiple constituents. They are those where government regulation, through its coercive powers, may actually pose fewer transaction costs than purely private market transactions. What is fascinating is that Coase's logic unwittingly leads in the same direction as that espoused by the leading twentieth-century welfare economist, A.C. Pigou,[39] whose work Coase initially set out to refute.[40] Carl Dahlman is the rare scholar who recognizes this crucial intersection:

> [T]he Coase analysis implies one of two corrective measures: (i) find out if there is a feasible way to decrease the costs of transacting between market agents through government action, or (ii) *if* that is not possible, the analysis would suggest employing taxes, legislative action, standards, prohibitions, agencies, or whatever else can be thought of that will achieve the allocation of resources we have already decided is preferred. . . . In this way, the Coase recommendations arrive at exactly the same policy implications that the correct Pigou analysis does. . . .[41]

In a later book, Coase even points out that the "world of zero transaction costs has often been described as a Coasian world. Nothing could be further from the truth. *It is the world of modern economic theory, one which I was hoping to persuade economists to leave.*"[42] Unfortunately, traditional law and economics has ducked the issue of transaction costs precisely because these economic realities are so messy—ironically, much to Coase's great and repeated chagrin:

> The world of zero transaction costs . . . is the world of modern economic analysis, and economists therefore feel quite comfortable handling the intellectual problems it poses, remote from the real world though they may be. . . . *A conclusion so depressing is hardly likely to be welcomed, and the resistance that my analysis has encountered is therefore quite natural.*[43]

Distinguished commentators have noted how "Coase's name is consistently attached to propositions that he has explicitly repudiated"[44] and how traditional law and economics "self-consciously sees its origins in his work."[45] Ignoring the subtleties and assumptions behind a major piece of work is unfortunately too common. Note, for example, how embedded Adam Smith's "invisible hand"[46] has become in the economic imagination. However, Smith's microeconomic theory, the very foundation of neoclassical economics, is only valid where there are "perfect liberty of exchanges"[47] and "competitors of equal wealth and luxury."[48] In other words, zero transaction costs have become to the Coase theorem what atomistic competition is to the "invisible hand": over time, drifting apart from their hypothetical roots, each has become misused ideological dogma—dogma that, ultimately, has fueled the tragic problems discussed in chapter 3.

3. Ignoring behavioral biases

Another strong assumption behind the Chicago school's analysis is the belief that humans as economic actors are rational maximizers of welfare. This notion is so pervasive that Richard Posner's influential treatise, *Economic Analysis of Law*, begins with it up front:

> As conceived in this book, economics is the *science of rational choice* in a world—our world—in which resources are limited in relation to human wants. The task of economics, so defined, is to explore the implications of *assuming that man is a rational maximizer* of his ends in life, his satisfactions—what we shall call his "self-interest."[49]

This passage is particularly illuminating for several reasons. First, even though a claim is made to scientific rigor, no evidence whatever is offered to substantiate the claim of rationality. After all, isn't the essence of scientific inquiry to propose hypotheses that can be tested empirically? Posner's assumption is remarkable in that the inherently nonfalsifiable claim of rationality is the bedrock upon which his opus rests.[50]

Not only is this assertion unproven, but recent work by economists is casting doubt on the notion that economic actors are, by definition, rational maximizers. An emerging branch of economics, behavioral economics, relies fundamentally on real-world experiments to ascertain how real people behave. Indeed, the core of the behavioral argument is not necessarily that people are irrational, as some commentators have suggested,[51] but rather that "assumptions about behavior should accord with empirically validated descriptions of actual behavior."[52] More precisely, behavioral economics can be conceptualized as a subset of empirical economics: while empirical economists use methods and data drawn from a variety of social science disciplines, behavioralists have successfully used cognitive psychology to challenge the assumptions of neoclassical microeconomics.

Two of the field's pioneers, Amos Tversky and the Nobel laureate Daniel Kahneman, summarize well the fundamental insight of behavioral economics: "[P]eople rely on a limited number of heuristic principles [rules of thumb] which reduce the complex tasks of assessing probabilities and predicting values to simpler judgmental operations."[53] "These heuristics[,]" they explain, "are highly economical and usually effective, but they lead to systematic and predictable errors."[54] In the emerging vocabulary of behavioral economics, "people exhibit bounded rationality, bounded self-interest, and bounded willpower."[55]

One common behavioral trait, for instance, is the "endowment effect," which states that people often demand more to give up a good than to purchase it.[56] This casts strong doubt on the idea that even in a world with minimal transaction costs, rights will be put to their most efficient use regardless of their initial allocation—a notion that Chicago school advocates are fond of citing. As Jennifer Arlen has pointed out,

> The endowment effect challenges the fundamental assumption of economics that, absent wealth effects, an individual's maximum willingness to pay for a good should equal his minimum sale price. *This assumption is at the heart of the conclusion that in markets with de minimis transactions costs, commodities will flow to the people who value them most.*[57]

Behavioral quirks also extend to firms as market actors. Many management teams desperately want to "build an empire" even where a rational utility maximizer would not. One article in the business press sums up the situation nicely: "All too often nowadays, corporate boards seem eager to rubber-stamp deals negotiated by empire-building CEOs."[58] It is why many companies, for example, overpay for acquisitions—as one commentator notes, "Despite 30 years of evidence demonstrating that most acquisitions don't create value for the acquiring company's shareholders, executives continue to make more deals, and bigger deals, every year."[59] It has also led companies in network industries to try unsuccessfully to build large proprietary networks. As the fate of companies like Apple in personal computers[60] and Wang in word processing[61] shows, this strategy typically ends up "irrationally" destroying shareholder value.

In the context of environmental regulation, Timothy Malloy captures reality when he notes that "what goes on inside the firm matters, and regulators should pay attention to this point in designing and

implementing regulation."[62] He adds, "The critical point here is that even
a perfectly efficient, profit-maximizing firm will not consist of a group of
profit-maximizing employees and managers. The sheer size and complexity of the modern firm virtually precludes it from using profit-maximization
as the driving goal for every firm participant."[63] As chapter 6 will explore,
regulation of corporations must, to a large extent, facilitate shareholder
oversight, which has become very difficult, given the dispersion of ownership and concentration of management in corporate America.

Whether it is applied to individuals or to firms, the field of behavioral economics is still in its infancy, and its implications are likely to be
refined and debated in the years to come. One thing can be stated with
reasonable certainty, however: often irrational market actors cast serious
doubt on the feasibility of standard Chicago school bromides.[64] As Coase
himself observes, somewhat somberly:

> The rational utility maximizer of economic theory bears no resem-
> blance to the man on the Clapham bus or, indeed, to any man (or
> woman) on any bus. There is no reason to suppose that most human
> beings are engaged in maximizing anything unless it be unhappi-
> ness, and even this with incomplete success.[65]

It is perhaps unsurprising that people and companies are not always rational actors maximizing utility in a world of perfect competition and
complete information; what is shocking is how little mainstream law and
economics has taken Coase's warning to heart.

4. Preordaining initial entitlements

If transaction costs and behavioral biases matter, then the initial distribution of entitlements does as well, since resources will not magically be
reassigned to their most valued use. But the Chicago school, perhaps
afraid to spoil its own party, is uncharacteristically silent on this issue. Its
commentators counsel parties to bargain to achieve an efficient result, but
curiously disallow any bargaining over the starting point. The status quo
is assumed to be the natural order of things. Again, Arthur Leff's almost
Orwellian critique of Posner's work is particularly biting:

> What all this means is that Posner has not played fair with the
> question of power, or inequalities thereof. He has made a very

common move: after something of value has been distributed he has defined taking as illicit and *keeping* (except when paid) as in tune with the express wishes of the universe. . . . Keepers keepers, so to speak. . . . The transfers that come about against a background of wealth inequality are fine; any that come about against a background of inequality in strength, or the power to organize and apply strength, are unjustifiable. *Some inequalities are apparently more equal than others.*[66]

Or, in Bruce Ackerman's words, "[Y]ou and I must confront the fact that we could never have bargained over some of the questions that most profoundly shape the course of our lives—most notably, those involving the distribution of initial endowments of wealth, education, and talent."[67]

One might argue, of course, that any discussion of initial wealth distribution is about justice, which should not be the focus of a discussion in economics. However, not only is separating the two problematic, but ignoring initial wealth distributions is arguably immoral. As Robert Ellickson has pointed out, "Until basic ground rules have been set, *no prices and no markets worthy of moral respect exist*. Cost-benefit entitlements cannot help a society decide how to confer basic entitlements because the numbers upon which this analysis relies come into existence only after those entitlements have been conferred."[68] Neoclassical law and economics would have autonomous actors bargain to put resources to their highest use based on their wealth, or ability to pay, but it conveniently takes existing wealth distributions as magically preordained.

Tellingly, even brilliant analysts not associated with the Chicago school nonetheless fall into the utilitarian trap of assuming away distributional and moral considerations. The most prominent of them is perhaps Steven Shavell, who justifiably observes that the wealth maximization mantra is "theoretically incoherent"[69] and quite correctly laments how "many of the advocates of the 'economic' position appear themselves to be ignorant of the fundamental definitions and concepts of welfare economics."[70] The great irony in Shavell's masterful work, however, is that in placing too much faith in the ability of the tax and transfer system to achieve distributional goals,[71] and in eschewing deontological concerns,[72] he too often ends up resorting to wealth maximization—the very norm he so eloquently criticizes.[73]

As Herbert Hovenkamp notes, "To date, no compelling argument has been made for a policy of maximizing satisfaction from a given starting point that says nothing about the location of the starting point. Until such an argument is made, the notion of 'allocative efficiency' is, at best, a trivial guide to policymaking."[74] One particularly poignant example is in the area of housing, where, as one scholar observes,

> When economic constraints and discrimination keep the poor and minorities from having the same mobility as wealthier and nonminority residents, they are less able to satisfy their preferences. . . . In light of the market's manifest failure to meet preferences, and meet them equally, the argument against government intervention loses force. If preferences are not met, then the goals of a market system are not met: social welfare is not maximized because individual preferences are not maximized. Liberty is not achieved if residents cannot realize preferences. . . . A misguided faith in the market should not stand in the way of initiatives to improve distributive equity.[75]

The mistake neoclassical economics makes is precisely to ignore the initial starting point—both in terms of financial resources and social attitudes—where many members of society must begin. To assume the market should ignore these woes is, as Ellickson points out, not morally respectable; to suggest the market or the tax system will magically redress them is either disingenuous or simply naive.

Mainstream law and economics thus ignores the initial distribution of wealth, and more broadly eschews equity considerations. It ignores the fact that Coase's seminal analysis is prefaced by four all-important words: "questions of equity apart."[76] Arguably, the greatest weakness of traditional economic analysis is that in its fascination with utilitarianism and efficiency, it ignores issues of justice that are central to our jurisprudence.[77] The presence of transaction costs and behavioral biases only adds insult to injury.

5. Normativity as science?

Thus, arguably the four most basic assumptions to the Chicago school's enterprise—that efficiency should rule, that transaction costs are insignificant, that economic agents are rational, and that initial entitlements do not matter—while couched in the metaphors of science, remain unsubstantiated. As George Priest observes:

A very large proportion of this [law and economics] work is scientistic and, in essence, alien to the sciences from which it seems to derive. More generally, I believe, the aim to construct a comprehensive theory of legal doctrine . . . represents, in our present state of knowledge, a perversion of the scientific enterprise.[78]

Arthur Leff is even more blunt: "[S]ubstituting definitions for both facts and values is not notably likely to fill the echoing void."[79] Indeed, Leff's caricature provides a masterful summary:

Richard Posner's hero is also eponymous. He is Economic Analysis. In the book [Posner's *Economic Analysis of Law*] we watch him ride out into the world of law, encountering one after another almost all of the ambiguous villains of legal thought, from the fire-spewing choo-choo dragon to the multi-headed ogre who imprisons fair Efficiency in his castle to keep for stupid and selfish reasons. In each case Economic (I suppose we can be so familiar) brings to bear his single-minded self, and the Evil Ones (who like most in the literature are in reality mere chimerae of some mad or wrong-headed magician) dissolve, one after another.[80]

More recently, distinguished critics have variously labeled traditional law and economics as the "never-never world of neoclassical economics,"[81] the "pop version of economics,"[82] and even a "remarkable array of alarming values, unexamined and implausible assumptions, circular arguments, and logical fallacies."[83] Jeanne Schroeder even "suggest[s] that the law and economics movement, which neither bases its policy suggestions on actual markets nor adequately comes to grips with its own ideal of the perfect market, is located in the Imaginary. It is the weaving of a series of fantasy images in a vain attempt to reconcile the Symbolic with the Real."[84] Pierre Schlag goes so far as to argue that traditional law and economics is "asking the wrong questions—questions that are unintelligible. There is, of course, something worse than asking unintelligible questions—and that is answering them."[85]

The issue remains, of course, why scholars as brilliant as Posner would choose to do this. One plausible explanation is that, given a state of imperfect knowledge, assumptions need to be made to push the thinking forward. As Douglas Baird points out,

The question is not whether economists' assumptions are unrealistic, but whether they capture enough of what is at work to allow us to see basic forces operating in an otherwise impenetrable maze. The wonder of modern price theory is how much can be derived from propositions that are so simple. For example, once one accepts that, as a general matter, demand decreases as price increases, much else follows. Graduate students sometimes reduce all of microeconomics to only four words—people maximize, markets clear.[86]

Even those of us who believe that "people maximize, markets clear" is all too reductionist a mantra should at least concede the simple elegance of the approach.

There is arguably, however, a less benign explanation—namely, that these facile assumptions have been carefully chosen to push forward a politically conservative agenda. Viewed in this light, the choreography is unsurpassed: extol efficiency and the common law while ignoring wealth distribution. Make this agenda appear inevitable by assuming away transaction costs and behavioral realities. The result is a bias away from government regulation and toward a nineteenth-century, almost Lochneresque[87] laissez-faire conception of the primacy of private law. Posner himself almost seems to admit as much when he remarks that

> conservative judges and business-oriented people found their voice and found there was a respectable body of academic thinking that they could use to support their predilections. But even if the main thing that economics does is give a *patina of academic respectability* to people's instincts or a vocabulary in which people can express their preferences, that contribution can have a big impact on policy.[88]

The ability of good rhetoric to make this all appear natural is remarkable. A vision of society is painted without making explicit its underlying assumptions and necessary trade-offs. As Bruce Ackerman points out,

> As good conservatives, these apologists for the new learning have sought to console the traditional lawyer by minimizing the challenge the lawyer-economist poses to traditional legal discourse. According to these Chicagoans, traditional private law is already instinct with an "implicit" economic logic.[89]

Other critics have variously labeled neoclassical law and economics as "avowedly anti-populist"[90] or as having an "oligarchic underside."[91] As a

serious economic endeavor, the Chicago school's brand of law and economics is a sequence of facile assumptions. As a normative agenda cloaked
in scientific positivism, it is brilliant.

RETHINKING CONTRACTARIANISM

The second major assault on regulation, the Virginia school's contractarianism, is similarly far from complete in either its descriptive or prescriptive
power. Traditional public choice fails to take into account a number of
realities. It assumes that government actors have self-interested motivations, without taking into account neither the distributive and ideological
functions of regulation nor the practical realities of regulating an industry. Empirically, its predictions do not match well with agency procedures
or the recent transformations of regulated industries that—while they can
be criticized on other grounds—nonetheless often occurred to the detriment of incumbents.

   As a threshold question, one must be cognizant of Mancur Olson's
sophisticated depiction of why interest group politics might be a positive
good. Referring to the work of economists such as John Commons, Olson
highlights not only the belief that different interest groups jockeying for
position tend to counterbalance each other,[92] but even the notion among
pluralists "that economic pressure groups were more representative of the
people than the legislatures based on territorial representation."[93] These
points can even be extended to argue that different government branches
and agencies should attempt to counterbalance each other.

1. Some inconsistencies

Even if one does not subscribe to this benign account of public choice,
one can argue that regulation at least does fulfill a distributive mandate.
In two early articles written primarily as a response to Stigler's public
choice argument,[94] none other than a young Richard Posner argued that
regulation effectively performs the function of taxation, and should thus
be treated as a branch of public finance.[95] Posner discusses how regulators
often cross-subsidize certain constituents by setting below-market rates,[96]
how "interests promoted by regulatory agencies are frequently those of
customer groups rather than those of the regulated firms themselves,"[97]
and how the same agency often has to regulate different firms with competing interests.[98]

Posner also finds fault with the view that common carrier and public utility regulation has served to benefit incumbents.[99] Nonetheless, he argues that even "if we assume that regulation is imposed primarily for the benefit of the regulated firms, it must be shown why other industries have not obtained the same kind of regulation as public utilities and common carriers."[100] Thus, the leading advocate of the Chicago school, while too easily claiming equivalence between public finance and regulation, has ironically nonetheless been able to mount a strong rebuke to public choice accounts of regulation.

Beyond ignoring distributive imperatives, public choice is vulnerable in assuming that the motivations of businesses coincide with the public good. The logical lapse is quite simple: while economists generally[101] consider competition to be beneficial, since it forces resources to be allocated to their most efficient use,[102] for a self-interested business competition means lower profits.[103] In the candid words of one article in the business press, "Businessmen, by and large, don't like free and open markets. From John D. Rockefeller on, they have found markets to be messy, chaotic, and insufficiently profitable."[104] As the former Federal Communications Commission (FCC) chairman Michael Powell—himself generally not a fan of regulation—warns, "Companies don't like competition. It's the biggest red herring and garbage I've heard in my life."[105] Tellingly, Powell adds that "[o]ne of the things I find as a regulator, the pattern is always the same. An innovator loves a free market—until they get big. Then they want to pull up the ladder. One of our more sacred responsibilities is to never take the heat off big companies."[106] Or, put simply in the words of one commentator:

> Today, the instinctive distrust of any governmental action, and the almost religious faith in free markets, which characterized the deregulatory movement, seem somewhat naïve. There is a growing recognition instead that unregulated markets do not necessarily operate perfectly, that successful, anticompetitive behavior by firms is in fact more plausible and common than we perhaps thought, and that the social costs of these phenomena are substantial.[107]

Given this painfully evident reality, it is rather puzzling that analysts continue to try to base public policy on trying to divine the "anticompetitive" or "competitive" intent of corporations[108]—rather than grapple with the essential task of actually having to analyze the structural characteristics of markets.

Just as business's motivations are not always benign, government's motivations are not necessarily distasteful. To begin with, empirical studies show that ideology is a better predictor of legislative votes than self-interest.[109] Stephen Breyer, for example, argues that public choice theories

> tend to overlook the extent to which nonpolitical factors affect the content of regulation. While some regulators are politicians, many are not; they are not elected; and they do not seek to maximize votes. . . . Similarly, one cannot in fairness view legislators as interested only in the political support of those who favor or oppose particular measures. The merits of those issues play an important role in political argument.[110]

Similarly, Farber and Frickey point out that "public choice ignores some other common sense observations about politics. Some crucial features of the political world do not fit the economic model. It does not account for ideological politicians like Reagan and Thatcher. Most notably, it does not account for popular voting."[111] Indeed, even politicians who may be intellectually averse to government intervention may pass consumer-friendly regulations precisely to secure the votes of consumers.[112]

Economics, voting, and ideology aside for a minute, the realities of managing a bureaucracy kick in. In his far-reaching study of the administrative state, Richard Stewart challenges the critics who assert "with a dogmatic tone that reflects settled opinion, that in carrying out broad legislative directives, agencies unduly favor organized interests."[113] In fact, Stewart offers an overarching practical explanation as to what might really be going on: given limited resources, regulators are dependent on the industries they regulate for cooperation and information.[114] Underfunded agency budgets only exacerbate the problem.[115] Another practical reality is the need for laws to evolve quickly. For example, there might be a law that is unwise today because it protects a powerful industry. But when the law was originally developed, years or even decades ago, it may have been with the good intentions of protecting a nascent industry.[116] The motivations, then, may not be invidious, just outdated. As Kip Viscusi points out, with some understatement, "[R]egulating an industry is a difficult task."[117]

Beyond the realities of regulatory implementation, agency capture theories do not accord with empirical reality. They do not predict regulations that have protected consumers or workers,[118] nor how regulators in many industries have taken an anti-incumbent, pro-competition stance. New Zealand's abolishing of its telecommunications regulator, followed by its reinstatement in the wake of abuses by the incumbent,[119] should make any observer cautious of loud cries to dismantle federal agencies and rely on some fuzzy combination of tort law, state agencies, and the private sector.[120] More generally, distinguished commentators have pointed out public choice's lackluster predictive power. Breyer observes that

> [i]nterest group theories, as causal explanations of either the historical origins of regulation or the actions of regulators, suffer several drawbacks. Where they are limited to producers, they are often inaccurate. They cannot fully explain environmental, health, safety regulation, or even traditional utility and transportation regulation. . . . If the theory is expanded beyond producers, it risks becoming nonpredictive and nonexplanatory. All regulatory rules and programs benefit some group or other.[121]

In addition, as Alfred Kahn notes, the composition of interest groups is fluid and constantly in flux.[122] In their analysis of the vast changes in regulation of transportation, telecommunications, and energy over the past twenty-five years, Joseph Kearny and Thomas Merrill remark:

> The public choice perspective is also vulnerable insofar as its central premise—that positive regulation is always inferior to market ordering—is usually advanced as an article of faith rather than by empirical demonstration. The history of the great transformation that we have recounted—in which regulatory agencies often led the charge for regulatory reform—should by itself be enough to give pause before one asserts any invariant hypothesis about the behavior of regulators. Contrary to the theory popular in the late 1960s and early 1970s, agencies do not always behave as the hopeless captives of their client industries.[123]

In their critique of the nondelegation doctrine, David Spence and Frank Cross argue that the public may in fact be better served by having an administrative bureaucracy. They conclude that "the empirical evidence on independent bureaucracies does not support the claims that independent bureaucrats advance their own interests at the expense of the commonwealth; to the contrary, greater independence may better promote the public interest."[124] Noting in particular that industry lobbyists typically rush to legislatures for favors, they conclude that "[n]o family of public choice models seems more irrelevant yet is more widely cited than capture models,"[125] and aptly observe the logical inconsistency in public choice where "capture theory is directly contradictory to the agency policy bias criticism, which suggests that agencies will over-regulate."[126] As Richard Parker points out, "If the traditional concern was that agencies would be captured by regulated interests and consequently, would regulate too little, the modern critique is led by charges that agencies—driven by technology, bureaucratic ambition, or 'public interest' pressures—are regulating too strictly and too much."[127]

In a somewhat similar vein, Steven Croley has compared public choice with the "messy participative details of agency behavior"[128]—namely, rule making[129] and agency adjudication[130]—and concludes that "strong claims about the undesirability of regulatory government (commonly associated with public choice theory) seem overstated."[131] Indeed, as Croley correctly points out, if "the relationship between legislators and regulation-seeking interest groups constitutes the real lynchpin of the public choice theory—then reforms in the area of campaign finance, for one example, might go far to alleviate the problems that lead public choice theorists to call for deregulation."[132] As Peter Schuck notes, "Today, the administrative agency is often the site where public participation in lawmaking is most accessible, most meaningful, and most effective."[133]

In sum, while public choice theory does provide some insight into the weaknesses of current regulatory paradigms, it is far from a complete depiction of the regulatory process. It ignores the reality that private actors simply do not like competitive markets, the distributional and ideological functions of regulation, the practical reality of regulating an industry, the agency rule-making process, and the creation of regulation that has benefited workers and consumers.[134]

2. Exalting the private

If we assume away public choice's theoretical and empirical weaknesses, we are seemingly left with its central message: advocacy for a "deregulated" world of private contracts, uninhibited by the strictures of government, versus a "regulated" world of government intervention. To begin with, such a stark choice is imaginary. As Cass Sunstein correctly observes:

> What "deregulation" really means is a shift from the status quo to a system of different but emphatically legal regulation, more specifically one of property, tort, and contract rights, in which

government does not impose specific public interest obligations but instead sets up initial entitlements and then permits trades among owners and producers. *This is a regulatory system as much as any other. . . . The issue is thus not whether to "deregulate," but whether one or another regulatory system is better than imaginable alternatives.*[135]

Indeed, chapter 3 tried to highlight the flagrant inconsistencies among those who vehemently argue against economic regulation, yet passionately support other government interventions such as restrictive zoning and intellectual property rights. Even what appears at first glance to be a change in private law—such as a move from tort liability to strict liability—can serve as a proxy for regulation.[136]

In addition, the privatization solution assumes efficient rearrangement of private property rights despite transaction costs and behavioral biases. It is currently fashionable to argue that society needs "to reduce the size of the public sector through accelerated privatization projects, reducing the size of bureaucracy primarily by contracting out public functions to private parties."[137] The idea is somehow to make the public sphere look more like the private sphere, while at the same time giving these powerful private actors a dose of public values.[138] One of the movement's most eloquent defenders, Jody Freeman, posits that "privatization can be a means of 'publicization.' "[139] The literature touts "information disclosure . . . [and] self-regulation."[140]

Leaving aside the serious constitutional questions that privatization raises under current state-action doctrine,[141] its impressive rhetoric rests on weak foundations. It relies on the assumption that private actors are somehow more "efficient" than government. We are told that the "governance model promotes more *efficient* organization of public life, *efficient* use of public dollars, and *effective* delivery of governmental services."[142] Of course, no reasons are offered as to why the private sector is more "efficient": is it because private firms can externalize their costs onto workers and society more easily than government agencies could? Or are the putative efficiencies illusory to begin with, as observers are beginning to realize?[143] If "efficiency" is a vapid concept, then the arguments put forth by privatization scholars must rely on something more tangible, notably contract.[144] Indeed, Freeman suggests we rely on "contract, not hierarchy"[145] in a world where "government might insist on detailed contractual terms and on supervising compliance with them, conceivably requiring information disclosure, public consultation, mandatory auditing, and the like."[146] Needless to say, little mention is made of the problems inherent in contractual or market-based conceptions of social welfare.[147] The new privatization arguments fail precisely where contractarianism does.

There is much to suggest that private contract, while generally a powerful tool to allocate resources, is far from complete as a mechanism to organize ourselves as a society. As Mark Lemley points out in his study of organizations that set private standards, "Legal theorists too often tend to exalt private ordering as perfect and denigrate public rules as incompetent, corrupt, or both. My empirical exploration does not reveal a perfectly functioning contractual system, a fact that advocates of private ordering will have to come to terms with."[148] In his study of path dependence—namely, the idea that entities are able to entrench themselves not necessarily because they are more efficient, but because they were there first—Mark Roe provocatively notes that "[t]hinking about path dependence tempts us toward greater government direction. . . . [I]t would be most satisfying to believe in evolution-toward-efficiency if we could believe that no important path could be inefficient, a belief the modern biological analogy does not support."[149]

Perhaps the most significant and overarching danger behind public choice theories is that government policy will be isolated from the political processes of a democracy. As Rudolph Peritz eloquently argues in his history of competition policy:

> In the last two decades, the political sphere has come to be identified as an economic domain—most zealously so under the influence of Chicago School economist George Stigler's market metaphor for government regulation and the Public Choice school that has reified Stigler's metaphor. Thus, the logic of unification produces one domain—whether political or economic—rather than the first logic's bipolar opposition. *But the purity produced by the logic of unification comes at a high price: Lost in the collapse is one sphere's ethical principles and social goals.* For example, equality may give way to liberty, as happened in the *Lochner* era, or equitable concerns may yield to wealth maximization. . . . In both theoretical and practical terms, competition policy comes to reflect only one rhetoric, one vision of society, untempered by its historical counterweight, because the

unifying logic of collapsing domains either ignores ethical and te-
leological differences between economic and political realms or
understands them as closed to negotiation.[150]

Not only is regulation sometimes necessary, but it should reflect, and be
formulated within, the broader social discourse of a public political system.[151] Democracy should not be privatized and reduced to monetary
exchanges. As Ezra Suleiman convincingly argues, "If our culture more
and more sees the individual as a mere consumer and undermines citizen-
ship, the bureaucracy will be ill-equipped to step in and provide the
society with a sense of itself as a collectivity."[152] To boot, public choice's
lionization of private contract must necessarily imply a poor opinion of
public servants. To the extent that it discourages qualified people from
entering government service or accepting public interest work, this perspective is doubly unfortunate. Contractarianism has no doubt fed the
environment behind Suleiman's observation that "[i]n almost all democratic societies we have witnessed over the past two decades an incontest-
able phenomenon: relentless attacks on and denigration of the state."[153] In
particular, "the attacks on the federal government, whether with a hammer or with a velvet glove, achieved none of the grandiose goals of reducing alienation, creating a sense of community, increasing participation,
or increasing trust in government."[154] In his chronicle of the collapse of
public bureaucratic institutions, Suleiman even makes the jarring point
that "[b]y and large, public administration may no longer be a field looking to become a discipline[.]"[155]

The bottom line is that while public choice theory is useful in
pointing out government's problems, its faith in private contract is not
even close to offering a complete solution. Perhaps the former Federal
Reserve chairman Paul Volcker puts it most succinctly: "Markets are ab-
solutely indispensable. . . . But I don't think they are God."[156] At its core
the privatization argument fails because government is necessary to supplement and protect market actors from transaction costs, inequities, and
behavioral biases.[157]

Given this reality, one major function of government is to grapple
with mechanisms to ensure fair and open participation in markets. As
Alfred Kahn perceptively observes, "[F]ree markets may demand governmental interventions just as pervasive and quite possibly more imaginative
than direct regulation; but its lesson is that those interventions should to

the greatest extent possible preserve, supplement, and enhance competition, rather than suppress it."[158] The challenge is thus not to abandon government, but to find ways to make it better, to go beyond and "create a regulatory superstructure that encourages the betterment of regulatory technology itself . . . for it is nothing less than the aspiration that government, like all things human, can improve."[159]

Chapter 5

. . . Toward New Research

Some understandably frustrated legal commentators—who might intuitively grasp the sleights of hand chronicled in chapter 4—find "stalemate in economic theory"[1] and discount the role of economics in informing public policy. Frederick Rowe summarizes the situation somewhat dramatically,

> Across the philosophical spectrum, thoughtful scholars lament a "Crisis in Economic Theory" that no longer explains, predicts, or fits. The malaise spreads from stale microeconomic models that misperceive how modern enterprise ticks. Essentially, and in conception, they ignore the interplay of governments and business organizations, neglect the spontaneous spark of innovation, and forget the "ultimate resource" of enterprise: the genius of the human mind which defies axioms, calculus, or quantification. Riddled by "externalities," "exogenous variables," and "market failures," *economic analysis tells more and more about less and less.*[2]

While acknowledging this frustration, I resist the temptation to dismiss the economic paradigm as an instrument useless for achieving social justice. Overcoming the malaise requires focusing the tools of economic analysis on messy real-world problems, rather than on mathematically elegant theories. What Paul Joskow observed over thirty years ago remains sadly true today:

> Somehow one gets the distinct feeling that the important messages are being carried by the informal theories, stories, and behavioral observations, and that the formal models are trotted out *ex post* to demonstrate that some kind of formal apparatus can explain or

incorporate some of what is actually being observed. The formal models often have great mathematical elegance and are fun to play with and teach, but at least from this author's vantage point their existence has had a negligible effect on applied research and policy analysis in the industrial organization area.[3]

Joskow's observation applies well beyond industrial organization (IO): the most beautiful mathematical model is of limited use in practice if its hypotheses cannot be tested against real-world behavior. Unrealistic assumptions, often made by distinguished economists,[4] often only serve to make scholars already leery of the economic paradigm even more cynical.

Fortunately however, new economics research focused on real-world effects, not facile assumptions, is shedding new light on possible justifications for regulation. Assessing the contributions of this new work—whether it be post-Chicago law and economics, core theory, or behavioral economics[5]—casts further doubt on simplistic theories that extol the virtues of private common law. For their part, new-economy industries—characterized by network effects, intellectual property, and path dependence—provide an especially compelling case for government oversight.

Post-Chicago Law and Economics

Ironically, as neoclassical economics continues to dominate the imagination of most law and economics scholarship, a new crop of economists, loosely called the "post-Chicago school"[6] is going beyond conventional static analyses of supply-and-demand equilibria to understand strategic interactions among economic actors. In particular, these economists are concerned about how and when private firms, left to their own devices, can interact over time to harm competition and consumers.[7]

The post-Chicago school has its roots in the tradition of IO, a branch of economics concerned with understanding market power,[8] most often through studying the decisions of oligopolists.[9] IO challenges neoclassical economics in two principal ways. First, beginning with William Baumol's early work showing how firms often try to maximize their size,[10] scholars have questioned the view that firms exist simply to maximize profits. Second, and more broadly, IO shifts the focus away from static supply-and-demand curves toward a more realistic interpretation of how firms actually behave with each other and consumers over time.[11] The principal tool IO economists have introduced from mathematics is game theory, which essentially "posits that firms' optimal actions incorporate the anticipated reactions of their competitors, and vice versa."[12] The IO tradition recognizes the irrelevance of price theory where "small numbers, hidden information, hidden actions, and incomplete contracts can turn markets into games."[13]

Game-theoretic approaches stand, of course, in sharp contrast to simple neoclassical models.[14] As one commentator points out,

> Neoclassical models tend to base their analysis on a static view of competition, which emphasizes the expected results of competition, but does not give serious attention to how the behavior of individual firms leads the market to those predicted equilibria. . . . The ultimate result is a model that is skeptical about the possibility of successful anticompetitive behavior or results, and *so tends to strongly oppose governmental intervention in markets as a means to "protect" or "foster" competition.*[15]

In contrast, as Ian Ayres observes, game-theoretic economics "runs against the *laissez-faire* policy prescriptions of the Chicago school of law and economics."[16] IO's overarching insight, through its deployment of game theory, is the proposition that markets need to be studied as interactions among actors over time, not simply as a point where supply and demand intersect—competitive dynamics and long-term market effects need to be understood. This insight has been instrumental in laying the foundations of the post-Chicago School, which in turn has shed new light on the desirability of regulatory intervention.

One relatively straightforward contribution of post-Chicago economics is the realization that many markets are not contestable,[17] often due to large sunk costs that can serve as potent barriers to entry.[18] In particular, many large-scale infrastructure industries—notably telecommunications,[19] transportation,[20] and energy[21]—are noncontestable due the enormous costs any new entrant must assume simply to begin operations.[22] Perhaps the best example of how simplistic contestability analysis has condoned anticompetitive behavior is the airline industry. Much of the impetus behind deregulation has been the idea that the airline business is contestable—that airplanes "can readily be moved from market to market."[23] Unfortunately, the airline industry has remained oligopolistic two decades after deregulation, and the realization has dawned that conventional contestability analysis is naive. Robert Willig, a leading intellectual behind contestability theory, admits that

> [t]oday, it is common knowledge that airport space at key network nodes is scarce, and that critical airport assets may be controlled in a concentrated fashion by particular carriers, which may possess market power over travelers as a result. The possibilities for entry or production substitution into particular routes cannot be determined without reference to the place of the routes in carriers' networks, and to the impediments carriers may face in extending their networks to those routes.[24]

Alfred Kahn, the economic architect of airline deregulation, now warns that "the contestability of airline markets does not afford travelers sufficient protection."[25] The sobering reality has similarly dawned on realistic economists that franchise bidding, made so prominent by Harold Demsetz as an alternative to natural monopoly regulation,[26] simply does not work due to the power of entrenched incumbents.[27]

Sunk costs are but one category of barriers to entry and exit that can squelch new entrants. Another barrier is simply the size of incumbents—the neoclassical school remains blissfully unaware of the reality that scale economies can present barriers to entry and exit.[28] In addition, Michael Spence has shown that the investment practices of incumbent firms—notably, the decision to carry excess capacity—create strategic interactions that deter potential rivals from entering a market.[29]

Once a rival has entered, of course, a larger firm can take advantage of its scale to raise its rival's cost of doing business.[30] Examples include engaging in a massive public relations campaign, filing litigation, or even using its influence to obtain preferential legislation.[31] Perhaps the most direct way to raise a rival's costs, however, is via exclusionary agreements. The classic example of exclusionary conduct is a vertical agreement or merger that can come in many flavors. One is "input foreclosure,"[32] where a powerful firm "may gain the ability to raise price by contracting [or merging] with input suppliers for the suppliers' agreements not to deal with the purchasing firm's competitors on equal terms."[33] The phenomenon, naturally, is broader than input foreclosure, and can include "customer foreclosure."[34] During the 1980s, Philippe Aghion and Patrick Bolton demonstrated that incumbents will sign long-term contracts with customers to prevent the entry of lower-cost producers.[35] Building on this insight, other commentators have shown how customer foreclosure plays itself out through a free-rider scenario: each individual customer, anticipating that no entry will occur, is willing to agree to sign an exclusivity contract with the incumbent firm in exchange for a small discount.[36] By serving to exclude rivals from the market, these agreements "severely constrain the dynamic process by which social wealth is created."[37] Post-Chicago analysis of exclusionary agreements provides yet another illustration of how private contracts—a subject of worship in conventional law and economics[38]—frequently need public oversight.

CORE THEORY

As if post-Chicago economics were not enough to point to new reasons for regulatory oversight, along comes core theory. It predicts that in some industries characterized by high fixed costs, competitive equilibrium is simply not possible: the fact that unregulated competition may be harmful invites the need for regulation. Core theory, like the post-Chicago school, stems from the IO tradition in its foundational reliance on cooperative game theory, which looks at dynamic strategic interactions among market participants.[39] At a basic level, a game or market is said to have a "core" if goods can be traded among participants such that the "final allocations are in the hands of those who value most what they get."[40] While this scenario might be valid where it is possible to disaggregate supply to meet changing demand, it becomes questionable in industries characterized by high fixed costs. As Stephen Pirrong points out, "[W]hen costs are characterized by indivisibilities (for example, avoidable costs) and demand is finely divisible, the core may be 'empty.' In other words, a competitive equilibrium frequently fails to exist, and, as a consequence, competitive interactions between firms cannot generate an efficient allocation of resources."[41]

At one level core theory further confirms why cutthroat competition can afflict industries characterized by high fixed costs:[42] stuck with fixed capacity, firms will try to recover whatever they can by "pricing at (or below) the incremental cost of production."[43] More importantly, it cleverly posits that faced with an empty core, "competition may require some cooperation in order to obtain efficiency"[44]—for instance, to better control capacity. To this point, core theory's arguments might appear interesting and counterintuitive, but as having very little to do with regulation. Core theorists, however, have made the link by studying the harmful effects that emerge when industries with high fixed costs are unregulated and subject only to antitrust. In particular, George Bittlingmayer's analysis of the wave of industrial mergers at the turn of the twentieth century shows that faced with antitrust's strict prohibition against cooperation, firms will do the next best thing: merge.[45] Many industries continue to consolidate, further lending credence to core theory's hypothesis; indeed, as core theory would predict, the pace of merger activity has been most frenetic in infrastructure industries with high fixed costs and overcapacity, such as airlines and telecommunications.[46]

Given that core theory predicts that under certain circumstances cartels, or other collusive devices, might be "efficient,"[47] it might be natural to discount the theory as yet another attack on government intervention. But a more nuanced interpretation is necessary. In the same way that the very existence of a firm is predicated on transaction costs that render market ordering ineffectual,[48] core theory suggests that "the difficulty associated with fixed costs can be thought of as one variety of market failure that requires a partial suppression of independence and the competitive mechanism."[49] This would suggest that there should be certain limited exemptions to the antitrust laws to allow government-monitored agreements among competitors where market mechanisms are inadequate. This approach is remarkably consistent with the intuition of prominent scholars who have made similar suggestions, but have done so without the benefit of core theory.[50]

As Bittlingmayer himself points out, the observations of core theory

> suggest that explicit cartelization, tacit collusion, and horizontal merger can be viewed, in many instances, as the noncompetitive arrangements that the firms in an industry must necessarily adopt. *Whether the resulting arrangements are in any sense optimal is another matter, and in some cases it may turn out to be correct to substitute government regulation or ownership for self-regulation.*[51]

As chapter 6 will argue, why not envision a public approach where government regulation manages those specific portions of industrial organization prone to an empty core, letting competition flourish elsewhere? Note that this approach does not necessarily imply a return to cartelization as the New Deal wrought. It does suggest, however, identifying which portions of an industry are prone to an empty core and regulating only those elements.[52]

BEHAVIORAL ECONOMICS

Chapter 4 has already explored how basic ideas from the emerging field of behavioral economics cast doubt on many of the Chicago school's assumptions. Behavioral economics has enjoyed some well-deserved recognition in the past decade, and a number of thoughtful treatments exist that cover the breadth of the topic.[53] The next step for behavioralists will be to help inform public policy. Roger Noll and James Krier have been among the first to point out the regulatory implications of this new line of research:

> The cognitive theory of choice under uncertainty offers two sorts of insights of some relevance to analysts interested in the regulation of risk. First, people take shortcuts (use heuristics) that lead them to make mistakes about variables (such as probability) relevant to evaluating risk. Second, putting the mistakes aside, they approach risk in ways that depart from the norms and assumptions of conventional decision analysis.[54]

More recently, Cass Sunstein has surfaced the broader policy questions inherent in the behavioral project:

> Is it possible for those involved in law to "debias" people, in the process, perhaps, lengthening human lives? What institutions work best at reducing the effects of biases? . . . Despite the amount of work done thus far, behavioral law and economics remains in its earliest stages, and much remains to be done in promoting its basic goals—*helping to produce new and improved understandings of the real-world effects of law, and ultimately better uses of law as an instrument of social ordering.*[55]

Sunstein and other behavioralists have started to develop this research agenda by providing new justifications for regulation based on the behavioral biases of people.[56] The regulatory economist Alfred Kahn has explored how, in unregulated markets, "[c]ompetition can in some circumstances make unrealistic demands on consumers as well—assuming a greater ability on their part to make complex choices, on pain of suffering penalties to which they had not previously been subjected, than they either have or are willing to take the trouble to acquire."[57] Another vibrant area of research is how law can steer individuals toward more rational choices, without appearing heavy-handed—something that Sunstein has labeled "libertarian paternalism,"[58] and other leading scholars have called "asymmetric paternalism."[59] These proposals typically emphasize a less-heavy-handed approach to regulation that offers choice to consumers—for example, via tweaking default rules, providing mandatory disclosure, and imposing "cooling off" periods.[60] Marketable rights that can be traded among companies, used primarily in the context of environmental regulation, are another example of less heavy-handed regulation.[61]

A related effort is the attempt to move game theory beyond its assumptions of rationality—and in doing so, add behavioral insights to those of the post-Chicago school. It is important to remember that the application of game theory to economics, despite its quantum improvement over conventional price theory, still has its roots in Nobel laureate John Nash's celebrated paper, *The Bargaining Problem*.[62] Nash idealizes the bargaining problem by assuming that the players "are highly rational, that each can accurately compare his desires for various things, that they are equal in bargaining skill, and that each has full knowledge of the tastes and preferences of the other."[63] Nash's insights, while pathbreaking, are also unfinished—modeling the behavior of individuals is not as simple as assuming rational actors to derive a Nash equilibrium. As Colin Camerer asks: "Is game theory meant to describe actual choices by people and institutions or not? It is remarkable how much game theory has been done while largely ignoring this question."[64] Camerer proposes a move toward behavioral game theory that "aims to replace descriptively inaccurate modelling principles with more psychologically reasonable ones, expressed as parsimoniously and formally as possible."[65] Scholars have already begun to propose a number of important adjuncts to traditional game theory, including an understanding of the role of fairness,[66] emotions,[67] culture,[68] and imperfect information.[69]

Beyond proposing less-heavy-handed regulation and incorporating human behavior into game theory, a third promising area of behavioral research explores new theories of the firm. Despite their seemingly sophisticated economics, existing theories have been complicit in poor public policy, as witnessed by recurring crises in corporate governance, most recently the Wall Street scandals chronicled in chapter 3. Research into three behavioral miscalculations—overconfidence, the self-serving bias, and herding—provides a useful starting point to modeling the firm in a more realistic manner.

The overconfidence bias has been well-studied in the context of individual decision-making.[70] Donald Langevoort remarks,

> One of the most robust findings in the literature on individual decisionmaking is that of the systematic tendency of people to over-rate their own abilities, contributions, and talents. This egocentric bias readily takes the form of excessive optimism and overconfidence, coupled with an inflated sense of ability to control events and risks.[71]

William Bratton's observation on the reasons behind the Enron fiasco applies equally well to any of the corporate scandals we have witnessed since the late 1990s:

> The firm [Enron] collapsed for the most mundane of reasons—its managers suffered the behavioral biases of successful entrepreneurs. They overemphasized the upside and lacked patience. They pursued heroic short-term growth numbers that their business plan could not deliver. That pursuit of immediate shareholder value caused them to become risk-prone, engaging in levered speculation, earnings manipulation, and concealment of critical information.[72]

The utility-maximizing business executive (of neoclassical fame) would not engage in such activity, but an overconfident one might. Closely related to the overconfidence bias is the "self-serving" bias, "the term used to describe the observation that actors often interpret information in ways that serve their interests or preconceived notions."[73] This bias, in turn, can help explain much puzzling corporate behavior, such as misleading investors regarding the prospects of the firm's future stock performance. Before the bulk of the current corporate fiascos erupted, Robert Prentice presciently argued that the self-serving bias even creates temptations for business service providers, such as public accountants:

> Auditors, like others, tend to act according to its [the self-serving bias's] dictates. They are more likely to falsify the numbers or simply

"look the other way" when it suits their purposes (e.g., allowing them to keep a lucrative client). They are more likely to resist client requests to fudge the numbers when that course of action serves their best interests (e.g., preventing unacceptable litigation risk). *Whether decisions to audit recklessly are conscious or (more often) subconscious, they are products of the self-serving bias.*[74]

The accounting scandals that rocked the corporate world a few months later confirm the warning. There is also the danger that group dynamics will exacerbate pernicious phenomena such as overconfidence and the self-serving bias. As Robert Shiller notes, "People who interact with each other regularly tend to think and behave similarly."[75] A phenomenon, typically labeled "groupthink" or "herding," emerges. This "groupthink causes members of a group to unconsciously generate shared illusions of superiority that hinder critical reflection and reality testing."[76] The mechanism that underlies this phenomenon is a desire by members of the group to be judged favorably by their superiors and peers,[77] leading to facile consensus at the expense of constructive dissent. Perhaps the herding bias sheds some light on why boards of directors—often composed of remarkably similar individuals—are often shockingly ineffective.[78]

Many of the distasteful activities we have witnessed firm actors perpetrate—fudging accounting statements, lying to employees and prosecutors, flaunting conflict-of-interest rules, and the like—are puzzling to laissez-faire interpretations of law and economics precisely because these activities cannot be explained through the lens of rational actors going about maximizing wealth or even utility. An understanding of overconfidence, the self-serving bias, and herding, however, starts to yield explanations that go well beyond the conventional wisdom. The next step will be to move from piecemeal behavioral analysis to "organizational behavioral economics"—an attempt to aggregate these individual biases into a coherent framework. Organizational economists at Carnegie Mellon University, led by the Nobel laureate Herbert Simon, conducted seminal research during the 1950s and 1960s.[79] During the 1980s and 1990s, Amitai Etzioni's brilliant critique of the neoclassical paradigm explored how organizations "cease to be efficient tools, if they ever were."[80] Yet the idea of combining organizational behavior and economics remains elusive. A starting point, building on Simon and Etzioni's work, might be to posit that firms develop counterproductive norms that are harmful not only to broader society but, ironically, also to the firm itself.[81]

Overall, emerging research in behavioral economics will continue to yield rich implications for regulatory policy. As Russell Korobkin and Thomas Ulen point out, the goal of behavioral economics "is to understand the incentive effects of law better than modern law and economics is able to do by enlisting more sophisticated understandings of both the ends of those governed by law and the means by which they attempt to achieve their ends."[82] To this objective, the "question for economics is not whether to include or exclude psychology, but rather what type of psychology to include."[83] Indeed, behavioral economics is part of a larger project in empirical economics that thankfully understands that "economic reality seldom adheres very closely to the textbook model of perfect competition."[84] Rather, as Korobkin and Ulen succinctly note, "The seminal insight that economics provides to the analysis of law is that people respond to incentives—a generalized statement of price theory."[85] A corollary is to recognize the particular strength of economics: a disciplined focus on looking, *ex ante*, at the costs and benefits of society's choices going forward—as if to say, utopian speculation if fine, but at the end of the day, who pays?[86] Developing hypotheses, then gathering real-world data to prove or disprove them, can unleash the true power of law and economics to address this question, and in doing so provide guidance on how to allocate resources in a manner that improves society. As Arthur Leff points out, "[I]f you were interested in a society, and with law as an operative variable within that society, you would have to find out something about that subject matter and those operations. You would, it seems, have to become an empiricist."[87] Donald Langevoort observes, "Nearly all interesting legal issues require accurate predictions about human behavior to be resolved satisfactorily. . . . [I]f these predictions are naive and intuitive, without any strong empirical grounding, they are susceptible to error and ideological bias."[88]

Contrast this plain reality with the purposeful ignorance of traditional law and economics as to how the real world actually works. Robert Bork, for instance, presents a vision of antitrust that "must avoid any standards that require direct measurement and quantification of either restriction, output or efficiency."[89] To be sure, neoclassicism's facile assumptions are remarkably elegant;[90] by contrast, empirical economics is messy and lacks grand predictive power.[91] Actual field research is difficult to do. As Robert Ellickson notes in the context of the stunning disregard of transaction costs by traditional law and economics:

[E]conomic theorists would need to add transaction costs to their equations to embark on the grubby (but essential) business of trying to monetize transaction costs in actual settings. This work is likely to be more difficult and less elegant than armchair theorizing about whether strategic behavior, or wealth effects, or nonconvexities, or what-not might undermine Coase-Theorem predictions about life in the never-never-world of zero transaction costs. Transaction costs themselves thus help explain why there has been little empirical work on transaction costs.[92]

To be sure, empirical methodologies are imperfect, but it is far better to debate methodology than simply to rely on nonfalsifiable assumptions that conveniently cut against regulation. And despite these challenges, empirical work is already yielding rich insights. In the area of consumer protection, behavioral research casts strong doubt on the argument that advertising serves merely to inform consumers so that they can make rational choices. Jon Hanson and Douglas Kysar have used empirical evidence to show how consumers are manipulated by marketers, and how "this manipulation has been successful and will continue to be so until policymakers take behavioralism as seriously as marketers do."[93] New research even suggests that consumers as a class are being systematically manipulated—as Jon Hanson and David Yosifon point out, "[E]ven though individuals and institutions may behave *as if* their goal were to maximize wealth, such behavior may actually reflect the social stage of interactions (the situation) more than it does the disposition of the actors."[94] Elizabeth Warren's research suggests that a re-regulation of consumer finance, especially the capping of allowable interest rates, would make for improved policy and a consequent reduction in bankruptcy rates.[95] She convincingly argues that a ceiling on interest rates would create a market-based solution: since lenders "would no longer be allowed to charge exorbitant interest rates to families with marginal credit records, it would become unprofitable for lenders to pursue families in financial trouble."[96] In a vastly different context, but based on his foundational work in experimental economics that seeks to test regulatory schemes before implementing them,[97] the Nobel laureate Vernon Smith has suggested the use of variable-rate (peak load) pricing as a means to resolving the seemingly intractable problems surrounding electricity deregulation.[98]

Other scholars are beginning to address many of the broader remaining questions using an empirical approach—for instance, whether Supreme Court precedent does in fact have an impact on the judiciary's review of administrative agency action,[99] or whether taxes or legal rules are the preferable means of redistributing wealth.[100] Of course, much of this research is still underdeveloped, and innovative economists not wedded to neoclassicism's strictures readily admit that much more work needs to be done.[101]

Going forward, interdisciplinary research will become even more critical. Both economists and other social scientists need to heed Amitai Etzioni's advice "to reintegrate economics and other social science disciplines."[102] As Coase himself warns in a retrospective on his own work, "None of the essays in this book deals with the character of human preferences, nor, as I have said, do I believe that economists will be able to make much headway until a great deal more work has been done by sociobiologists and other noneconomists."[103]

SPECIAL PROBLEMS OF NEW-ECONOMY INDUSTRIES

New-economy industries typically involve initial large investments in intellectual property that are then commercialized on a large scale, often over networks—high-technology industries such as computer software and Internet-based products and services are prototypical examples. Confronted with the special difficulties of these industries, commentators who espouse a laissez-faire ideology throw up their hands and predictably suggest government get out of the way.[104] Of course, this belies the reality that government intervention has often been necessary to spur innovation.[105] Indeed, new economic research suggests that public regulation may be especially appropriate in new-economy industries, where intellectual property rights, network effects, and path dependence can result in profoundly uncompetitive markets. Dynamic market analysis as envisioned by post-Chicago economics is a must in these industries with short product cycles.[106] There are, however, at least three additional complications that render simplistic neoclassical analyses problematic.

The first is that many incumbents protect their positions using ever-expanding intellectual property (IP) rights. On the one hand, there are the well-touted Schumpeterian gales of "creative destruction"[107] that can uproot competitive advantages in high-technology markets. On the other, there exists the real possibility that an incumbent can use its intellectual property rights to maintain a proprietary stranglehold that slows technological innovation.[108] At the very least, policy makers must recognize that IP is a counterintuitive form of regulatory intervention that not only

exalts the private over the public, but rewards activities with high development (fixed) costs and low distribution (variable) costs.[109] IP in itself
thus creates a scale effect that presents a barrier to entry.[110]

Second, network effects only make things more complicated by
serving as an additional barrier to entry. These effects can be conceptualized as demand-side economies of scale, where "products for which the
utility that a user derives from the consumption of the good increases
with the number of other agents consuming the good."[111] They are
demand-side analogies to the role scale and sunk costs play on the supply
side.[112] Such effects apply both to real networks, such as telecommunications[113] and transportation systems,[114] and to virtual networks, such as the
"network of Apple Macintosh users, the network of users of Microsoft
Excel, or the network of users in DVD machines."[115] In a market exhibiting network effects, consumers will be reluctant to switch to a techno-
logically superior product offered by a new entrant: in addition to the
usual switching costs, the new product might be incompatible with the
installed base the existing technology enjoys.[116]

Third, network effects are also eerily reminiscent of free-rider problems engendered by exclusionary agreements: "[I]f consumers expect a
seller to be dominant, then consumers will be willing to pay more for the
firm's product, and it will, in fact, be dominant."[117] To further limit competition with their networks, incumbent firms too often oppose open
standards that ensure compatibility.[118] Without countervailing regulation,
network effects and intellectual property can combine forces to entrench
incumbents. Robert Pitofsky summarizes the matter as follows:

> Because of the nature of markets characterized by intellectual prop-
> erty, there is a tendency to drift to single-firm dominance and even
> monopoly for two reasons. First, in order to encourage initial in-
> vestments, the law provides intellectual property protection (prima-
> rily via patent and copyright law) and, in effect, precludes competition
> within the scope of the intellectual property for a period of time.
> Second, products and services based on intellectual property fre-
> quently exhibit "network effects."[119]

As Pitofsky succinctly puts it, "[T]here remains the concern that consumers will be exploited while we wait for the future to arrive."[120] New research is also helping to grasp the forces that underlie network effects.
For instance, building from the foundational notion that, with a good

exhibiting a network effect, an extra unit of production actually enhances the value of units already in existence, the network effects problem might be reconceptualized as the inverse of the durable goods problem antitrust economics has faced for decades.[121] Looking beyond the strictures of neoclassical price theory also shows that network effects can often combine with overexpansive intellectual property rights to lock in customers, thereby exacerbating path dependencies.[122] Incumbents are able to entrench themselves not because they are more innovative or valuable, but simply because they were there first. In network industries, the central question will become how regulators can protect consumers by creating an environment that prevents incumbency from squelching innovation.[123]

SOME COMMONALITIES

Robert Ellickson remarks, "The mark of a true economist is not fealty to the classical rational-actor model, but rather openness to any technique that would improve understanding of complex human behavior."[124] To become relevant to debates on social justice, law and economics must begin to address a series of uncomfortable questions concerning inequalities in wealth and bargaining power.[125] As Alfred Kahn candidly observes in his landmark treatment, *The Economics of Regulation*,

> The regulatory power is in principle virtually unlimited. How vigorously and intelligently it will be exercised (and the rate of pay, financial support, and quality of administrative personnel is obviously one aspect of this same phenomenon) will depend on the basically political question of how power is distributed between producer and consumer interests, between public officials and private managers, and how aggressive are the interventions of public officials in asserting their conception of the public interest.[126]

Perhaps surprisingly, the issues that Kahn raises are strikingly similar to those that critical legal theorists have been raising for nearly three decades,[127] and that remain central to contemporary "outsider" scholarship such as critical race, feminist, and gay legal writing. Much of this work uncovers how seemingly innocuous legal forms and assumptions can make the status quo appear natural. Similarly, new economic research—the post-Chicago school, core theory, behavioral law and economics, and an understanding of the special problems of new-economy industries—remains loyal to the behavioral and empirical roots of economics, while, perhaps unknowingly, heeding the critical school's warning that basic assumptions can unwittingly legitimate inequality. Economics should not be hijacked as a tool to legitimate public policy that perpetuates social inequalities. Instead, emphasis must squarely remain on framing the problem, disentangling assumptions, and gathering data. The analyst should not be allowed to hide behind the legitimating veneer of reassuring neoclassical assumptions.

To be sure, even the most advanced, most socially-minded economics is not a panacea—it is merely an input to democratic discourse into which noneconomic factors must necessarily enter. As Herbert Hovenkamp argues,

> [E]conomists—even free market economists—have recognized an important difference between theoretical economics and public policymaking, particularly if the policies are being made in a democratic State. The public purpose of theoretical economics is not to eliminate distributive justice as a public policy concern. Rather, it is to enable policymakers to make some judgments about the cost or effectiveness of a particular policy.[128]

Put succinctly in Alfred Kahn's words, "What economists are good at, in politics, is pointing out the benefits of economically efficient arrangements."[129] A willingness to incorporate new economics research into public policy is merely a step forward in making these difficult judgments. So far, each new stream of work has uncovered additional limitations to private contract, and a consequent need to reinvigorate public law as either a supplement or an alternative. By contrast, conventional law and economics scholarship continues to hide behind the cloak of its neoclassical assumptions and reassuring mathematical models. Perhaps it is no surprise that over the past two decades, traditional law and economics research has created mounting frustration among scholars focused on social justice. Indeed, those wedded to further mathematical refinement of neoclassical assumptions might be wise to heed Gary Becker's warning:

> The problem with having a discipline that is too theoretical is that you begin to discuss the problems raised by other theorists rather than the problems raised by trying to understand the world out there. To some extent that is happening in Law and Economics. If that is not corrected, there is a greater likelihood the field will

become sterile and will not grow like other fields that have a closer interaction between data and various forms and theory.[130]

Merton Miller, who like Becker is a Nobel laureate in economic sciences, is even more blunt: "I don't think I could find many cases where the mathematical modeling actually led to new truths."[131] If there is a supervening similarity among the new research methodologies outlined above, it is that each is usefully focused on discovering what is really going on in the world. As part 3 will explore, however, these new developments do not simply suggest a return to "command and control" regulation as it has been historically practiced. They do suggest, however, a careful rethinking of our existing paradigms for regulation and deregulation.

Part III

A Path Forward

Chapter 6

Substantive Reform

By this point, it should be clear that the conventional polarized debate surrounding regulation is incomplete, and that new economic research suggests a path forward. Raising consciousness, shifting the dialogue away from a simplistic trashing of regulatory policy, and focusing efforts on pragmatic reforms constitute the very important next step.[1] The operative question remains how to harmonize the difference between what the welfare economist A.C. Pigou has called "*the value of the marginal private* and *the value of the marginal social net product*."[2]

The natural question that emerges, therefore, is how to begin minimizing the difference between public and private benefits, or surplus. What are some policy prescriptions to get started on substantive regulatory reform? My suggestions are first centered on two of the most difficult questions facing social and economic regulation, respectively: measuring the health, safety, and environmental benefits of agency action, and allowing access to bottleneck resources. The chapter then argues that the overarching challenge toward achieving reform will be to rekindle "publicness" in regulation. It concludes by using the concept of publicness to address arguably the most pressing issue in regulatory theory today—how to reform the regulation of public corporations.

Social Regulation: Rescuing Cost/Benefit Analysis

In the realm of social regulation there is a desperate and urgent need for agencies to make better use of cost/benefit analysis. Such a proposal will at first blush no doubt strike some readers as strange; after all, in a book that attempts to show how traditional law and economics has alienated those concerned with social justice, it would seem bizarre to argue for more economics. The apparent paradox, however, dissolves quickly: as seen repeatedly throughout the book, analysis trumpeted by antiregulation advocates as "economic" is too often nothing more than ideology under the guise of science.

Objective cost/benefit analysis, rather surprisingly, is a rarity in administrative decision-making—more often, it is either ignored or performed incorrectly. Take, for instance, the core of contemporary social regulation, which is standard setting—something "aimed at objectives as diverse as increasing workplace and product safety, producing a cleaner environment, and providing consumers with better information."[3] Stephen Breyer's observations, made over twenty years ago, unfortunately still ring true today. Succinctly put, his conclusion is that agencies typically do not "begin setting standards under a new regulatory program by first conducting a cost/benefit analysis to establish priorities."[4] Consider the National Highway Traffic Safety Administration's (NHTSA) attempt at setting automobile safety standards to save lives:

> NHTSA, for example, did not simply consider how it might best save lives. Had it used even a very rough cost/benefit analysis to do so, instead of starting with head restraints, it might have worked on mandating special devices to stop illegal speeding, such as flashing lights on the outside of a car that would indicate a speed above 60 mph. A cost/benefit analysis might also have suggested that instead of mandating an elaborate new truck brake technology, NHTSA should have tried to improve brake maintenance. Yet auto and truck technology, not speed control or repair shops, formed the context of the political debate out of which NHTSA emerged, and it is not surprising that NHTSA turned to that debate for an initial agenda.[5]

Of course, it is more than fair for those readers focused on social justice to ask whether cost/benefit analysis will help or hurt the cause, given the plethora of regulatory "scorecards" putatively showing how the costs of regulation vastly outweigh the benefits. Little faith, however, should be placed in these antiregulation studies. In a detailed, eye-opening study of three of the most prestigious of these scorecards—those by John Morrall at the Office of Management and Budget (OMB), Robert Hahn at the American Enterprise Institute (AEI)–Brookings Joint Center for Regulatory Studies, and John Graham and Tammy Tengs of the Harvard Center for Risk Analysis—Richard Parker concludes that these often-trumpeted studies represent "deeply flawed analyses which fail to prove their own conclusions."[6] The errors Parker finds are almost too numerous to name. The scorecards

- alter agency numbers in undisclosed and arbitrary ways;

- draw on biased samples of regulation;

- undervalue the benefit of reducing risk to life and health;

- misrepresent ex ante guesses as actual cost-benefit measurements;

- falsely assume that regulations will never be eased or modified;

- disregard major categories of quantified and monetized benefits;

- disregard all unquantified costs and benefits;

- ignore important non-linearities of risk and risk preferences, as well as cumulative and distributive impacts;

- assume that savings from regulations foregone will be redirected to save lives, even though no mechanism for accomplishing such a redirection exists; and

- conceal important uncertainties, as well as virtually all the omissions and alterations discussed above.[7]

In showing that these scorecards "fail badly"[8] Parker convincingly demonstrates the shoddiness of the "empirical foundation for the anti-regulatory fervor that has gripped Congress, academia, and millions of Americans for over a decade."[9]

Once the importance of conducting accurate cost/benefit analysis is appreciated, attention can be focused on bettering the tool itself.[10] As Howard Gruenspecht and Lester Lave note, "Any systematic approach to reforming HSE (health, safety, environmental) regulation requires that both benefits and costs be quantified. Laying out the costs is relatively straightforward, although far from trivial. *Quantifying the benefits is much more difficult.*"[11] Indeed, "[p]erhaps the most glaring feature in regulatory practice is the wide divergence of opinion as to the benefits of externality control."[12] A first step to narrowing the uncertainty would be to assign the quantification task to scientists and engineers—today, too often politicians and economists try to quantify the benefits of social regulation, but inevitably bring with them ideological bias.[13] Also, recall from chapter 1 that social regulation is often a response to externalities—quantifying the benefits of regulation thus gives insight into the costs of the externality. Once this link is made, a new opportunity for regulatory reform emerges: expanding the notion of tradable rights to externalities by defining new markets in externalities, beyond their initial deployment in environmental law.[14] Alfred Kahn persuasively says,

> I believe that the most productive regulatory reform activity in the next several years will be in introducing marketlike techniques that will enable us to achieve given regulatory goals at minimum cost. . . . Here is a cause to which both proponents and opponents of environmental and other kinds of social and protective regulation could fruitfully subscribe, if only they could submerge their mutual distrust about each other's ultimate intentions, and concentrate instead on these innovative regulatory techniques.[15]

Indeed, correct cost/benefit analyses could start to address the central puzzle externalities present in welfare economics: "the lack of markets for such goods or bads."[16]

Once economics begins "pursuing the valuation of nonmarket goods and services[,]"[17] then nonquantifiable and distributional factors can be added to the mix.[18] Good social science is a first step to better law. Gruenspecht and Lave show that not only does the general public desire health, safety, and environmental regulation, but that it is prepared to pay for it—opposition stems "from frustration with their heavy-handed and inefficient manner of operation rather than from opposition to their goals."[19] They note that "[w]hen a movement as sweeping and important as the environmentalist-consumerist movement occurs, economists should not be complaining two decades later that government programs are not efficient; we should have done more to show how to improve the efficiency and effectiveness of these social programs."[20] New solutions in social regulation will only emerge if we are willing to get beyond rhetoric and ideology and move toward empirical methods.[21] In the realm of social regulation, perhaps more directly than anywhere else, attention to empirical economic analysis is a critical first step to achieving goals of social justice. Meaningful cost/benefit analysis would be a good place to start.

ECONOMIC REGULATION: GAINING ACCESS TO BOTTLENECKS

Network industries—telecommunications, transportation, energy, and the like—are doubly important to economic regulation. First, they provide, as Posner puts it, "the essential infrastructure of modern industrial society."[22] Second, network industries are the testing ground for the thorniest problems in regulatory policy, since they often present both supply-side economies of scale and demand-side network effects, giving incumbents advantages that are insurmountable unless consumers and new entrants receive regulatory relief.

The traditional method to protect consumers from being exploited by natural monopolies inherent in many network industries has been retail rate regulation. But this regulatory tool has been susceptible to a never-ending barrage of often justifiable criticism, beginning with Averch and Johnson's seminal article.[23] Faced with these difficulties, Stephen Breyer's trailblazing book *Regulation and Its Reform* suggested the metaphor of "less restrictive alternatives,"[24] and laid out "a framework that sees classical regulation as a weapon of last resort and looks for less restrictive ways to deal with problems thought to call for regulation."[25] Breyer's paradigm proved to be quite prescient: as the 1980s and 1990s unfolded, technological innovation dramatically narrowed the scope of natural monopoly in a variety of industries. For example, long-haul telecommunications networks and the generation of electricity can now be separated from local telephone and electricity wires—with competition possible on the former, regulation can be limited to the latter. As Joseph Kearney and Thomas Merrill point out,

> The original [rate regulation] paradigm was created because of widespread perceptions of market failure in regulated industries, most prominently the presence of natural monopolies. In recent decades, however, advances in technology have eliminated many of the natural monopoly features of these industries, or at least have significantly reduced their scope.[26]

Or, simply put in Paul Joskow and Roger Noll's words, "The fact that components of the network have natural monopoly characteristics does not necessarily imply that every part of the industry ought to be a monopoly."[27]

As a consequence, the locus of attention must move away from simply setting retail rates and controlling the entry and exit of players, and toward improving the narrow regulation of bottlenecks where it is prohibitively expensive for new entrants to compete with incumbents. In telecommunications, for example, the bottleneck is typically the last mile of cable or copper wire going into subscribers' homes.[28] Eli Noam even suggests that "[i]n a competitive regime, interconnection rights will achieve most of the goals that lie behind common carriage."[29] In the electricity and natural gas industries, the high fixed costs of transmission and local distribution represent bottlenecks to competition.[30] As Paul Joskow persuasively argues, "A retail competition program must start by unbundling competitive services (generation service supplies and their associated costs) from regulated monopoly services (transmission, distribution, and designated stranded-cost charges)."[31] Similarly, Curtis Grimm and Clifford Winston discuss "the problems that could arise when shippers must depend on only one railroad—a growing possibility as the industry consolidates[,]"[32] suggesting the unbundling of railroad network elements as one option to overcome the problem.[33] Bottlenecks, however, are not limited to communications or transportation networks—they can arise whenever supply-side economies of scale or demand-side network effects give incumbents the upper hand. Computer operating systems, airport landing slots, and computerized airline-reservation systems are but three other examples. In each case, competition would be possible but for the fact that the larger or more established firms control an essential input to the end product.

To address this problem—rather than regulating rates, or the "output," of a monopolist—competitors should be allowed access to these critical "inputs" that are costly to duplicate. This new approach is effective, since it allows competition to flourish in the nonbottleneck portions of the network, while protecting consumers from monopoly rents in the bottleneck portions. William Rogerson echoes Breyer's suggestion when he points out that "[r]egulating narrowly defined inputs instead of outputs is one approach regulators can use to attempt to confine regulation to as small a sphere as possible, and thereby allow the benefits of competition to infuse more segments of an industry."[34] To be sure, some regulatory mandates have tried to implement this lesson. In the telecommunications sector, Congress has required incumbents to unbundle their local networks to allow access to new entrants.[35] The Federal Energy Regulatory Commission (FERC) has similarly ordered electric utilities to open their transmission lines to competition.[36] Unfortunately, however, regulatory agencies have to this point approached the unbundling of incumbents' networks with precious little economic discipline.

There are several reasons why existing attempts to allow access to bottlenecks have been a mixed success. First, and most simply, regulators have missed the bottleneck. As chapter 5 discussed in the context of contestability theory, the problems surrounding airline deregulation can be traced to the fact that many deregulators did not realize that airport landing slots and gates, rather than the airplanes themselves, are the bottleneck.[37] Second, regulators have calculated the access price incorrectly. The most notable case is the FCC's attempt to foster competition in local telephony by allowing new competitors access to incumbents' local networks at the incremental cost of a maximally efficient network.[38] The result has been protracted litigation by incumbents in court, as well as a slew of bankruptcies among new entrants. Fortunately, economists have developed solutions to the pricing problem, notably by basing access pricing on the opportunity cost to the incumbent of not being able to use the input itself.[39]

The third, and most complex, reason why implementation has been problematic is counterintuitive: regulators have sometimes tried to unbundle too much of the network. The most egregious example perhaps is the FCC's repeatedly poor implementation of its congressional mandate to provide competitive access to the "necessary" elements of incumbents' networks.[40] As Justice Breyer has insightfully noted in the context of the FCC's overly expansive unbundling of local telephone networks,

> Increased sharing by itself does not automatically mean increased competition. *It is in the unshared, not in the shared, portions of the enterprise that meaningful competition would likely emerge.* Rules that force firms to share *every* resource or element of a business would create not competition, but pervasive regulation, for the regulators, not the marketplace, would set the relevant terms.[41]

Most poignantly, in the context of broadband competition, overly expansive unbundling at too low a price created a great irony. Put simply, the FCC's poor methodology hurt the new telecommunications competitors it was supposed to encourage. New entrants had the usual business incentives to expand, but were not forced to develop any competitive advantage. As Jerry Hausman has argued, these broadband competitors "spent large sums of money on marketing, but customer churn remained high because none of the companies had a superior product to sell. . . . [Eventually,] equity values . . . plummeted and capital markets became closed to them. The result was bankruptcy. Faulty regulation led to a large expenditure of money with little remaining in terms of real assets."[42]

But what limiting principle can be used? The essential facilities doctrine from antitrust law can help address the problem. The doctrine carves out an exception to the general rule that a firm has no obligation to deal with its competitors; it states that in certain circumstances, a refusal to deal is subject to a monopolization claim under the antitrust laws.[43] The clearest judicial articulation of the doctrine is perhaps in *MCI Communications v. AT&T*,[44] where the United States Court of Appeals for the Seventh Circuit developed a four-part test that must be met to invoke the essential-facilities doctrine. The test consists of showing "(1) control of the essential facility by the monopolist; (2) a competitor's inability practically or reasonably to duplicate the essential facility; (3) the denial of the use of the facility to a competitor; and (4) the feasibility of providing the facility."[45] Essential facilities thus typically tend to be "capital assets that cannot be economically duplicated given the size of the market—a communications network, a central terminal facility, stadium, or energy transmission facilities."[46] These are precisely the elements that have infuriated regulators.

Despite its broad applicability, however, the essential facilities doctrine currently inhabits the fringes of antitrust law. For starters, while several United States Supreme Court cases implicitly seem to support the doctrine,[47] the Court has never explicitly endorsed it.[48] More dramatically, prominent antitrust commentators have roundly criticized the doctrine. Philip Areeda calls it "less a doctrine than an epithet";[49] Herbert Hovenkamp believes it is "troublesome, incoherent, and unmanageable";[50] and Michael Boudin goes so far as to label it a doctrine of "dubious character" and "embarrassing weakness."[51] Much of the disdain stems from the discomfort of forcing competitors to share, something Keith Hylton calls the "potential for parasitism in the essential facilities doctrine."[52] This criticism is based on the underlying popular premise that competitors should compete based on their own facilities. For example, the former FCC chairman Michael Powell believes that "facilities-based" competition—where a new entrant creates its own infrastructure—may be the only tenable form of telecommunications competition.[53] This point of view ignores, of course, the often prohibitive costs and inefficiencies of duplicating infrastructure.[54] By and large, competitors who have tried this route have failed miserably—imagine trying to create your own electricity distribution grid or build your own airport. Additionally, some critics argue that new technologies will make such natural monopolies obsolete,[55] but this is often wishful thinking. Basic infrastructure, whether it be telephone lines or electricity lines or railroad track, remains important.[56] If it were not, incumbents would not devote so much time and money to keeping their infrastructure off-limits to competitors. As Joskow and Noll plainly summarize the matter, "[N]owhere in the world are there working examples of a structurally competitive, facilities-based local access industry."[57]

The fundamental, often overlooked, cause behind the discomfort eminent antitrust scholars feel maybe has nothing to do with the economics of essential facilities; rather, it has to do with the reality that the doctrine is difficult to implement within the confines of antitrust's traditional institutions. Examining why provides an excellent illustration of how economics and institutions are intertwined. In their detailed study of the doctrine, Abbott Lipsky and Gregory Sidak "conclude that mandatory access remedies, such as the essential facilities doctrine, do not fit comfortably within antitrust law. They are the stuff of regulatory bodies, not courts."[58] As they point out, successfully deploying the essential facilities doctrine requires a hands-on approach, since

> [c]ourts must be prepared (1) to command that access be provided to others, (2) *to regulate the prices, terms, and conditions for the provision of such access*, (3) to command the capacity expansion required to make such access feasible, and (4) to command that the service of the facility—as expanded to make access feasible—actually be provided to those who demand it.[59]

Perhaps the most famous example of a structural remedy is the breakup of AT&T, which introduced competition into the telecommunications market. Though not couched in the language of essential facilities, the effort succeeded precisely because

> [t]he fundamental theory underpinning the Modification of Final Judgment (MFJ) . . . is that regulated monopolies have the incentive and opportunity to monopolize related markets in which their

monopolized service is an input, and that *the most effective solution to this problem is to "quarantine" the regulated monopoly segment* of the industry by separating its ownership and control from the ownership and control of firms that operate in the potentially competitive segments of the industry.[60]

To be sure, AT&T's breakup required long-term supervision by U.S. District Court Judge Harold Greene[61] for precisely the reasons Lipsky and Sidak enunciate, but the problem seems to be more with the administrative difficulties of the essential facilities doctrine than with its inherent incoherence. If the idea is taken out of conventional antitrust, and implemented by a regulatory body, then these issues recede and the doctrine can enter the mainstream. More generally, as chapter 7 will argue, there is no reason why courts should be the frontline purveyors of regulation. Furthermore, while the principle of essential facilities—isolate the bottleneck and make it available to competitors while allowing competition to flourish elsewhere—is illustrated in the AT&T breakup, the remedy need not involve divestiture, thereby reducing administrative headaches. For instance, one particularly promising application of the essential facilities doctrine could be in high-technology industries where there are conflicting concerns. On the one hand, it is critically important to make sure incumbents do not exploit scale, intellectual property, and network effects to squelch competition; on the other hand, remedies such as divestiture might be too drastic in industries characterized by innovation and Schumpeterian creative destruction. Allowing new competitors access to bottleneck portions of an incumbent's network that cannot be duplicated—such as an operating system—would be far less drastic, while at the same time giving smaller players a chance to compete. As just one example, it seems that after years of litigation and countless court cases, the outcome of the Microsoft antitrust litigation has moved away from divestiture[62] to emerge along the lines of access. Though not presented under the rubric of essential facilities, the final court settlement at least seeks to force Microsoft to allow software developers interconnection rights to its operating systems.[63]

Finally, various strands of the new economic research discussed in chapter 5 further buttress the importance of allowing access to incumbents' bottlenecks. In the language of post-Chicago law and economics, essential facilities are a quintessential barrier to entry. Moreover, denying access to a bottleneck facility is at heart nothing but an extreme example of foreclosure. As Patrick Rey and Jean Tirole note, "[F]oreclosure refers to a dominant firm's denial of proper access to an essential good it produces, with the intent of extending monopoly power from that segment of the market (the bottleneck segment) to an adjacent segment (the potentially competitive segment)."[64] What seems unappreciated in the literature to this point, however, is that the essential facilities doctrine is also congruent with core theory, which stipulates that competition is often ill-advised when supply is indivisible due to large fixed costs.[65] This is precisely the situation at the bottleneck—by mandating access, regulatory law can devise a public solution to the problem of the empty core.[66] The upshot is isolation of the bottleneck (barrier) to allow access to new entrants, allowing competition to flourish elsewhere (where the core is not empty). Consumers typically get cheaper, more innovative products and services in a competitive and diverse environment; after all, as two former members of the Department of Justice have pointed out, "[C]ompetition tends to drive markets to a more efficient use of scarce resources."[67] Regulators must, however, create an environment where such competition can thrive.

Confining regulation to essential facilities thus can provide a useful, generalizable framework. As Glen Robinson argues, "[A]cademics and practitioners ought to be searching for ways to define and limit the obligation to deal with competitors. Ultimately, the best way to accomplish this is to use a narrowly defined essential facilities doctrine as the sole foundation for imposing such a duty."[68] It also has the added benefit of limiting the scope of regulation, ushering in a new, more focused regulatory paradigm.[69] As Kearney and Merrill summarize the matter,

> If one conceives of the regulator under the original paradigm as a sort of ice cap, covering all aspects of the regulated industry, then the objective under the new paradigm is to melt away the sphere of regulatory oversight to the smallest industry segment possible—the so-called bottleneck monopoly.[70]

Ironically, administrative realities suggest that the essential facilities may be more germane in the regulatory context than within traditional antitrust doctrine. Emerging commentary is beginning to recognize this reality, and some distinguished academics have even enhanced the four-part essential facilities test when recommending it in the regulatory context.[71] As Kearney and Merrill cogently argue, regulatory agencies would improve their lot by becoming "limited-jurisdiction enforcer[s] of antitrust principles, applying a version of the 'essential facilities' doctrine in a single industry."[72] To achieve this goal, however, the doctrine must be implemented as a form of economic regulation.

REACHIEVING PUBLICNESS

1. Basic principles

Quantifying the benefits of social regulation and ensuring competition in network industries are, of course, important goals. Yet addressing these vexing problems is only the tip of a larger project: the desperate need to reinfuse regulatory law with a sense of public purpose. Three proposals for reform strive toward this larger goal: emphasizing consumer welfare, reinvigorating the public trust doctrine, and placing greater emphasis on background liability rules.

Perhaps the single most important change will be to rethink the vague "public interest" standard in administrative law, which all too often has entrenched private interests at the expense of the public. The ubiquitous mandate from Congress to virtually every regulatory agency is to protect the "public interest." As just one example, under the Communications Act of 1934, the FCC must rule as "public convenience, interest, or necessity requires"[73]—indeed, as FCC Commissioner Copps has observed, "[T]he term 'public interest' appears over 110 times in the Communications Act."[74] On one level, this all sounds good: after all, protecting the public should be a central mandate of government agencies, and very often, regulators have the best intentions to help the public.[75] But skirting over the term belies a number of interpretative quandaries. To begin with, how does one measure the "public interest"? Who should determine it? Thomas Hazlett puts it bluntly when he laments that "not even the government's own experts can define what it means, or what action it rules out."[76]

As a result of this fuzziness, the public interest mandate has gone awry.[77] The public welfare can become secondary to the narrow interests of some politicians whose authority is ensured by the presence of powerful incumbents. As Hazlett illustrates in the context of telecommunications spectrum allocation,

Private spectrum rights . . . were "purchased" by broadcaster subsidies to "public interest" concerns, a tax which initially amounted to little more than nominal acquiescence to (and political support for) a federal licensing authority but would, over time, include significant payments to unprofitable local programming, "fairness doctrine" regulation, extensive proof of commitment to "community" in station renewals, and the avoidance of broadcasting content offensive to the political party in power.[78]

Even worse, the FCC's free allocation of prime bandwidth to broadcasters in exchange for fulfillment of "public interest" obligations has too frequently been a mechanism to entrench private interests. In fact, the high market values broadcasters enjoy are largely due to this giveaway—a fact recognized nearly fifty years ago by Ronald Coase in his classic article on the FCC.[79] One estimate is that spectrum assigned, for free under the "public interest" banner, to commercial TV broadcasters approaches a market value of $400 billion[80]—something that the business press has called "the biggest handout of public assets since the land grants to the railroads."[81]

Other examples abound. For instance, in one infamous case an entire neighborhood was condemned in order to clear land for a General Motors plant. The Michigan Supreme Court noted that "[t]he power of eminent domain is to be used in this instance primarily to accomplish the essential *public purposes* of alleviating unemployment and revitalizing the economic base of the community. *The benefit to a private interest is merely incidental.*"[82] Similarly, in the copyright realm, one is left wondering how incessant expansion of private rights in copyright law could possibly be in the public interest.[83] Pronouncements from regulatory officials can also be perplexing. For instance, when former FCC Commissioner Kathleen Abernathy comments that "[t]oday the Commission uses its broad discretion in crafting service rules in the *public interest* to grant far more flexibility *to our licensees*[,]"[84] one is left wondering how granting more power to private parties necessarily equates to enhanced benefits for the public. Lawrence White justifiably complains that the public interest "banner" has been used to establish "far too many protectionist, anti-competitive, anti-innovative, inflexible, output-limiting regulatory regimes."[85] Richard Stewart remarks, "To the extent that belief in an objective 'public interest' remains, the agencies are accused of subverting it in favor of the private interests of regulated and client firms."[86] The problem, unfortunately, is not new. Over forty years ago, Charles Reich sounded the alarm bell in a famous law review article when he lamented that "[s]omehow the idealistic concept of the public interest has summoned up a doctrine monstrous and oppressive."[87]

When an administrative law standard designed to protect the public devolves into protecting private interests, it provides ammunition for public choice theorists. All is not lost, however, since there are ways for administrative law to put teeth into its "public interest" mandate. New research avenues in regulatory theory can help redefine "public interest" to mean something that actually benefits consumers at large. Foremost among these—recognizing that the "public interest standard relegates consumer welfare to one interest competing among many"[88]—is to reshape the nebulous "public interest" standard into one of "consumer welfare." One must be careful, of course, to ensure that the term "consumer welfare" actually means what it says. In particular, some well-known commentators associated with the Chicago school have, in a rhetorical tour de force, managed to equate "consumer welfare" with overall economic efficiency.[89]

Prominent economists, notably Jerry Hausman, have explored a consumer welfare approach in the context of telecommunications reform,[90] but the idea is applicable across different areas of administrative law. For instance, Ian Ayres and John Braithwaite have proposed a consumer monopsony[91] standard, where governments "emulate what a monopsonist consumer would do,"[92] by "studying and at times emulating the practices of these quintessentially empowered consumers."[93] For example, in a proposed merger, the question becomes whether the "additional competitors are likely to reduce an industry's prices"[94] or even "whether a downstream monopsonist would be willing to subsidize upstream entry."[95] Such questions refocus the debate on the harms and benefits to consumers. Another alternative is for local government to emphasize its role not as grantor of exclusive franchise rights to private companies under the "public interest" banner, but rather as a competitor itself. For instance, evidence suggests that competition from municipal cable companies forces private cable franchisees to lower their prices significantly,[96] as witnessed, for example, by the sharp opposition of telecommunications incumbents to municipalities wishing to provide broadband access to their citizens.[97] Note also that during the California electricity debacle, Los Angeles County, which has a municipal electricity provider, was one of the few areas unaffected by price gouging.[98] Some scholars even go so far as to suggest transferring a portion of some profit-making businesses, such as banking and insurance, to local government control.[99]

While finding ways to make the "public interest" congruent with "consumer welfare" is perhaps the most important way to reachieve publicness in regulatory law, other reforms will also help the cause. One important idea is to revitalize the public trust doctrine, which conceives the regulatory state as a custodian of public assets. The doctrine traces its roots to the Justinian notion that certain resources—such as fish, wild animals, and rivers—should not be owned privately.[100] Its earliest American manifestations include the New Jersey Supreme Court case of *Arnold v. Mundy*[101] and the United States Supreme Court case of *Martin v. Wadell's Lessee*.[102] Before the turn of the twentieth century, in *Illinois Central Railroad Co. v. Illinois*,[103] the United States Supreme Court again used the public trust doctrine to uphold the Illinois legislature's revocation of a grant of a large portion of submerged lands at Chicago's waterfront to the railroad. The Court noted that its decision "follows necessarily from the public character of the property, being held by the whole people for the purposes in which the whole people are interested."[104] The best-known modern application of the public trust doctrine is the *Lake Mono*[105] case, where the Supreme Court of California allowed the California Water Resources Board to revoke a 1940 permit allowing the Los Angeles Department of Water and Power to appropriate the flow from several streams into Lake Mono.

Consistent in every opinion that relies on public trust is the desire to entrust the management of scarce resources to the state. To the extent the resources belong to the people, the state should be more concerned with what is beneficial to society than with what will benefit private interests that are profiting from these public resources, such as the logging companies and ranchers described in chapter 3. Those who argue that giving government this flexibility unnecessarily creates uncertainty forget that managing risk is part and parcel of every business. As Louis Kaplow observes,

> For purposes of analyzing risk and incentive issues, the source of the uncertainty is largely irrelevant. A private actor should be indifferent as to whether a given probability of loss will result from the action of competitors, *an act of government*, or an act of God, except to the extent that the source of the risk will affect the likelihood of compensation or other relief.[106]

Allowing government the freedom to protect the public by taking action such as revoking grants takes the air out of public choice arguments that, ultimately, are obsessed with protecting private actors.

As society has evolved, more resources have become scarce: we need to worry not only about our natural resources, but also about things like access to telecommunications, power, and safe medications. As Joseph Sax has persuasively argued,

> The central idea of the public trust is preventing the destabilizing disappointment of expectations held in common but without formal recognition such as title. The function of the public trust as legal doctrine is to protect such public expectations against destabilizing changes, just as we protect conventional private property from such changes.[107]

If the regulatory state is viewed as the custodian of the public assets—rather than merely as protecting some ill-defined "public interest"—then its ability to protect public over private interests is sharply enhanced.[108]

It is one thing to speak of "publicness" when regulators themselves are acting directly, and another for regulators also to set background rules that benefit the public even when private actors are bargaining for resources among themselves. I propose greater use of "liability" rules to overcome many of the problems inherent in private contracting identified in chapter 4, precisely because liability rules force economic actors desirous of resources to reveal their worth publicly. Here a little legal background might be helpful. In a classic law review article, Guido Calabresi and Douglas Melamed distinguish between two types of legal entitlements.[109] An entitlement "is protected by a *property rule* to the extent that someone who wishes to remove the entitlement from its holder must buy it from him in a voluntary transaction in which the value of the entitlement is agreed upon by the seller."[110] But "[w]henever someone may destroy the initial entitlement if he is willing to pay an objectively determined value for it, an entitlement is protected by a *liability rule*."[111] Property rules thus give an absolute right to exclude; with a liability rule, another party is allowed to encroach on the entitlement provided he or she is willing to pay.

The conventional wisdom is that property rules encourage contracting. Building on Calabresi and Melamed's work, however, Ian Ayres and Eric Talley have challenged this concept:

The ability of Solomonic entitlements such as untailored liability rules to facilitate Coasean trade is starkly at odds with the accepted wisdom that property rules are "market-encouraging" when transaction costs are low. Property rules and liability rules may thus run neck and neck in a Coasean horse race, even when transaction costs are low; and when private information is the major source of inefficiency, liability rules and other divided entitlement forms may hold the lead. . . .

. . . Our conclusion that uncertain and weakly protected entitlements might produce more efficient trade than undivided property rights runs counter to deeply held but possibly unexamined beliefs.[112]

A central reason for this reality is that with a liability rule, the entitlement owner is forced to reveal what the entitlement is worth to him or her, thereby sharply curtailing strategic bargaining and holdouts. As Ayres and Talley note, "[D]ivided entitlements can enhance welfare by promoting greater revelation of information during bargaining."[113] Conventional wisdom, however, suggests that liability rules are inferior, because the state has to set the amount that needs to be paid.[114] As Calabresi and Melamed themselves argue, "[L]iability rules involve an additional stage of state intervention: not only are entitlements protected, but their transfer or destruction is allowed on the basis of a value determined by some organ of the state rather than by the parties themselves."[115] But Louis Kaplow and Steven Shavell's economic analysis suggests that "if a court sets damages equal to its best estimate of harm—the average harm for cases characterized by the facts the court observes—the outcome under the liability rule will be superior, on average, to the outcome under property rules."[116] As chapter 7 will argue, it would be better to have a regulatory agency, rather than a court, set damages, but this does not change the overall point.

In fact, liability rules are particularly effective where there are collective action problems. Conceptualize, for example, a number of rights vested collectively in citizens: the right to enjoy clean air or vibrant forests, for example. Under a property rule regime, corporations who want to infringe on those rights would need to bargain with the public at large. Of course, this is virtually impossible. The corporation could bargain directly with the state to cede those rights (which, sadly enough, is happening today), but unless it hides behind nebulous "public interest" mandates, the state is not in a position to give the rights away—they belong to the people. Liability rules, on the other hand, would force the corporation to pay for infringement. This conception dovetails nicely with the public trust doctrine and the notion of creating marketable rights in externalities: the state is acting as custodian for the public's rights, and even those permitted to infringe on those rights must nonetheless pay for use rather than grabbing a free ride.

Any attempt at reform of regulatory law must reachieve publicness instead of merely hiding behind facile bromides such as the "public interest."[117] A consumer welfare standard, the public trust doctrine, and liability rules are merely some starting suggestions.

2. Reforming the regulation of public corporations

Given the spate of corporate scandals America has suffered through, perhaps the most pressing and visible area for reform is rethinking the way the law regulates public corporations—today done primarily through basic corporate law, securities regulation, and antitrust. The overarching challenge will be to find ways of implementing notions of publicness so that there is created firm oversight. For its part, corporate law is to a large extent based on the "firm as contract" mantra,[118] which of course brings with it all of the fallacies of the contractarian ideology discussed in chapter 4. As one commentator points out, the "dominant contemporary view of corporate law is contractarian, meaning that corporate constituencies are assumed to be best able to determine their mutual rights and obligations by way of voluntary arrangement."[119] Doctrines assume, for example, that parties to the corporate contract are rational actors with equal bargaining power.[120] Consistent with the most fundamental notion that corporations derive their advantages and protections from the state, lawmakers need to move away from these simplistic assumptions and treat corporate law more as a form of public law.

Revamping fiduciary duties, rethinking the importance of default rules, and putting in place mechanisms to foster more diverse discourse within the firm are some specific proposals that would go a long way toward curing corporate law's ills. Current corporate law couches the fiduciary duties of firm insiders to shareholders in vague terms. Yet, as behavioral economics would suggest and Donald Langevoort notes, "What does seem likely is that highly indeterminate legal standards—such as those based on 'reasonableness' or 'good faith'—will have a less direct impact on firm behavior than we would like to think. The managerial bias is to perceive the firm's actions as both reasonable and in good faith."[121] Perhaps more importantly, the business judgment rule gives managers almost unlimited protection: as one commentator points out, "The purported duty of managers to maximize shareholder wealth can be almost meaningless because the business judgment rule gives corporate managers enormous discretion in deciding how to try to generate profits."[122] The result of these choices is a group of insulated managers and directors who enjoy enormous legal leeway. As Lucian Bebchuk notes,

> The weakness of shareholders vis-à-vis boards of directors in publicly traded companies is often viewed as an inevitable corollary of the modern corporation's widely dispersed ownership. But this weakness is partly due to legal rules that insulate management from shareholder intervention. Changing these rules would reduce the extent to which boards can stray from shareholder interests and would much improve corporate governance.[123]

In such a permissive legal environment, it is perhaps no surprise that some insiders would place their own interests above those of their shareholders, let alone above those of the broader community. As one observer points out in his critique of agency law in the corporate context, "For these modern princes, including corporate CEOs, the term quasi-principal may be coined to capture their double lives—agents for others (their corporations and shareholders) *and de facto principals who hold vast authority and power*."[124] Beyond eminently reasonable proposals to give shareholders greater say in corporate elections,[125] one way out of this mess is to give fiduciary duties much greater teeth while de-emphasizing the business judgment rule. There are a multitude of reasons that support this perspective, provided one is willing to move beyond the facile assumptions of a contractual, entirely private vision of the firm. As Thomas Hazen points out:

> The fiduciary paradigm is a necessary limitation on the right to contract within the corporate setting. This limitation on freedom of contract is warranted because of the recognition of the relative unequal power positions of the various corporate constituencies. *The fiduciary principle also is applicable because a corporation is not only*

an economic institution but is also a powerful political and social insti-tution. As such, the corporate paradigm must be evaluated in light of societal values rather than the allegedly neutral economic model. Finally, corporate managers make decisions concerning the deployment of shareholders' capital. Corporate managers are in fact managing other people's money. This is yet a further reason for retaining the fiduciary paradigm.[126]

Reformers also need to focus on the pernicious aspects of corporate culture and to design laws to change behavior.[127] A few illustrative examples should hopefully drive the point home. If directors are overconfident and tend to dismiss early warnings of trouble for the firm, then corporate law could impose a fiduciary duty to warn of impending trouble such as bankruptcy.[128] To begin remedying vast and increasing income inequality within the corporate hierarchy, the law might further rethink the composition and processes of board compensation committees.[129] If the corporate ethos does not take conflicts of interest seriously, then the law needs to restrict events like related-party transactions.[130] If the behavioral biases of managers prevent bad news from reaching the top of the corporate food chain, then the law might relax the knowledge (scienter) requirements for fraud liability.[131]

Corporate governance mechanisms also need to counteract the behavioral reality of herding. Cass Sunstein's observation, made in the context of the public organizations, applies with equal force to private firms: "[C]ohesive groups of like-minded people whose members are connected by close social ties often suppress dissent and reach inferior decisions, whereas heterogeneous groups, building identification through focus on a common task rather than through other social ties, tend to produce the best outcomes."[132] Recent corporate scandals have made this dynamic all too apparent, especially at the board level.[133] Corporate law must understand this tendency, and encourage differing viewpoints in corporate discourse. For example, it should develop mechanisms to ensure that at least one board member at each meeting actively encourages alternative viewpoints.[134] Board diversity also needs to be increased,[135] perhaps even to include employee representatives.[136] Corporate law's attempt to improve firm decision-making thus needs to be twofold: focus relentlessly on creating legal safeguards, and at the same time encourage the selection of decision-makers who are less insular. Each time, the process is the same: focus on the organizational behavioral problem, then design countervailing public policy.[137] This methodology should be vastly more productive than one that simply assumes a group of rational actors with equal bargaining power happily going about making contracts.

Alongside the reform of corporations, there exists a need to rethink securities regulation. Two needs stand out: active public oversight of markets, and a counterweight to the obsessive norm of short-term performance. A threshold issue—hopefully apparent by this point in the book— is to recognize that markets need rules. As Coase himself points out,

> It is not without significance that these [commodity and stock] ex- changes, often used by economists as examples of a perfect market and perfect competition, are markets in which transactions are highly regulated (and this quite apart from any government regulation that there may be). It suggests, I think correctly, that for anything ap- proaching perfect competition to exist, an intricate system of rules and regulations would normally be needed.[138]

Unfortunately, private regulation of securities markets has not worked. One article in the business press sounds the alarm bell when it recounts how "Wall Street's self-regulators have missed virtually all of the major securities scandals of the past two decades—from troubles that brought down Kidder Peabody, to analysts' conflicts, to favoritism in awarding initial-public-offering shares, to trading abuses at the Nasdaq Stock Market."[139] The reasons for this failure should hopefully be evident by now: to the extent that self-regulation is a private "legal" system that relies upon contractual arrangements, it brings with it all the problems of private contract discussed in chapter 4. The reason why private regulation of securities markets does not work is directly related to the limitations of public choice: to assume that economic activity can be organized sim- ply via private contract is hopelessly naive. One business journalist sums it up: "Markets are a great way to organize economic activity, but they need adult supervision."[140]

The second driver behind corporate malfeasance is the allowance in current securities regulation to worship at the altar of short-term perfor- mance, to the detriment of long-term corporate value. William Bratton is able to cut through the clutter and refocus the discourse by recognizing this driver:

But in the transfer from theory to practice, the set of economic instructions diffuses into a norm. . . . As the norm becomes more capacious it takes on a dark side. . . . For equity investors in recent years, the practice of shareholder value maximization has not meant patient investment. Instead, it has meant obsession with short-term performance numbers. For managers, the shareholder value norm has come to mean more than astute investment and disinvestment. It also means aggressive management of reported figures responsive to the investment community's demands for immediate value.[141]

The metric of choice to game is earnings per share:[142] as one financial journalist puts it, "The cult of the number [earnings per share] distorted the U.S. economy in ways that will take years to fix."[143] Viewed through this lens, a number of proposals for corporate reform make eminent sense. One is simply to expense stock options, something which has just begun—as Paul Krugman notes, "Companies might have issued fewer options, and accounting fraud might have been less of a problem, if accounting rules had required companies to count the issue of stock options as a cost, rather than pretending they were somehow free."[144] Another is to hold gatekeepers—bankers, lawyers, accountants, and the like—strictly liable "for material misstatements and omissions in offering documents and remove any due-diligence based defenses from securities regulation."[145] Other ideas worth discussion have been proposed, including de-emphasizing shelf registration,[146] eliminating the safe harbor doctrine,[147] and insisting on greater oversight of private credit rating agencies.[148]

But these proposals are incomplete—regulatory change must go further. For example, Jill Fisch and Kenneth Rosen provide an insightful critique of section 307 of the Sarbanes-Oxley Act (requiring lawyers to report evidence of corporate wrongdoing to corporate leaders) based on the near futility of looking "to private service providers from outside the organization to transform corporate governance."[149] Correctly suggesting that " 'first best' solutions should focus on the heart of corporate governance . . . directors and officers,"[150] Fisch and Rosen suggest a host of changes, such as "[r]equiring additional personal certifications of the contents of corporate communications and reports,"[151] increasing the risk of criminal liability for corporate leaders, and establishing a legal audit committee.[152]

The problems, however, run deeper than even what these commentators envision. Bill George, the former CEO of Medtronic, sums up our current sad state of affairs:

One thing's clear: Tossing corporate leaders in the slammer and passing Sarbanes-Oxley isn't enough to eradicate corporate scandals. First we have to address the root cause: an exaggerated and unbalanced emphasis on serving the short-term interests of shareholders, quarter after quarter. *This mania for making Wall Street's numbers is at the heart of why some CEOs cheat and others have simply mismanaged.*[153]

True reform of securities law will require severely weakening this cult of short-term performance. Currently, short-term changes in share prices are driven by a game. First, corporations selectively release information prior to declaring official quarterly results, allowing financial analysts to develop a "consensus estimate" of what earnings will be. Then, as if by magic, corporations typically exceed this estimate by exactly one cent. If they do not, then the firm can suffer wild fluctuations in share price. The name of the game, then, becomes managing Wall Street's expectations more than delivering fundamental value to shareholders. Reforming this scenario requires two steps. First, public regulators must work with accountants to revamp the way financial performance is calculated or, more precisely, miscalculated. Second, public regulators must work with corporations, equity research firms, financial markets, and the business media to change the format and timing of how performance is reported. One place to start would be to consider re-regulating brokerage commissions.[154] Until we move away from the existing charades, we will never have true securities reform.

Along with basic corporate law and securities regulation, antitrust is an area ripe for regulatory reform. Even the simplest improvement to the analysis—namely, the insight from IO that firms often maximize size, not profits[155]—suggests that attempts to leverage adjacent products, such as tying, do present real anticompetitive danger. As Louis Kaplow notes,

> This theory [that management may trade off size for profits] has striking implications for much of antitrust. For example, virtually all of the practices connected with the leverage issue operate to increase the sales or growth of the firm. Comments concerning tying often note the immediate effect in shifting sales of the tied product from other firms to the tying firm. Long-run growth in the market for the tied product, and entry barriers, as in the case of tying, vertical mergers, and a number of other restrictions, all concern future growth in the firm's sales. Thus, to the extent firms depart from profit maximization in the manner here described, one might observe widespread use of the restrictive practices [enunciated above].[156]

The emerging study of the behavioral quirks of organizations, discussed in chapter 5, provides further justification for reinvigorating antitrust. To the extent that many overconfident, self-serving CEOs push for mergers that do not make economic sense, antitrust law should be particularly strict when looking at both horizontal and vertical combinations. To the extent that firms fall prey to social pressures, defection from a cartel may actually be more difficult than standard economic theory would predict. One commentator who has studied the inner workings of organizations aptly summarizes the situation:

> (1) Cartels are much more stable than classical microeconomics would predict; (2) Managers frequently will not seize even highly profitable opportunities to cheat on a cartel, whether those opportunities need to be taken in secret or can be grasped openly; (3) The co-optation of a new entrant into the cartel is much easier than one would suppose; and (4) Price-fixing or market-division cartels can diminish competition and have adverse economic effects even where the members of the cartels collectively lack market power.[157]

In a world where overconfident entrants may ignore barriers to entry, then antitrust policy should focus on encouraging the survival of innovative competitors after they have entered—for instance, by seriously considering any claims of predatory pricing that might not increase an incumbent's short-term profits, but are designed to ensure its long-term hegemony.[158]

Finally, to create disincentives for activities that may lead to future scandals, regulatory agencies need to change the way they punish corporations for violation of corporate law, securities regulation, and antitrust. As Dan Kahan has shown in the context of street crime, an "order-maintenance" strategy—one in which law enforcement places an emphasis on visible responses to criminal activity[159]—is both cheaper and more effective "than simply 'raising the price' of serious crimes through either investments in law enforcement or longer terms of imprisonment."[160] The underlying reason for this rather puzzling anomaly, one that contradicts basic tenets of neoclassical economics, is behavioral—order-maintenance conveys a message about the social unacceptability of criminality:

> The level of crime, this account suggests, turns not just on the price of crime but also on the direction of social influence. A strategy of

low-certainty/high-severity can create social meanings that point social influence toward criminality. This is so because of what a low probability of conviction does to the norms of law-breakers and what severe punishments express to law abiders.[161]

Today, the law by and large tries to deter corporate malfeasance with a low-certainty/high-severity punishment regime. Perhaps it is little surprise that this strategy has had, at best, mixed success. Agencies should move to a high-certainty/low-severity regime whose "beneficial effects . . . on the direction of social influence might well compensate for what appears to be a greater-than-optimal investment in certainty of conviction."[162]

Changing the punishment regime is only an additional initiative. The broader point is experimenting with regulations to instill a culture among firms that respects, rather than vilifies, the law. What Robert Lane observed in 1953 remains unfortunately still true today:

> Since violation is a product, in part, of social pressure and community attitudes, government and business should jointly seek to build respect for law—even distasteful law enforced by a repugnant administration. Government cannot do this alone; business cannot do this without a record of fair dealing by the government. It is a task for both elements of society.[163]

Over fifty years later, these problems persist;[164] fortunately, however, we are finally developing the tools to understand and imbue "social pressure and community attitudes" with a sense of publicness. Reinvigorating corporate law, securities regulation, and antitrust would be a good place to begin reforming the regulation of public corporations. This success, in turn, would go a long way toward rescuing regulation.

Chapter 7

Institutional Changes

To the extent that some of the substantive reforms suggested in chapter 6 might be compelling, one important question remains: within which institutional framework should these changes be implemented?[1]

LIMITED AGENCIES

The central insight underlying institutional reform is to recognize that it is impossible for regulatory agencies to occupy successfully the role of "command and control" überregulators who seek to override markets. As Alfred Kahn notes, with a touch of humor, traditional regulation has the unfortunate tendency "to micromanage the process; to prescribe the results that, it is anticipated, the Almighty would have produced if He or She were in full possession of the facts; [and] to handicap the competitive process to produce visible competitors."[2] Ironically, the bureaucracies in chapter 1 that emerged from the New Deal collapsed over time under their own expansive weight. As John Duffy notes, "[T]he failure [of Progressive-era agencies] occurred because the Progressives constructed heroic institutions that, with their broad delegations, long-tenured officials, absence of effective constraints on self-interested activity, and impossibly ambitious regulatory agenda, were doomed to fail."[3] It is one thing to realize the impossibility of having an omniscient regulatory commission micromanage a vast array of command-and-control edicts. It is quite another to use this observation as an excuse to trash regulatory agencies—which is precisely where the antiregulatory rhetoric of conventional law and economics leads the unwary.

The alternative path is to find ways to improve, not simply abandon, our regulatory institutions. The challenge is to develop carefully circumscribed public agencies capable of addressing specific market failures *ex ante*, while subject to limited delegations of duty.[4] The overarching idea is for government to ensure a free and open market rather than try to supplant it with "command and control" edicts. Here, history is instructive. The framework I propose harkens back to what Richard Stewart describes as the "traditional model of administrative law"[5] that emerged during the late nineteenth century: the agency only enjoys a limited delegation of power, and is further limited by judicial review.[6] While obtaining funding for resources is obviously essential, it must not overshadow the need to deploy limited resources intelligently—as one article in the *Wall Street Journal* rightly asks in the context of New York Attorney General Eliot Spitzer's indictment of corporate miscreants, "How did the SEC's staff of more than 3,000 allow Mr. Spitzer's investor-protection staff of 84 to grab the enforcement torch?"[7]

One model of a limited agency that has operated fairly successfully for over two hundred years is the United States Patent and Trademark Office (PTO). As Duffy points out, "Unlike the sweeping delegations conferred in the Progressive and New Deal eras, the delegations of governmental power for the patent system were, and still are, extraordinarily narrow."[8] Duffy has suggested an insightful reform of the FCC based on this model. Partly analogizing from Duffy's vision for the FCC,[9] I have proposed a new institutional structure to address cross-industry issues of competition policy. I suggest a Competition Office of limited powers— partly financed through user fees rather than general tax revenues[10]—to streamline antitrust enforcement that is currently scattered among the Department of Justice, Federal Trade Commission, and a variety of sector-specific industry regulators.[11] Similarly, other commentators have suggested that "[w]hat's needed to control the costs and to provide basic health and hospitalization coverage for all Americans is *an independent agency* that would set national health care policy, collect medical fees, pay claims, reimburse doctors fairly, and restrain runaway drug prices."[12] In the wake of recent drug safety scandals, some commentators have similarly suggested an independent drug safety board.[13] In the context of the regulation of financial markets, one analyst convincingly argues that "only by amending its [financial] regulatory system and adopting unitary regulation of financial services can the US ensure it will maintain its supremacy as the home of global financial services participants."[14] The idea of having a unified agency is thus applicable across a variety of industries.

Cabining regulatory agencies under limited delegations of power is only a start. It could be combined with agencies taking "steps to better assess and describe regulatory benefits"[15] and Congress establishing "an independent 'ombudsman' to investigate alleged regulatory failures (and failures to regulate) one intervention at a time—mixing ordinal and quantitative analysis to produce a full picture of costs, benefits, distributive impacts, and all relevant uncertainties."[16] The need over the longer term, of course, is to have the courage to begin a systematic study of regulatory agencies. In his classic article on administrative law reform, Richard Stewart suggests that

> [a]dministrative agencies might be classified by their function, structure, powers, environment, and the nature and quantities of discretion exercised. . . . Such a classification of agency functions and institutional contexts might be paralleled by a similar classification of the various techniques for directing and controlling administrative power, including judicial review, procedural requirements, political controls, and partial abolition of agency functions.[17]

Are regulatory agencies getting appropriate authority under their enabling statutes or putting available resources to their best use? What checks are there on legislative and administrative power? Once we understand the complexity of the problem and the lopsidedness of the rhetoric of mainstream law and economics, new possibilities will emerge. As John Duffy aptly warns, "The better point is that we should resist the temptation to replace the fallen heroes of the Progressive era with new idols. Unchecked pessimism in the administrative form is as unjustified as the unbridled optimism of the Progressives."[18] If as a society we are willing, our regulatory agencies can be improved.

SOME OBJECTIONS

Even a carefully circumscribed role for regulatory agencies is sure to draw ire from several camps. Below, I try to respond to three objections that might emerge in response to my proposal.

1. Aren't government actors biased?

Chapter 4's critique of the Chicago school and public choice theory has tried to debunk the most common arguments that denigrate public administrative law and extol the primacy of private common law. Any serious attempt at institutional reform, however, must directly address a more sophisticated version of antigovernment rhetoric that is beginning to emerge.

The claim—typically made in response to behavioral economists who suggest that government might have a role to play in remedying behavioral biases[19]—is that government officials themselves are prone to bias. For instance, Richard Posner criticizes "proposals for entrusting risk regulation to insulated bodies of civil servants (shades of the Progressive era and the New Deal) without explaining why these civil servants could be expected to be immune from cognitive quirks and weakness of will."[20] Stephen Bainbridge argues that a "welfare economics model that posits legal intervention as a solution to market failure ignores the fact that regulators are themselves actors with their own self-interested motivations."[21] In the context of securities regulation, other distinguished scholars ask: "[I]f everyone suffers from cognitive defects, doesn't that also include the commissioners and staff of the SEC?"[22] There are several responses to this more nuanced attack on public law.

First, government cares about different things than the private sector does. As Daryl Levinson points out, "Markets and politics are different institutions with different goals and mechanisms."[23] As a consequence, he finds that "making governments pay money is not an especially promising approach. . . . [G]overnment behavior responds to political, not market, incentives."[24] With echoes of public choice theory's desire to reduce civic life to a private contractual arrangement, commentators who disfavor government regulation imbue their argument with the rhetoric of the market. Note, for instance, how Stephen Choi and Adam Pritchard believe that current "market forces are unlikely to correct the biases affecting monopolistic regulators"[25] and propose instead a new world that would "subject securities regulation to the forces of market competition."[26] Such rhetoric belies the reality that "[u]sing market criteria to evaluate the fairness or efficacy of democratic processes simply will not do."[27] As the noted political scientist James Q. Wilson observes, "The currency of the marketplace may be wealth, which is divided unequally, but the currency of politics is votes, which are distributed equally."[28]

Second, government institutions—even carefully cabined ones—serve an important function as the public face of society's mores, and hence as a deterrent to antisocial behavior. This tendency is well studied in the context of criminal law, where one of the principles of effective crime control is to make police presence as visible as possible.[29] Dan Kahan notes,

> When public deterrence predominates, individuals are much less likely to perceive that criminality is widespread. Moreover, when they feel reassured that law enforcement is adequate, law-abiders are *more* likely to view private precautions as worthwhile, and less likely to see such precautions as signs that those around them lack confidence in the efficacy of law. These attitudes are likely to sustain norms of private behavior that reduce the need for expenditures on public deterrence. In short, a mix tilted toward public law enforcement rather than private precautions would be more likely to generate a low crime-rate equilibrium at any given price of crime.[30]

Even beyond the criminal law, government serves an expressive function as the arbiter of what is wrong and right. As Robert Prentice points out, "When Congress outlaws racial discrimination or insider trading, people's views of the acceptability and even morality of those actions change. One theory is that legislation changes what people believe about approval patterns in their society and because people value approval, their new beliefs affect their behavior."[31]

Third, new research in game theory suggests that "law does not enter simply to help players arrive at the cooperative equilibrium but is also required to sustain that equilibrium."[32] Paul Mahoney and Chris Sanchirico conclude,

> Thus, although law—meaning centralized commands backed by force—may constitute only a small portion of the total rule-making and enforcement system, it is a necessary one. Without it, the remaining parts of the system may unravel in the face of uncertainty about whether all players continue to expect one another (and expect that others expect, and so on) to continue to comply with the extant norms.[33]

Rather than engage in superficially appealing, yet fundamentally incoherent, antigovernment bashing, energy should be directed at developing an institutional framework within which to improve public law. We must eschew what Lawrence Lessig has identified as our "self-indulgent 'anti-governmentalism.' "[34] Especially in an era in which corporate scandals have made market failures glaringly apparent and often even shattered confidence in the system, regulatory agencies must evolve to better protect the public—consumers, employees, and the broader citizenry.

2. Why not courts as frontline arbiters?

Another objection to my proposal might be that courts should play a more direct role as regulators. However, there are several problems with having courts occupy the front lines of regulatory policy. First, regulatory enforcement via common law is inherently an *ex post* method of adjudication. To a very large extent, decisions are made after the alleged harm has already occurred, offering little prospective guidance to market participants. As A. D. Woozley points out in his philosophical critique of laws that retrospectively affect conduct, "The case here against retroactive law is simply that it frustrates planning."[35] Somewhat amusingly, even Richard Posner, generally unflappable in his praise of the common law, admits that laws with " 'common law' (that is, judge-made) character" suffer from "considerable fluidity in the meaning and application of the law, and uncertainty about its effects."[36]

A second issue with entrusting regulatory law to common law evolution is that judges are by definition generalists. With the notable exception of judges like Justice Stephen Breyer who taught administrative law for decades, few judges will have the necessary expertise to fill in for the gamut of administrative agencies. One way to alleviate this problem is to set up specialized courts; for example, Thomas Hazlett has suggested a "Network Interconnection Court" to adjudicate disputes in network industries such as telecommunications.[37] Another possibility is greater use of special masters and technical experts.[38] While perhaps valuable improvements to judicial process, such proposals remain captive to the *ex post* limitations of common law.

Beyond the difficulties of trying to create regulatory law through a generalist judiciary that must decide cases *ex post*, there are other obstacles to achieving justice. As Richard Stewart points out, a collective action problem exists

> where the impact of a decision is widely diffused so that no single individual is harmed sufficiently to have an incentive to undertake

litigation, and where high transaction costs and the collective nature of the benefit sought preclude a joint litigating effort, even though the aggregate stake of the affected individuals would justify it.[39]

Expanding, rather than limiting, citizen-suit provisions such as those in the Clean Air Act could begin to remedy this limitation.[40] Another criticism is that judicial remedies are often messy[41]—courts should not pretend they are legislatures or administrative agencies.

More broadly, it is important to ask whether the institutional limitations of courts continue to hold back the implementation of sophisticated economic research. After all, to the extent judges should even be expected to function as economists, it is understandably much easier for a generalist judge to interpret supply-and-demand curves than to delve into the game-theoretic models of post-Chicago or behavioral law and economics. Steven Salop and Craig Romaine point out in the context of anticompetitive behavior that

> to the extent that it is concluded that judges or juries are not competent to deal with these issues in a judicial context, then that forum must be replaced with some other venue for deciding the case. The answer cannot be that the issues are too complicated for judges and juries so, therefore, monopolists should be unconstrained.[42]

Indeed, though a simple desire to limit administrative regulation likely drives most of the Chicago's school's advocacy for the common law,[43] one cannot also help wonder to what extent the Chicago school also likes courts for offering a safe forum wherein the economics can stay simple.[44]

Even though courts cannot and should not serve as the frontline arbiters of regulatory policy, one point cannot be overemphasized: the judiciary does have a critical role to play through judicial review of agency decisions. As Justice Breyer writes, "[R]eview by generalist judges is important, both because technical agency decisions are often of great importance to the general public and because the law forbids agencies, in the name of technical expertise, to wrest themselves free of public control."[45] Courts need to step in where the elected branches do not. As Charles Haar says in his study of American suburbanization,

> The proposition I advance here is that courts are obliged to intervene—to undertake the coercive reordering of major social institutions—when a wrongful social practice either impairs a group's ability

to participate in the political process or when another branch of government is systematically delinquent in carrying out the mandates of the constitution.[46]

Federal District Court judge William Dwyer—who famously issued an injunction against timber sales from old-growth forests in the Pacific Northwest—eloquently sums up the role of judges when he states that the "problem here has not been any shortcoming in the laws, but simply a refusal of administrative agencies to comply with them. . . . This invokes a public interest of the highest order: the interest in having government officials act in accordance with law."[47]

Judicial review must thus serve as a countermajoritarian check on legislative and agency power, or in Haar's words, "a safety valve when the rest of the governmental system is clogged."[48] As Farber and Frickey point out, "Democracy cannot be equated with pure majority rule, because pure majority rule is incoherent. Rather, a viable democracy requires that preferences be shaped by public discourse and processed by political institutions so that meaningful decisions can emerge."[49] Generalist judges are an integral part of this discourse—but it is quixotic to argue that *ex post* common law should occupy the front lines of regulatory policy.[50]

3. Isn't this giving up on participatory democracy?

A different, and vastly more sophisticated, critique of my proposal would be to argue that an administrative state, albeit a limited one, still creates a bureaucracy that runs counter to the ideals of participatory democracy. After all, as Gerald Frug points out in his perceptive deconstruction of the stories woven to legitimate bureaucracy, the models that justify both private and public bureaucracy are nothing but "attempts to escape from the problems of face-to-face human relationships; all of them promise us that human relationships—even relationships built on hierarchy and separation—can be made unthreatening through some organizational arrangement."[51]

Over the long term, rethinking democracy might be the only solution to curing the ills of administrative law. As Richard Stewart suggests,

> The only conceivable way out of the labyrinth would seem to be a new and comprehensive theory of government and law that would successfully reconcile our traditional ideals of formal justice, individual autonomy, and responsible mechanisms for collective choice,

with the contemporary realities of decentralized, uncoordinated, discretionary exercises of governmental authority and substantial disparities in the cohesiveness and political power of private interests.[52]

A corollary to this notion is that the law, as expressed through our existing bureaucratic institutions, cannot possibly achieve social justice. Consider William Widen's thought-provoking analysis of the Enron scandal:

> The cultural problem revealed by Enron ultimately is not subject to correction by teaching lawyers more accounting, fine tuning rules governing the use of "gatekeepers" in corporate matters, or requiring and expecting more from independent directors, though all these measures would help in a small way. *The problem is that corporate and legal culture has lost all sense of right and wrong.* Norms of business behavior have evolved so that compliance with the positive law is the sole standard of ethical conduct—a role for which the positive law is ill-suited.[53]

Widen concludes by warning ominously that the "decline in business and legal ethics in our large corporations, if unchecked, may signal the beginning of the end of actual capitalist markets, not merely its theoretical death."[54]

But how to reform "corporate and legal culture"? What will substitute for the bureaucracy that public law brings with it? Ideally, the public interest will be exercised through the discourse inherent in participatory democracy. As Frug points out, "Acting together, we could begin to dismantle the structure of bureaucratic organizations—not all at once, but piece by piece. In their place we could substitute forms of human relationship that better reflect our aspirations for human development and equality."[55] Central to all these noble ideas is the notion of social discourse. Jürgen Habermas describes it as follows:

> Here the social substratum for the realization of the system of rights consists neither in spontaneous market forces nor in the deliberate measures of the welfare state but in the *currents of communication and public opinion that, emerging from civil society and the public sphere, are converted into communicative power through democratic procedures.*[56]

In a similar vein, Amitai Etzioni's pathbreaking work "seeks to provide a different approach to moral issues by drawing new, shared moral understandings, drawn from moral dialogues, rather than by relying on hierarchical dictates. The approach emphasizes convincing people to change their ways rather than enacting coercive laws to force them to do so."[57] This path has much to commend it and may indeed be ideal over the longer term.[58] Such a project would admirably include emphasis "on the formation of preferences side, via moral education, peer culture, community values, and the mobilization of appropriate public opinion."[59] An informed populace could in turn counteract, even prevent, the dangerous norms that a small number of actors would try to impose upon the rest of society. After all, even the best-intentioned legislators, judges, and bureaucrats cannot conceivably be everywhere at once.

Currently, however, the polity too often disengages from issues of public policy. An overarching culprit for this sorry state of affairs—and the concomitant decline of "publicness" that chapter 3 laments—is the unfortunate stubbornness of the public/private distinction. Oversimplified, the idea is that citizens should concern themselves with their private lives and businesses, and except perhaps for voting every few years, not participate in public life. As Morton Horwitz notes, the distinction is surprisingly recent:

> [O]nly in the nineteenth century was the public/private distinction brought to the center of the stage in American legal and political theory. . . . One of the central goals of nineteenth century legal thought was to create a clear separation between constitutional, criminal, and regulatory law—public law—and the law of private transactions—torts, contracts, property, and commercial law.[60]

It is no coincidence that traditional law and economics has fueled the public/private distinction. As Herbert Hovenkamp points out, neoclassical law and economics "represents a sharp turn from the essentially republican vision of government that dominated Progressive legal thought, to a more classical liberal view emphasizing the uniqueness and centrality of individual preference, the efficiency and robustness of private markets, and the many imperfections of public processes."[61]

Unsurprisingly, much like its ally traditional law and economics, the public/private distinction cannot withstand critical scrutiny. Early twentieth-century legal realists were the first to point out that the very concept of private property is only meaningful in relation to public enforcement of rights.[62] Today, it is hard to find a private function that does not have a public counterpart, and vice versa; for example, the provision of traditional public services has often become privatized—security guards, utilities, letter couriers, jails, and even the military, to name just a few.[63] Duncan Kennedy even bemoans that "one simply loses one's ability to take the public/private distinction seriously as a description, as an explanation, or as a justification of anything."[64]

Despite its logical inconsistency, the public/private distinction is inextricably linked to the liberal dislike of having any intermediate social structures mediate individual choice. Perhaps many liberals are uncomfortable with administrative law precisely because, as Frug points out, agencies represent "the merging of concepts of public and private into the idea of expertise."[65] In the words of one commentator, the distinction symbolizes the "inherent conflict between individualism and collective control that informs the liberal perspective. . . ."[66] Achieving participatory democracy thus becomes an immense project that runs counter to deeply ingrained tenets of liberalism. The central long-term challenge will be to find ways to overcome the false public/private distinction and motivate the public to participate in civic life.

A first step would be to make citizens aware of the structures that allow private parties to manipulate government. As Etzioni points out,

> The economic literature is replete with distortions the government causes in the markets. Comparable attention should be paid to manipulations of the government by participants in the market, and the effects of these manipulations on the internal structures of markets. A major way these manipulations are carried out is for corporations, banks, farmers, and labor unions to use their *political* power to significantly and systematically affect the outcomes of market transactions.[67]

A variety of proposals could help improve public attention to regulatory law. More emphasis on publicizing government misbehavior,[68] as well as greater encouragement of public participation in agency decision-making via notice and comment rule making would be fruitful measures.[69] Even more direct participation, such as the public's monitoring of agencies, in much the way shareholders should oversee corporations, is a possibility.[70] Some commentators have even proposed experimenting with the election of administrative agency members,[71] although, such a scheme would be susceptible to the dangers of interest-group representation.[72] Whether we want to adopt any of these proposals should be hotly debated, but the more important point is at least to begin the civic debate.

Yet participative democracy can only evolve if two challenges are met. First, citizens must have the capacity to be active participants. Habermas himself warns:

> Communicative freedom exists only between actors who, adopting a performative attitude, want to reach an understanding with one another about something and expect one another to take positions on reciprocally raised validity claims. The fact that communicative freedom depends on an intersubjective relationship explains why this freedom is coupled with illocutionary obligations.[73]

As a consequence, as Michael Froomkin warns, "some discourses—many, maybe all, discourses—do not meet Habermas's conditions."[74] Thus, while participatory democracy is a laudable goal—and, in the abstract, superior to even a limited government bureaucracy—it requires enfranchising a broad spectrum of society.[75] Second, even enfranchised citizens must be given incentives to participate in social discourse. Mancur Olson's work on group behavior warns us that "[o]nly when groups are small, or when they are fortunate enough to have an independent source of selective incentives, will they organize or act to achieve their objectives."[76] As a consequence,

> *The high degree of organization of business interests, and the power of these business interests, must be due in large part to the fact that the business community is divided into a series of (generally oligopolistic) "industries," each of which contains only a fairly small number of firms.* . . . [T]he multitude of workers, consumers, white-collar workers, farmers, and so on are organized only in special circumstances, but business interests are organized as a general rule.[77]

Given these substantial hurdles, we cannot simply do away with public law—rather, we need to harness it to create the preconditions for the emergence of participatory democracy. The central question will be how to create a legal regime that allows citizens to achieve Habermasian "illocutionary obligations" through Olson's "selective incentives"—in other words, to use the discipline of economics to fulfill the vision of participatory democracy.

Even if participatory democracy is achieved, society will still need rules and regulations. As Ellickson reminds us, "To achieve order without law, people must have continuing relationships, reliable information about past behavior, and effective countervailing power. . . . *Legal rules can influence all these attributes of social structure and thereby promote—or impede—informal cooperation.*[78] Public law also has a central role to play by serving as a countervailing force to the norms that small, powerful groups play in society. As Ellickson admits, "An especially valuable function of government is to supply laws designed to override the parochial norms of close-knit subgroups within it. A norm of 'honor among thieves' may well be welfare maximizing for thieves, but welfare diminishing for society at large."[79] Furthermore, there is substantial evidence to suggest that private norms can reduce even the welfare of the group that has developed the norm.[80] In the end, regulation is entirely consistent with aspirations for participatory democracy. As Ezra Suleiman points out in his recent study of public institutions necessary to democracy, "[T]he maintenance of a democratic order" requires "a trained, nonvenal bureaucratic machine."[81]

AFTERWORD

Rescuing Regulation has been an attempt to show how good economic and institutional analysis can help save regulation. In doing so, it has tried to suggest not only ways to improve our regulatory machinery, but also an outline of how social science can inform normative legal discourse. At one level, I have tried to engage in a variety of specific analyses and prescriptions to incorporate the latest economics and revamp our regulatory institutions. At this level of abstraction, the agenda is about deconstructing the messy reality of barriers to entry, network effects, economies of scale, and the like. It involves reconstructing the law using a variety of new concepts with intimidating names like "core theory," "consumer monopsony," and "dynamic market analysis."

At a more profound level, however, I hope the reader sees beyond the clutter to three broader themes. The first is the need for regulatory reformers to look beyond strict methodological and doctrinal boundaries. To a large extent, regulation is in a rut because of an unwillingness or inability to learn from the sea change underway in economics and other social sciences. The unfortunate bifurcation between antitrust and regulation not only has slowed the development of promising analytical tools, but more importantly has also allowed policymakers enamored of simplistic deregulation to assuage critics by sloughing off responsibility to antitrust enforcement. If antitrust is made part and parcel of regulation, it becomes more difficult for regulatory pundits to pass the buck when things go awry. Responsibility just might breed reform.

The second is that remaking the regulatory state requires looking beyond the pitched economic and institutional battles that at first blush paint a simple caricature of "more" versus "less" regulation—the real trend may be toward privatization, not deregulation per se. If nothing else, a pragmatic approach suggests that blanket policy prescriptions are dangerous. Arguments for regulation cannot be made in a vacuum and depend on contextual details.[1] For instance, a market where expansive intellectual property can combine with network externalities to cut against innovation is very different than a commodities market that competes on volume and cost. In some cases regulation needs to be more aggressive; in others less so. As Amitai Etzioni notes, "Among the dichotomies that hinder serious intellectual examination few are as detrimental as the notion that free markets are 'good' and governments are 'bad,' both because some measure of rule-setting and enforcement is clearly needed, and too much is harmful."[2] Dissenting in *Lochner v. New York*,[3] Justice Holmes warned that "a constitution is not intended to embody a particular economic theory, whether of paternalism and the organic relation of the citizen to the State or of *laissez faire*."[4] As Holmes suggests, reality is much more subtle, and replete with unintended consequences. The doctrinal suggestions that I have outlined are only an illustrative beginning. Flexibility, and a willingness to experiment with new regulatory paradigms should be a touchstone. While the basic challenge will be to limit government intervention to assure free and open markets,[5] government behavior cannot always be neatly categorized into "competition-enhancing" versus "competition-suppressing" compartments, as many of deregulation's most eloquent defenders have tried to do.[6] While theoretically elegant and conceptually useful in the broadest sense, it is simply too crude a dichotomy. Though usually government should work to enhance competition, sometimes it must suppress it.

The third, and most important, theme is that overcoming regulation's current malaise necessarily requires getting beyond the seduction of neoclassical economics.[7] Underneath the veneer of elegance and simplicity lie nonfalsifiable assumptions, blind faith in the ability of self-interested private parties to make public policy, and a consequent disregard for the law's distributional goals. Naive methodological assumptions underlie a masterful rhetoric that all but ignores consumer and employee interests. When examined critically, the arguments in favor of blind deregulation rest on facile assumptions: that transaction costs are negligible, that equity is unimportant, that economic actors are rational, and above all, that it is perfectly fine to devolve public deliberation into a monetary transaction. Unfortunately, these basic assumptions are rarely stated explicitly.[8] As Professors Laffont and Tirole have observed, "[D]eregulatory fervor is often guided more by a gut feeling that competition is efficient than by a clear conceptual framework embodying the specificities of these industries."[9]

I have tried to begin sketching out an alternative vision of regulatory law—avowedly less elegant, but significantly more realistic. It rests on economics that are pragmatic, empirical, and behavioral. It tries to pay attention to the social interactions that underlie economic phenomena and struggles with the need to develop public institutions reflective of a democracy rather than simply collapses political discourse into the realm of private contract. During the 1970s and 1980s, laissez-faire law and economics scholars cleverly disseminated their vision of impeccable supply-and-demand schedules and magically efficient common law. Twenty years later, recovering from a cynical post-Enron world demands that a new generation of scholars offer a modernized economic and institutional vision of administrative law. We must direct our efforts at improving, not trashing, our regulatory system. Nothing less than capitalism's survival may be at stake.

NOTES

PREFACE

1. *See, e.g.*, Jacob M. Schlesinger, *What's Wrong? The Deregulators: Did Washington Help Set Stage for Current Business Turmoil? Wall St. J.*, Oct. 17, 2002, at A1.

CHAPTER 1. TRADITIONAL PERSPECTIVES

1. Stephen Breyer, *Regulation and Its Reform* 7 (1982).

2. *See, e.g.*, David P. Baron, *Design of Regulatory Mechanisms and Institutions* in *Handbook of Industrial Organization* 1349 (Richard Schmalensee & Robert D. Willig eds., 1989). ("Regulation involves government intervention in markets in response to some combination of normative objectives and private interests reflected through politics.").

3. W. Kip Viscusi et al., *Economics of Antitrust and Regulation* 297 (3d ed. 2000).

4. *Id.* at 297.

5. *See also id.* at 3 ("The government has two types of mechanisms at its disposal to address these departures from the perfectly competitive model. The first mechanism is price incentives. We can impose a tax on various kinds of activities in order to decrease their attractiveness. . . . An alternative to taxes is to try to control behavior directly [via regulation].").

6. Breyer, *Regulation, supra* chap. 1, note 1, at 160. *Cf. U.S. Dep't of Justice, Overview: Antitrust Division* 1–2 (2002), *available at* http://www.usdoj.gov/atr/overview.html.

7. Breyer, *Regulation, supra* chap. 1, note 1, at 160.

8. *Id.* at 156–57.

131

9. Herbert Hovenkamp, *The Areeda-Turner Treatise in Antitrust Analysis*, 41 *Antitrust Bull.* 815, 832 (1996) (emphasis added). *See also* Hovenkamp, *Federal Antitrust Policy* 699 (2d ed. 1999).

10. Paul L. Joskow, *Mixing Regulatory and Antitrust Policies in the Electric Power Industry: The Price Squeeze and Retail Market Competition*, in *Antitrust and Regulation* 173 (Franklin M. Fisher ed., 1985). *See also* Paul L. Joskow, *Transaction Cost Economics, Antitrust Rules and Remedies*, 18 *J.L. Econ. & Org.* 95, 98 (2002).

11. George Bittlingmayer, *The Economic Problem of Fixed Costs and What Legal Research Can Contribute*, 14 *Law & Soc. Inquiry* 739, 744 (1989).

12. Glen O. Robinson, *On Refusing to Deal with Rivals*, 87 *Cornell L. Rev.* 1177, 1184 (2002).

13. Thomas Gale Moore, *Introduction* to *Antitrust and Economic Efficiency: A Conference Sponsored by the Hoover Institution*, 28 *J.L. & Econ.* 245, 245 (1985).

14. Peter J. Hammer & William M. Sage, *Antitrust, Health Care Quality, and the Courts*, 102 *Colum. L. Rev.* 545, 637 (2002). Ironically, in some markets such as broadband, regulation plays an even more important role in fostering competition than antitrust. *See, e.g.*, Lawrence A. Sullivan, *An Inquiry Into Antitrust, Intellectual Property, and Broadband Regulation as Applied to the "New Economy,"* 52 *Case W. Res. L. Rev.* 41, 75 (2001).

15. William J. Baumol & J. Gregory Sidak, *Toward Competition in Local Telephony* 27 (1994).

16. Jean-Jacques Laffont & Jean Tirole, *Competition in Telecommunications* 277 (2000).

17. The benefits of such cross-fertilization can be substantial. One example where antitrust can inform conventional economic regulation is the essential facilities doctrine, discussed in chapter 6. Others involve defining markets and identifying anticompetitive behavior. *See, e.g.*, Inquiry Concerning the Commission's Merger Policy under the Federal Power Act: Policy Statement, Order 592, Issued Dec. 18, 1996, 77 FERC ¶¶ 61, 263 (bringing the Federal Energy Regulatory Commission's merger guidelines more in line with those of the Department of Justice); News Release, Federal Communications Commission, FCC Sets Limits on Media Concentration 9 (June 2, 2003), *available at* http://hraunfoss.fcc.gov/edocs_public/attachmatch/DOC-235047A1.pdf (creating a media diversity index "modeled on the Herfindahl-Hirschmann [*sic*] Index (HHI) which is used in antitrust analysis to measure the degree concentration [*sic*] in an economic market."); Federal Communications Commission, Ninth Annual Assessment, of the Status of Competition in the Market for the Delivery of Video Programming ¶ 28 (2002), *available at* http://hraunfoss.fcc.gov/edocs/public/attachmatch/FCC-02-338A1.pdf (noting significant barriers to entry in cable marketing, notably "(a) predatory conduct including 'predatory pricing'; (b) strategic behavior by an

incumbent to raise its rival's costs by limiting the availability of certain popular programming as well as equipment. . . .").

18. For a concise history of economic regulation, see Viscusi et al., *supra* chap. 1, note 3, at 301–07.

19. Air Commerce Act of 1926, Pub. L. No. 69-254, 44 Stat. 568 (1926).

20. *See, e.g.*, Howard K. Gruenspecht & Lester B. Lave, *The Economics of Health, Safety, and Environmental Regulation*, in *Handbook of Industrial Organization, supra* chap. 1, note 2, at 1509. The Bureau of Chemistry eventually transformed into the FDA in 1931. For a comprehensive timeline of the foundation and transformation of regulatory agencies, see Clifford Winston et al., *Explaining Regulatory Policy*, 1994 *Brookings Papers on Econ. Activity: Microeconomics* 1.

21. *See, e.g.*, Reza Dibadj, *Saving Antitrust*, 75 *Univ. Colo. L. Rev.* 745, 763–64 (2004).

22. Alfred E. Kahn, *The Political Feasibility of Regulatory Reform*, in *Reforming Social Regulation: Alternative Public Policy Strategies* 252 (Le Roy Graymer & Frederick Thompson eds., 1982). *See also* 1 Alfred E. Kahn, *The Economics of Regulation* 10 (1970); Alfred E. Kahn, *Lessons from Deregulation: Telecommunications and Airlines after the Crunch* 11 (2004).

23. The faith stemmed from the Progressives' identification with the legal realist tradition. *See, e.g.*, Herbert Hovenkamp, *Knowledge About Welfare: Legal Realism and the Separation of Law and Economics*, 84 *Minn. L. Rev.* 805, 854 (2000).

24. Breyer, *Regulation, supra* chap. 1, note 1, at 350–51 (emphasis added).

25. *See, e.g.*, Eugene V. Rostow, *The New Sherman Act: A Positive Instrument of Progress*, 14 *U. Chi. L. Rev.* 567 (1947). *See also* Spencer Weber Waller, *The Antitrust Legacy of Thurman Arnold*, 78 *St. John's L. Rev.* 569 (2004). For an excellent discussion of the "new" Sherman act, see Joel B. Dirlam & Alfred E. Kahn, *Fair Competition: The Law and Economics of Antitrust Policy* (1954). For a survey of the political shifts in antitrust since the adoption of the Sherman Act, see, e.g., Robert A. Skitol, *The Shifting Sands of Antitrust Policy: Where It Has Been, Where It Is Now, Where It Will Be in Its Third Century*, 9 *Cornell J.L. & Pub. Pol'y* 239 (1999); Laurence Zuckerman, *How the Antitrust Wars Wax and Wane, N.Y. Times*, Apr. 11, 1998, at B7.

26. Viscusi et al., *Economics of Regulation, supra* chap. 1, note 3, at 637.

27. For a thoughtful summary of macroeconomic conditions prevailing at the time, notably "stagflation," see Alfred E. Kahn, *Can Liberalism Survive Inflation? Economist*, Mar. 7, 1981, at 3.

28. Kahn, *Political Feasibility, supra* chap. 1, note 22, at 247.

29. *Id.* at 253.

30. *Id.* at 256.

31. *See, e.g.*, Sullivan, *Broadband Regulation, supra* chap. 1, note 14, at 47.

32. Although Baxter was instrumental in the antitrust action that led to the dissolution of AT&T. *See, e.g.*, Howard A. Shelanski & J. Gregory Sidak, *Antitrust Divestiture in Network Industries*, 68 *U. Chi. L. Rev.* 1, 1 (2001).

33. Paul L. Joskow & Nancy L. Rose, *The Effects of Economic Regulation*, in *Handbook of Industrial Organization, supra* chap. 1, note 2, at 1497. *See also* Viscusi et al., *Economics of Regulation, supra* chap. 1, note 3, at 302.

34. *See also* Gruenspecht & Lave, *Health, Safety, and Environmental Regulation, supra* chap. 1, note 20, at 1513.

35. Per-Olov Johansson, *An Introduction to Modern Welfare Economics* 60 (1991). *See also* Breyer, *Regulation, supra* chap. 1, note 1, at 15.

36. *See, e.g.*, Breyer, *Regulation, supra* chap. 1, note 1, at 15.

37. *See, e.g.*, Ronald R. Braeutigam, *Optimal Policies for Natural Monopolies*, in *Handbook of Industrial Organization, supra* chap. 1, note 2, at 1292 ("The traditional story thus hinges on the existence of economies of scale (or increasing returns to scale) in an industry.").

38. *See, e.g.*, Richard A. Posner, *Natural Monopoly and Its Regulation*, 21 *Stan. L. Rev.* 548, 548 (1969) ("If the entire demand within a relevant market can be satisfied at lowest cost by one firm rather than by two or more, the market is a natural monopoly, whatever the actual number of firms in it.").

39. Viscusi et al., *Economics of Regulation, supra* chap. 1, note 3, at 314.

40. Johansson, *Welfare Economics, supra* chap. 1, note 35, at 7. *See also* Breyer, *Regulation, supra* chap. 1, note 1, at 15.

41. Roger Noll, *Economic Perspectives on the Politics of Regulation*, in *Handbook of Industrial Organization, supra* chap. 1, note 2, at 1255–56.

42. *See, e.g.*, Joskow & Rose, *Economic Regulation, supra* chap. 1, note 33, at 1454.

43. Noll, *Politics of Regulation, supra* chap. 1, note 41, at 1256.

44. Breyer, *Regulation, supra* chap. 1, note 1, at 23.

45. *Cf.* Viscusi et al., *Economics of Regulation, supra* chap. 1, note 3, at 314 ("An *externality* exists when the actions of one agent, say agent A, affect the utility or production function of another agent, say agent B, *and* agent A does not care how his behavior affects B's welfare.").

46. *See, e.g.*, Noll, *Politics of Regulation, supra* chap. 1, note 41, at 1256.

47. Johansson, *Welfare Economics, supra* chap. 1, note 35, at 7.

48. *See, e.g.*, Reza Dibadj, *Rescuing Broadband in America Requires a New Path*, L.A. Daily J., Sept. 30, 2004, at 6.

49. Johansson, *Welfare Economics*, *supra* chap. 1, note 35, at 7 (emphasis added).

50. James Q. Wilson, *Bureaucracy* 347 (1989).

51. Breyer, *Regulation*, *supra* chap. 1, note 1, at 27.

52. Noll, *Politics of Regulation*, *supra* chap. 1, note 41, at 1256. *See also* Johansson, *Welfare Economics*, *supra* chap. 1, note 35, at 68.

53. Viscusi et al., *Economics of Regulation*, *supra* chap. 1, note 3, at 8. *See also* Breyer, *Regulation*, *supra* chap. 1, note 1, at 34; Gruenspecht & Lave, *Health, Safety, and Environmental Regulation*, *supra* chap. 1, note 20, at 1508.

54. Braeutigam, *Natural Monopolies*, *supra* chap. 1, note 37, at 1299.

55. Breyer, *Regulation*, *supra* chap. 1, note 1, at 22.

56. *See, e.g.*, Thomas G. Krattenmaker, *The Telecommunications Act of 1996*, 29 Conn. L. Rev. 123, 142–45 (1996); Robert W. Crandall & Jerry A. Hausman, *Competition in U.S. Telecommunications Services: Effects of the 1996 Legislation*, in *Deregulation of Network Industries* 81 (Sam Peltzman & Clifford Winston eds., 2000).

57. *See, e.g.*, Jim Rossi, *The Common Law "Duty to Serve" and Protection of Consumers in an Age of Competitive Retail Public Utility Restructuring*, 51 Vand. L. Rev. 1233, 1321 (1998).

58. *See, e.g.*, News Release, Federal Communications Commission, FCC Sets Limits on Media Concentration 1 (June 2, 2003), *available at* http://hraunfoss.fcc.gov/edocs_public/attachmatch/DOC-235047A1.pdf.

59. Breyer, *Regulation*, *supra* chap. 1, note 1, at 22. *See also* Noll, *Politics of Regulation*, *supra* chap. 1, note 41, at 1257.

60. *See, e.g.*, Dibadj, *Saving Antitrust*, *supra* chap. 1, note 21, at 755–59.

61. Johansson, *Welfare Economics*, *supra* chap. 1, note 35, at 70. *Cf.* Gruenspecht & Lave, *Health, Safety, and Environmental Regulation*, *supra* chap. 1, note 20, at 1531 ("Paternalism, not market failure, is the primary motivation behind much HSE regulation.").

62. J. Gregory Sidak & Daniel F. Spulber, *Deregulation and Managed Competition in Network Industries*, 15 Yale J. on Reg. 117, 118 (1998).

63. *See, e.g.*, Viscusi et al., *Economics of Regulation*, *supra* chap. 1, note 3, at 313.

64. *Cf.* Noll, *Politics of Regulation*, *supra* chap. 1, note 41, at 1254–55.

65. Viscusi et al., *Economics of Regulation, supra* chap. 1, note 3, at 315–16.

66. *See, e.g.*, David Hume, *A Treatise of Human Nature* 469 (L.A. Selby-Bigge ed., Oxford University Press 2d ed. 1978) (1740) ("when of a sudden I am surpriz'd to find, that instead of the usual copulations of propositions, *is*, and *is not*, I meet with no proposition that is not connected with an *ought*, or an *ought not*") (emphasis added).

67. Edward L. Rubin, *New Directions: Law and the Methodology of Law*, 1997 *Wis. L. Rev.* 521, 545–46.

68. *Cf.* Joskow & Rose, *Economic Regulation, supra* chap. 1, note 33, at 1452.

CHAPTER 2. LAMBASTING REGULATION

1. Alfred Kahn helpfully groups the movements to undo NPT under the rubric of "revisionist scholarship." *See* Kahn, *Political Feasibility, supra* chap. 1, note 22, at 249.

2. R. H. Coase, *The Problem of Social Cost*, 3 *J.L. & Econ.* 1 (1960).

3. Harvey Averch & Leland L. Johnson, *Behavior of the Firm Under Regulatory Constraint*, 52 *Am. Econ. Rev.* 1052 (1962).

4. George J. Stigler, *The Theory of Economic Regulation*, 2 *Bell J. Econ. & Mgmt. Sci.* 3 (1971).

5. Coase, *Social Cost, supra* chap. 1, note 2, at 8.

6. *Id.* at 14 (emphasis added).

7. *Id.* at 15.

8. *Id.* at 18.

9. *See* Averch & Johnson, *supra* chap. 1, note 3, at 1062–68. *See also* Paul L. Joskow & Roger G. Noll, *The Bell Doctrine: Applications in Telecommunications, Electricity, and Other Network Industries*, 51 *Stan. L. Rev.* 1249, 1269 (1999).

10. *See* chapter 6 for an alternative to retail rate regulation.

11. Stigler, *Economic Regulation, supra* chap. 2, note 4, at 9.

12. *See id.* at 13–17.

13. *Id.* at 3.

14. For good overviews of Chicago school economics, see, e.g., William H. Page, *The Chicago School and the Evolution of Antitrust: Characterization, Antitrust Injury, and Evidentiary Sufficiency*, 75 *Va. L. Rev.* 1221 (1989); Ron Harris, *The Uses of History in Law and Economics*, 4 *Theoretical Inq. L.* 659, 661–74 (2003).

15. For a discussion of different types of efficiency, including "productive efficiency" and "dynamic efficiency," see Shelanski & Sidak, *supra* chap. 1, note 32, at 18.

16. *See, e.g.*, Harold Demsetz, *Toward a Theory of Property Rights*, 57 *Am. Econ. Rev.* 347, 349 (1967).

17. For a lionization of the common law, see Richard A. Posner, *Economic Analysis of Law* 271–90 (5th ed. 1998).

18. *See, e.g.*, William M. Landes, *An Economic Analysis of the Courts*, 14 *J.L. & Econ.* 61 (1971); Richard A. Posner, *An Economic Approach to Legal Procedure and Judicial Administration*, 2 *J. Legal Stud.* 399 (1973).

19. Chicagoans, of course, did not originate the economic analysis of antitrust. *See* Herbert Hovenkamp, *Antitrust Policy After Chicago*, 84 *Mich. L. Rev.* 213, 223 (1985).

20. Tying is "an agreement by a party to sell one product but only on the condition that the buyer also purchases a different (or tied) product, or at least agrees that he will not purchase that product from any other supplier." *Northern Pacific Railway Co. v. United States*, 356 U.S. 1, 5–6 (1958).

21. *See, e.g.*, Ward S. Bowman, *Tying Arrangements and the Leverage Problem*, 67 *Yale L.J.* 19 (1957) ("Analysis of the situations in which sellers find tie-ins useful casts doubt upon the validity of the statement that the only purpose of tie-ins is monopolistic exploitation."); Keith N. Hylton, *Antitrust Law* 308 (2003) ("The core of the Chicago School critique is that tying cannot be used to enhance monopoly profits when the market for the tied good is competitive."); Louis Kaplow, *Extension of Monopoly Power Through Leverage*, 85 *Colum. L. Rev.* 515, 515–16 (1985) (noting the traditional Chicago school view that "antitrust law should be indifferent to the exploitation of monopoly power because extant power is a fixed sum and thus will result in the same damage regardless of how it is deployed.").

22. *See* Robert H. Bork, *The Antitrust Paradox* (1978). For a similar take on antitrust law, see Richard A. Posner, *Antitrust Law* (2d ed. 2001).

23. *Cf.* Alfred E. Kahn, *Whom the Gods Would Destroy, or How Not to Deregulate* 39 (2001) (noting that the Chicago school has "virtually written predation out of the antitrust laws").

24. Bork, *supra* chap. 2, note 22, at 406. Of course the criticism of vigorous antitrust enforcement predates Bork's book. For a perceptive critique of the early opponents of antitrust, see Dirlam & Kahn, *supra* chap. 1, note 25, at 284 (lamenting that antitrust's critics "would, on the strength of inconclusive economic analysis that does not show what they say it shows, amend a law that does not say what they say it says, in such a way as to jeopardize social, political and economic values that all of us are intent on preserving.").

25. Harold Demsetz, *Why Regulate Utilities?* 11 *J.L. & Econ.* 55, 56 (1968).

26. *Id.* at 65.

27. Posner, *Natural Monopoly, supra* chap. 1, note 38, at 549.

28. *Id.* at 635.

29. *Id.* at 639.

30. Richard A. Posner, *The Social Costs of Monopoly and Regulation,* 83 *J. Pol. Econ.* 807, 821 (1975). He even later professes that the "small businessman usually is helped rather than hurt by monopoly." Posner, *Antitrust Law, supra* chap. 2, note 22, at 2.

31. Larissa MacFarquhar, *The Bench Burner, New Yorker,* Dec. 10, 2001, at 78.

32. Laura Kalman, *The Strange Career of Legal Liberalism* 78 (1996).

33. Robert C. Ellickson, *Bringing Culture and Human Frailty to Rational Actors: A Critique of Classical Law and Economics,* 65 *Chi.-Kent. L. Rev.* 23, 26 (1989).

34. *See* Posner, *Economic Analysis, supra* chap. 2, note 17.

35. *Id.* at vii.

36. For an overview of these efforts, see Jeffrey Rosen, *The Unregulated Offensive, N.Y. Times Mag.,* Apr. 17, 2005, at 42. *See also* Richard A. Epstein, *Classical, Liberal, Rational, Wall St. J.,* Sept. 5, 2003, at A8.

37. In fact, these efforts have been so successful that one prominent foundation has closed its doors, essentially declaring victory. *See* Jason DeParle, *Goals Reached, Donor on Right Closes Up Shop, N.Y. Times,* May 29, 2005, § 1, at 1.

38. Elizabeth E. Bailey, *Contestability and the Design of Regulatory and Antitrust Policy,* 71 *Am. Econ. Rev.* 178, 178 (1981). *See also* Elizabeth E. Bailey & William J. Baumol, *Deregulation and the Theory of Contestable Markets,* 1 *Yale J. on Reg.* 111, 113 (1984).

39. A sunk cost is "an outlay that cannot be recouped without substantial delay." Bailey & Baumol, *supra* chap. 2, note 38, at 113–14.

40. *Id.* at 123. *See also* William J. Baumol et al., *Weak Invisible Hand Theorems on the Sustainability of Multiproduct Natural Monopoly,* 67 *Am. Econ. Rev.* 350, 360 (1977); William J. Baumol, *Contestable Markets: An Uprising in the Theory of Industry Structure,* 72 *Am. Econ. Rev.* 1, 14 (1982).

41. Bailey & Baumol, *supra* chap. 2, note 38, at 111.

42. Baumol, *Uprising, supra* chap. 2, note 40, at 14 (emphasis added).

43. *See, e.g.,* Harold Demsetz, *Barriers to Entry,* 72 *Am. Econ. Rev.* 47 (1982).

44. Daniel A. Farber & Philip P. Frickey, *Law and Public Choice: A Critical Introduction* 44 (1991).

45. *See, e.g.*, James M. Buchanan, *Politics, Policy, and the Pigovian Margins*, 29 *Economica* 17 (1962).

46. James M. Buchanan, *A Contractarian Paradigm for Applying Economic Theory*, 65 *Am. Econ. Rev.* 225, 229 (1975).

47. *Id. See also* James M. Buchanan, *Contractarian Political Economy and Constitutional Interpretation*, 78 *Am. Econ. Rev.* 135 (1988).

48. For example, the mainstream press regularly uses public choice ideas to explain the failures of regulatory agencies. *See, e.g.*, Gardiner Harris, *At F.D.A, Strong Drug Ties and Less Monitoring*, N.Y. *Times*, Dec. 6, 2004, at A2; David Willman, *The National Institutes of Health: Public Servant or Private Marketer?* L.A. *Times*, Dec. 22, 2004, at A1; Eric Schlosser, *The Cow Jumped over the U.S.D.A.*, N.Y. *Times*, Jan. 2, 2004, at A17.

49. *See, e.g.*, *The Federalist No. 10*, at 57 (James Madison) (Jacob E. Cooke ed., 1961).

50. Mancur Olson, *The Logic of Collective Action* 128 (1971) (emphasis added).

51. Some of Buchanan's followers may have taken his insights to an extreme. For instance, it is one thing to say that gains-from-trade should be included in public policy. It is quite another to say that all other considerations should be disregarded. *Cf.* Howard Banks, *A Talk with the Nobel Laureate*, *Forbes*, Nov. 17, 1986, at 108.

52. For a good description of this phenomenon, *see* Viscusi et al., *Economics of Regulation*, *supra* chap. 1, note 3, at 10.

53. *See also id.* at 314–21.

54. Michael C. Jensen & William H. Meckling, *Can the Corporation Survive?* 78 *Fin. Analysts J.* 31, 32 (1978). *See also* Michael C. Jensen, *The Debasement of Contracts and the Decline of Capital Markets*, in *The World Capital Shortage* 73 (Alan Heslop ed., 1977).

55. Jensen & Meckling, *supra* chap. 2, note 54, at 32. *See also id.* at 33 (listing a parade of horribles associated with regulation).

56. *See* Gregory Sidak & Daniel F. Spulber, *Deregulatory Takings and Breach of the Regulatory Contract*, 71 *N.Y.U. L. Rev.* 851 (1996).

57. Thomas W. Hazlett, *Explaining the Telecommunications Act of 1996: Comment on Thomas G. Krattenmaker*, 29 *Conn. L. Rev.* 217, 239 (1996).

58. *See, e.g.*, Bork, *Antitrust Paradox*, *supra* chap. 2, note 22.

59. *See, e.g.*, Posner, *Antitrust Law*, *supra* chap. 2, note 22.

60. *See, e.g.*, Milton Friedman, *Capitalism and Freedom* 132 (1962).

61. Fred S. McChesney & William F. Shughart II, *The Unjoined Debate*, in *The Causes and Consequences of Antitrust: The Public-Choice Perspective* 349 (Fred S. McChesney & William F. Shughart II eds., 1995).

62. Fred S. McChesney & William F. Shughart II, *Preface to The Causes and Consequences of Antitrust, supra* chap. 2, note 61, at ix–x.

63. *See, e.g.*, Fred S. McChesney, *Be True to Your School: Chicago's Contradictory Views of Antitrust and Regulation*, in *The Causes and Consequences of Antitrust, supra* chap. 2, note 61, at 324.

64. Hovenkamp, *Knowledge About Welfare, supra* chap. 1, note 23, at 809–10.

Chapter 3. Where Is Society Left?

1. *See, e.g.*, Reza Dibadj, *Deregulation: A Tragedy in Three Acts*, Wash. Post, Sept. 13, 2003, at A21.

2. *Deregulated*, Consumer Rep., July 2002, at 30.

3. *Id.*

4. *See, e.g.*, Steven A. Morrison & Clifford Winston, *The Fare Skies: Air Transportation and Middle America*, 15 Brookings Rev. 42 (1997) (claiming that deregulation was responsible for a 20% drop in fares between 1976 and 1993).

5. *See, e.g.*, Kahn, *Lessons from Deregulation, supra* chap. 1, note 22, at 3.

6. Alfred E. Kahn, *Deregulation: Looking Backward and Looking Forward*, 7 Yale J. on Reg. 325, 344 (1990).

7. E. Han Kim & Vijay Singal, *Mergers and Market Power: Evidence from the Airline Industry*, 83 Am. Econ. Rev. 549, 550 (1993). *See also* Robert D. Willig, *Antitrust Lessons from the Airline Industry: The DOJ Experience*, 60 Antitrust L.J. 695, 701 (1992); David R. Graham et al., *Efficiency and Competition in the Airline Industry*, 14 Bell J. Econ. 118, 137 (1983).

8. *See* Alfred E. Kahn, *Deregulatory Schizophrenia*, 75 Cal. L. Rev. 1059, 1062–64 (1987).

9. *See* Alfred E. Kahn, *Air Travel's Free Market Works*, L.A. Times, Sept. 16, 2004, at B11. *Cf.* Patrick Smith, *Travel Plans*, N.Y. Times, Dec. 22, 2004, at A31 (noting the low employee pay at upstart airlines, as well as characteristically poor service across the entire airline industry).

10. *See, e.g.*, John W. Berresford, *Mergers in Mobile Telecommunications Services: A Primer on the Analysis of Their Competitive Effects*, 48 Fed. Comm. L.J. 247

(1996); Robert Kuttner, *AT&T and Comcast: A Bad Deal for Almost Everybody*, Bus. Wk., May 20, 2002, at 26.

11. *See, e.g.*, Reza Dibadj, *Toward Meaningful Cable Competition: Getting Beyond the Monopoly Morass*, 6 N.Y.U. J. Legisl. & Pub. Pol'y 245 (2003); William Safire, *Regulate the F.C.C.*, N.Y. Times, June 16, 2003, at A19; William Safire, *On Media Giantism*, N.Y. Times, Jan. 20, 2003, at A19.

12. Walter Adams & James W. Brock, *Antitrust, Ideology, and the Arabesques of Economic Theory*, 66 U. Colo. L. Rev. 257, 317 (1995). *See also* Ronald J. Gilson & Mark J. Roe, *Understanding the Japanese Keiretsu: Overlaps Between Corporate Governance and Industrial Organization*, 102 Yale L.J. 871, 877–78 (1993).

13. Kahn, *Deregulation*, *supra* chap. 3, note 6, at 338.

14. Kahn, *Deregulatory Schizophrenia*, *supra* chap. 3, note 8, at 1059. *See also* Kahn, *Lessons from Deregulation*, *supra* chap. 1, note 22, at 47 ("Deregulation shifts the major burden of consumer protection to the competitive market, and therefore, in important measure, to the enforcement of the antitrust laws.").

15. Kahn, *Deregulation*, *supra* chap. 3, note 6, at 350–51.

16. *See, e.g.*, Dan Benson, *Petri Targets "Rogue Movers,"* Milwaukee J.-Sentinel, Mar. 4, 2003, at 4B.

17. *See, e.g.*, Michelle Cole & Brent Walsh, *Mad Cow Case Reveals Food Safety System Flaws*, Sunday Oregonian, Feb. 1, 2004, at A1; Anita Manning & Elizabeth Wise, *Who Is Minding the USA's Food Store*, USA Today, Jan. 27, 2004, at 1D.

18. Marilyn Geewax, *The Theory of Deregulation Proves Deadly in Practice*, Atlanta J. & Const., July 5, 1991, at A15. *See also* William Rice, *Safe to Eat? Consumers Stand Last in Line on the Safe-food Battlefront*, Chi. Trib., May 16, 1991, at C1.

19. *See, e.g.*, Tina Borgatta, *After Energy Jolt, Cities Think Small*, L.A. Times, May 26, 2002, at B1.

20. *See, e.g.*, Lorraine Mirabella & Dan Thanh Dang, *Utilities Add Blackout to Woes*, Baltimore Sun, Aug. 24, 2003, at 1D.

21. *See, e.g.*, Rebecca Smith, *States Seek Ways to Curb Surging Electricity Bills*, Wall St. J., Feb. 28, 2006, at A1; Rebecca Smith, *Texas Electricity Deregulation Hasn't Aided Small Power Users*, Wall St. J., May 5, 2005, at A2; Rebecca Smith, *Hard Line: How a Texas Power Company Got Tough with Consumers*, Wall St. J., Mar. 22, 2005, at A1.

22. Kathryn Kranhold, *Short-Term Debt for Energy Industry Is Long-Term Problem*, Wall St. J., Nov. 6, 2002, at C1.

23. William W. Bratton, *Enron and the Dark Side of Shareholder Value*, 76 *Tul. L. Rev.* 1275, 1282 (2002).

24. *See, e.g.*, Reza Dibadj, *Excesses of Burst Economic Bubble Persist in After-math*, L.A. *Daily J.*, Sept. 23, 2003, at 6.

25. *See, e.g.*, Deborah Solomon & Ian McDonald, *Spitzer Decries Lax Regu-lation over Insurance*, Wall St. *J.*, Nov. 17, 2004, at C1; Monica Langley & Theo Francis, *Insurers Reel from Spitzer's Strike*, Wall St. *J.*, Oct. 18, 2004, at A1.

26. Kurt Eichenwald, *Could Capitalists Actually Bring Down Capitalism?* N.Y. *Times*, June 30, 2002, § 4 (The Week in Review), at 1 (emphasis added).

27. *See, e.g.*, Mark Maremont & Deborah Solomon, *Behind SEC's Failings: Caution, Tight Budget, '90s Exuberance*, Wall St. *J.*, Dec. 24, 2003, at A1.

28. *See, e.g.*, Scott J. Paltrow & Ianthe Jeanne Dugan, *State-Based Regula-tion Gets Scrutiny*, Wall St. *J.*, Oct. 18, 2004, at A15.

29. Schlesinger, *The Deregulators*, *supra* Preface, note 1, at A12.

30. Critics even suggest that, in exchange for liquidity, the Federal Reserve loosened its oversight of the banks it regulates, leading to "complicity by Fed-regulated banks in the recent corporate scandals." Greg Ip, *The Deregulator: A Less-Visible Role for the Fed Chief; Freeing Up Markets*, Wall St. *J.*, Nov. 19, 2004, at A1.

31. *See, e.g.*, Alex Berenson, *The Number* 85–87 (2003).

32. *See, e.g.*, Schlesinger, *The Deregulators*, *supra* Preface, note 1, at A12.

33. Steven Pearlstein, *Regulation vs. Competition: No Winner Yet*, Wash. Post, Nov. 2, 2002, at A14.

34. James Hansen, *Deregulation: Nothing Short of Disastrous*, Rocky Mountain News, Feb. 23, 2002, at 4W.

35. *See, e.g.*, Robert A. Moffitt & Peter Gottschalk, *Trends in the Transitory Variance of Earnings in the United States*, 112 Econ. *J.* C68 (2002); Sanford M. Jacoby, *Are Career Jobs Headed for Extinction?* 42 Cal. Mgmt. Rev. 123, 140 (1999); Dan Roberts & Christopher Swann, *America's Dilemma: As Business Retreats from its Welfare Role, Who Will Take Up the Burden?*, Fin Times, Jan. 13, 2006, at 17; Jacob S. Hacker, *Call It the Family Risk Factor*, N.Y. *Times*, Jan. 11, 2004, § 4, at 15; Jonathan Krim & Griff Witte, *Average-Wage Earners Fall Behind*, Wash. Post, Dec. 31, 2004, at A1.

36. Peter G. Gosselin, *If America Is Richer, Why Are Its Families So Much Less Secure?* L.A. *Times*, Oct. 10, 2004, at A1 (emphasis added). *See also* Peter G. Gosselin, *Corporate America Pulling Back Pension Safety Net*, L.A. *Times*, May 15, 2005, at A1; Dale Russakoff, *Retirement's Unraveling Safety Net*, Wash. Post, May 15, 2005, at A1; Peter G. Gosselin, *The New Deal: The Poor Have More Things Today—Including Wild Income Swings*, L.A. *Times*, Dec. 12, 2004, at A1.

37. *See, e.g.,* Debora Vrana, *Health Insurance Costs Jump 11.2%, L.A. Times,* Sept. 10, 2004, at A1. *Cf.* Janny Scott, *Life at the Top in America Isn't Just Better, It's Longer,. N.Y. Times,* May 16, 2005, at A1; Daniel Costello, *At What Cost? To Keep Health Coverage, More Workers Are Cutting Back on Food, Heat and Other Necessities, L.A. Times,* Apr. 4, 2005, at F1.

38. Donald L. Bartlett & James B. Steele, *The Health of Nations, N.Y. Times,* Oct. 24, 2004, § 4 (The Week in Review), at 11 (emphasis added).

39. A classic scheme is "Loan to Own" where lenders have been found "deliberately issuing mortgages to families that could not afford them, with the ultimate aim of foreclosing on these homes." Elizabeth Warren & Amelia Warren Tyagi, *The Two-Income Trap: Why Middle-Class Mothers and Fathers Are Going Broke* 136 (2003). *See also* Sandra Fleishman, *From Foreclosure to the Cleaners, Wash. Post,* Dec. 25, 2004, at A1.

40. *See* Warren & Tyagi, *supra* chap. 3, note 39, at 132–34. *See also* Patrick McGeehan et al., *Soaring Interest Is Compounding Credit Card Woes for Millions, N.Y. Times,* Nov. 21, 2004, § 1, at 1.

41. Which has become increasingly difficult, given recent bankruptcy reform. *See, e.g.,* Paul Krugman, *The Debt-Peonage Society, N.Y. Times,* Mar. 8, 2005, at A23.

42. *See, e.g.,* David Cay Johnston, *Richest Are Leaving the Rich Far Behind, N.Y. Times,* June 5, 2005, § 1, at 1.

43. *Where's The Stick? Economist,* Oct. 11, 2003, at 13. *See also* Dibadj, *Burst Economic Bubble, supra* chap. 3, note 24, at 26; Bob Herbert, *We're More Productive. Who Gets the Money? N.Y. Times,* Apr. 5, 2004, at A21.

44. *See, e.g.,* William Dietrich, *From American Ethic to Global Imperative, the World of Work Turns, Seattle Times,* July 25, 2004, at 14.

45. *See, e.g.,* Janny Scott & David Leonhardt, *Class in America: Shadowy Lines that Still Divide, N.Y. Times,* May 15, 2005, § 1, at 1 ("mobility, which once buoyed the working lives of Americans as it rose in the decades after World War II, has lately flattened out or possibly even declined, many researchers say."); David Wessel, *As Rich-Poor Gap Widens in the U.S., Class Mobility Stalls, Wall St. J.,* May 13, 2005, at A1. Not to mention that the growing wealth gap disproportionately affects Hispanics and African Americans. *See, e.g.,* Miriam Jordan, *Wealth Gap Widens in U.S. Between Minorities, Whites, Wall St. J.,* Oct. 18, 2004, at A2.

46. Gary Becker, *quoted in* Wessel, *supra* chap. 3, note 45, at A7 (emphasis added). For statistics regarding trends in income and poverty, see U.S. Census Bureau, *Income, Poverty, and Health Insurance Coverage in the United States: 2004* (Aug. 2005), *available at* http://www.census.gov/prod/2005pubs/p60-229.pdf.

47. Robert Kuttner, *The Road to Enron, Am. Prospect,* Mar. 25, 2002, at 2.

48. John Cassidy, *Striking it Rich: The Rise and Fall of Popular Capitalism*, *New Yorker*, Jan. 14, 2002, at 63 (emphasis added).

49. Peter G. Gosselin, *Private Prosperities, Public Breakdowns: The '90s Private Boom Stingy on Public Good*, L.A. *Times*, Aug. 5, 2001, at A1 (emphasis added).

50. *Id.*

51. Peter G. Gosselin, *Private Prosperities, Public Breakdowns: Amid Nationwide Prosperity, ERs See a Growing Emergency*, L.A. *Times*, Aug. 6, 2001, at A1.

52. Gosselin, *Stingy on Public Good*, supra chap. 3, note 49, at A1.

53. *Id.*

54. American Society of Civil Engineers, Report Card for America's Infrastructure: 2003 Progress Report 1, *available at* http://www.asce.org/reportcard/. The twelve categories are: roads, bridges, transit, aviation, schools, drinking water, wastewater, dams, solid waste, hazardous waste, navigable waterways, and energy. *See id. See also* Timothy Aeppel, *U.S. Waterway System Shows Its Age*, Wall St. J., Feb. 8, 2005, at A2.

55. Torie Osborn, *Nonprofits Can't Take the Place of Government*, L.A. *Times*, Dec. 13, 2003, at B27.

56. *Quoted in* Gosselin, *Stingy on Public Good*, supra chap. 3, note 49, at A1. *See also* Reza Dibadj, *Government Is Bad, Isn't It?*, S.F. Chron., Sept. 8, 2005, at B9.

57. *See, e.g.*, Reza Dibadj, *Regulatory Givings and the Anticommons*, 64 *Ohio St. L.J.* 1041, 1077–80 (2003).

58. Eli M. Noam, *Before the U.S. Senate Committee on Commerce on Radio Spectrum Allocations and Valuation*, 104th Cong. (July 25, 1995) (prepared testimony of Eli M. Noam), *at* http://www.citi.columbia.edu/elinoam/articles/spectrum_allocation_testimony.htm.

59. For a critique of the movement to privatize electromagnetic spectrum, see Dibadj, *Regulatory Givings*, supra chap. 3, note 57.

60. *See, e.g.*, Richard Stroup & John Baden, *Externality, Property Rights, and the Management of Our National Forests*, 16 *J.L. & Econ.* 303 (1973).

61. *See, e.g.*, Paul Stanton Kibel, *Reconstructing the Marketplace: The International Timber Trade and Forest Protection*, 5 *N.Y.U. Envtl. L.J.* 735 (1996).

62. *See, e.g.*, Perri Knize, *The Mismanagement of the National Forests*, *Atlantic Monthly*, Oct. 1991, at 98.

63. *See, e.g.*, Paul Roberts, *The Federal Chain-Saw Massacre*, *Harper's Mag.*, June 1997, at 37; Curt Anderson, *Timber Sales Lost Millions in 1997*, *Chattanooga Times*, June 11, 1998, at C6.

64. R. Brent Walton, *Ellickson's Paradox: It's Suicide to Maximize Welfare*, 7 *N.Y.U. Envtl. L.J.* 153, 183 (1999).

65. Charles M. Haar, *Suburbs Under Siege: Race, Space, and Audacious Judges* 208 (1996).

66. *Id.* at xiii.

67. For an example of a typical zoning ordinance, *see S. Burlington County NAACP v. Township of Mount Laurel*, 336 A.2d 713, 719–20 (N.J. 1975) (Mt. Laurel I).

68. Kenneth T. Jackson, *Crabgrass Frontier* 219 (1985).

69. Sullivan, *Broadband Regulation, supra* chap. 1, note 14, at 89.

70. *See, e.g., State St. Bank & Trust Co. v. Signature Fin. Group*, 149 F.3d 1368, 1373 (Fed. Cir. 1998); Maureen A. O'Rourke, *Toward a Doctrine of Fair Use in Patent Law*, 100 *Colum. L. Rev.* 1177, 1178–79 (2000).

71. *See, e.g.*, Jack M. Balkin, *Don't Use Those Words: Fox News Owns Them*, *L.A. Times*, Aug. 14, 2003, at B15.

72. *See* Sonny Bono Copyright Term Extension Act of 1998, Pub. L. No. 105–298, § 120(a), 112 Stat. 2827 (1998) (codified at 17 U.S.C. §§ 301–304 (2000)).

73. *See* Digital Millennium Copyright Act (DMCA), Digital Millennium Copyright Act, Pub. L. No. 105–304, § 103(a), 112 Stat. 2863 (1998) (codified at 17 U.S.C. § 1201(a)–(b) (2000)).

74. Ruth Okediji, *Givers, Takers, and Other Kinds of Users: A Fair Use Doctrine for Cyberspace*, 53 *Fla. L. Rev.* 107, 179–80 (2001). *See also* Jed Rubenfeld, *The Freedom of Imagination: Copyright's Constitutionality*, 112 *Yale L.J.* 1 (2002).

75. *Cf.* Justin Hughes, *The Philosophy of Intellectual Property*, 77 *Geo. L.J.* 287, 323 (1988).

76. Edward R. Johnson, *The Law Against Sharing Knowledge*, *Chron. Higher Educ.*, Feb. 14, 2003, at B14.

77. *See, e.g.*, R.G. Edmonson, *Stuck in the Doldrums: Cargo-liability Reform Bogs Down at New York Meeting*, *J. of Com.*, May 31, 2004, at 21; Ron Lent, *Ship Reform Act Leaves Underwriters at Sea*, *J. of Com.*, Sept. 1, 1999, at 8.

78. *See e.g.*, Bob Keefe, *Some Not Ready to Toss Lifelines to All Those Ailing*, *Atlanta J. & Const.*, Oct. 5, 2001, at A8.

79. Christopher Oster et al., *After Storms, Florida Wakes Up to New Insurance Reality*, *Wall St. J.*, Sept. 7, 2004, at A1 (emphasis added).

80. *Id.*

81. *See* Keefe, *supra* chap. 3, note 78, at A8.

82. *See, e.g.,* Peter Coy, *How the Game Was Played—and Why Long-Term Lost,* Bus. Wk., Oct. 12, 1998, at 40.

83. *See* Gary H. Stern & Ron Feldman, *Big Banks, Big Bailouts,* Wall St. J., Jan. 27, 2004, at A14.

84. Alan Freeman & Elizabeth Mensch. *The Public-Private Distinction in American Law and Life,* 36 Buff. L. Rev. 237, 248–49 (1987) (emphasis added).

85. Felix Rohatyn, *Free, Wealthy and Fair,* Wall St. J., Nov. 11, 2003, at A18 (emphasis added).

86. Kahn, *Liberalism, supra* chap. 1, note 27, at 6.

87. *Id.*

88. *Quoted in* Louis Uchitelle, *Looking for Ways to Make Deregulation Keep Its Promises,* N.Y. Times, July 28, 2002, at C12 (emphasis added). *Cf.* Irwin Stelzer, *Deregulation: It's Their Loss and Your Gain,* Sunday Times, Aug. 25, 2002, at 4.

CHAPTER 4. BEYOND FLAWED ASSUMPTIONS . . .

1. Contestability theory and the Averch-Johnson hypothesis, the two other principal contributors to this demise, are addressed in chapters 5 and 6, respectively.

2. Posner, *Economic Analysis, supra* chap. 2, note 17, at 14.

3. *Id.* (emphasis added).

4. Hovenkamp, *After Chicago, supra* chap. 2, note 19, at 245–46.

5. *See* Amartya Sen, *The Impossibility of a Paretian Liberal,* 78 J. Pol. Econ. 152 (1970).

6. *See also* Johansson, *Welfare Economics, supra* chap. 1, note 35, at 100.

7. *See* Posner, *Economic Analysis, supra* chap. 2, note 17, at 13–14.

8. *See id.* at 503.

9. Joseph William Singer, *Legal Realism Now,* 76 Cal. L. Rev. 467, 527 (1988) (book review). *See also* Anthony D'Amato, *Post-Revolutionary Law and Economics: A Foreword to the Symposium,* 20 Hofstra L. Rev. 757, 759 (1992).

10. Posner, *Economic Analysis, supra* chap. 2, note 17, at 27. *See also* Richard A. Posner, *quoted in* Douglas Baird, *The Future of Law and Economics: Looking Forward; Introduction,* 64 U. Chi. L. Rev. 1129, 1153 (1997).

11. Peter Huber, *Law and Disorder in Cyberspace: Abolish the FCC and Let Common Law Rule the Telecosm* xv (1997).

12. *Id.* at 206.

13. *See, e.g.,* John F. Duffy, *The FCC and the Patent System: Progressive Ideals, Jacksonian Realism, and the Technology of Regulation,* 71 *U. Colo. L. Rev.* 1071, 1077 (2000). For an impressionistic discussion of why Posner feels the common law is more efficient, see Posner, *Economic Analysis, supra* chap. 2, note 17, at 274–75. *See also* Mark M. Hager, *The Emperor's Clothes Are Not Efficient: Posner's Jurisprudence of Class,* 41 *Am. U. L. Rev.* 7, 16 (1991).

14. *See* George L. Priest, *The New Scientism in Legal Scholarship: A Comment on Clark and Posner,* 90 *Yale L.J.* 1284, 1290–91 (1981).

15. Hovenkamp, *After Chicago, supra* chap. 2, note 19, at 254–55.

16. *See* Susan Rose-Ackerman, *Progressive Law and Economics—and the New Administrative Law,* 98 *Yale L.J.* 341 (1988). *See also* Ellickson, *Rational Actors, supra* chap. 2, note 33, at 52.

17. Frederick M. Rowe, *The Decline of Antitrust and the Delusions of Models: The Faustian Pact of Law and Economics,* 72 *Geo. L.J.* 1511, 1549 (1984) (emphasis added).

18. Friedman, *Capitalism and Freedom, supra* chap. 2, note 60, at 3.

19. Posner, *Economic Analysis, supra* chap. 2, note 17, at 11.

20. Coase, *Social Cost, supra* chap. 2, note 2, at 3.

21. *See id.,* at 8.

22. Carl J. Dahlman, *The Problem of Externality,* 22 *J.L. & Econ.* 141, 148 (1979). *See also* A. Mitchell Polinsky, *An Introduction to Law and Economics* 12 (2d ed. 1989); Robert C. Ellickson, *The Case for Coase and Against "Coaseanism,"* 99 *Yale L.J.* 611, 615 (1989).

23. *See* Olson, *supra* chap. 2, note 50, at 128.

24. *See* chapter 1.

25. *See, e.g.,* William A. Fischel, *The Economics of Zoning Laws: A Property Rights Approach to American Land Use Controls* (1985).

26. Yochai Benkler, *Overcoming Agoraphobia: Building the Commons of the Digitally Networked Environment,* 11 *Harv. J.L. & Tech.* 287, 389 (1998).

27. *See, e.g.,* Huber, *Cyberspace, supra* chap. 4, note 11.

28. Laffont & Tirole, *Telecommunications, supra* chap. 1, note 16, at 34.

29. *See, e.g.,* Lawrence J. White, *"Propertyzing" the Electromagnetic Spectrum: Why It's Important, and How to Begin,* 9 *Media L. & Pol'y* 19, 32 (2000).

30. Robert C. Ellickson, *Order Without Law* 280–81 (1991).

31. *See, e.g.,* R.H. Coase, *The Firm the Market and the Law* 7 (1988).

32. *See* R.H. Coase, *The Nature of the Firm*, 4 *Economica* 386 (1937).

33. For an overview of transaction cost economics, *see* Howard A. Shelanski & Peter G. Klein, *Empirical Research in Transaction Cost Economics: A Review and Assessment*, 11 *J.L. Econ. & Org.* 335, 337 (1995).

34. Oliver E. Williamson, *Transaction-Cost Economics: The Governance of Contractual Relations*, 22 *J.L. & Econ.* 233, 233 (1979).

35. D'Amato, *supra* chap. 4, note 9, at 761.

36. Oliver E. Williamson, *Franchise Bidding for Natural Monopolies—in General and with Respect to CATV*, 7 *Bell J. Econ.* 73, 74 (1976).

37. Coase, *Social Cost, supra* chap. 2, note 2, at 15 (emphasis added). *See also* Williamson, *Franchise Bidding, supra* chap. 4, note 36, at 74 n.2.

38. Coase, *Social Cost, supra* chap. 2, note 2, at 18.

39. *See* A.C. Pigou, *The Economics of Welfare* (4th ed. 1932).

40. *See* Coase, *Social Cost, supra* chap. 2, note 2, at 28–29.

41. Dahlman, *supra* chap. 4, note 22, at 160. *See also* Fischel, *supra* chap. 4, note 25, at 121.

42. Coase, *Firm Market Law, supra* chap. 4, note 31, at 174 (emphasis added).

43. *Id.* at 15 (emphasis added). *See also* Dahlman, *supra* chap. 4, note 22, at 161.

44. Ellickson, *Coaseanism, supra* chap. 4, note 22, at 611.

45. Jules L. Coleman, *Afterword: The Rational Choice Approach to Legal Rules*, 65 *Chi.-Kent L. Rev.* 177, 188 (1989).

46. Adam Smith, *An Inquiry into the Nature and Causes of the Wealth of Nations* 345 (1900).

47. *Id.* at 43.

48. *Id.* Of course, the great equilibrium theorists, notably Walras and Debreu, made similar assumptions. *See* Amitai Etzioni, *The Moral Dimension* 200 (1988).

49. Posner, *Economic Analysis, supra* chap. 2, note 17, at 3–4 (emphasis added).

50. *See also* Arthur Allen Leff, *Economic Analysis of Law: Some Realism About Nominalism*, 60 *Va. L. Rev.* 451, 456 (1974); Mario J. Rizzo, *The Mirage of Efficiency*, 8 *Hofstra L. Rev.* 641, 643 (1980); Gregory Scott Crespi, *The Mid-Life Crisis of the Law and Economics Movement: Confronting the Problems of Nonfalsifiability and Normative Bias*, 67 *Notre Dame L. Rev.* 231, 239–240 (1991).

51. *See, e.g.,* Gregory Mitchell, *Taking Behavioralism Too Seriously? The Unwanted Pessimism of the New Behavioral Analysis of Law,* 43 *Wm. & Mary L. Rev.* 1907, 2021 (2002).

52. Christine Jolls et al., *A Behavioral Approach to Law and Economics,* 50 *Stan. L. Rev.* 1471, 1489 (1998). *Cf.* Etzioni, *Moral Dimension, supra* chap. 4, note 48, at xi.

53. Amos Tversky & Daniel Kahneman, *Judgment Under Uncertainty: Heuristics and Biases,* 185 *Sci.* 1124, 1124 (1974). *Cf.* Etzioni, *Moral Dimension, supra* chap. 4, note 48, at 166–77.

54. Tversky & Kahneman, *Heuristics, supra* chap. 4, note 53, at 1131.

55. Jolls et al., *supra* chap. 4, note 52, at 1471. *See also id.* at 1477–79.

56. The classic experiment in this context surrounds the exchange of coffee mugs. People who were initially given the mugs wanted twice as much to give them up as those who didn't have a mug were willing to pay. *See id.* at 1483–85.

57. Jennifer Arlen, Comment, *The Future of Behavioral Economic Analysis of Law,* 51 *Vand. L. Rev.* 1765, 1771 (1998) (emphasis added).

58. Michael Arndt, *Let's Talk Turkeys, Bus. Wk.,* Dec. 11, 2000, at 44.

59. Robert G. Eccles et al., *Are You Paying Too Much for that Acquisition? Harv. Bus. Rev.,* July–Aug. 1999, at 136. *See also* Dennis K. Berman, *Mergers Horror II: The Rhetoric, Wall St. J.,* May 24, 2005, at C1.

60. *See, e.g., Sculley Placed All Bets on the Proprietary Mac Way, InfoWorld,* Feb. 17, 1997, at 53. Apple has, of course, tried to reinvent itself by developing products that work on various computer platforms, notably the iPod. *See, e.g.,* Nick Wingfield, *Apple's Products Continue to Pay Off, Wall St. J.,* July 14, 2005, at A3.

61. *See, e.g., The Innovator that Quit Innovating, U.S. News & World Rep.,* Aug. 31–Sept. 7, 1992, at 23.

62. Timothy F. Malloy, *Regulating by Incentives: Myths, Models, and Micromarkets,* 80 *Tex. L. Rev.* 531, 536 (2002).

63. *Id.* at 558.

64. *See also* Harris, *supra* chap. 2, note 14, at 665.

65. Coase, *Firm Market Law, supra* chap. 4, note 31, at 3–4.

66. Leff, *supra* chap. 4, note 50, at 480–81 (second emphasis added). *See also* Singer, *supra* chap. 4, note 9, at 514.

67. Bruce A. Ackerman, *Foreword: Talking and Trading,* 85 *Colum. L. Rev.* 899, 904 (1985).

68. Ellickson, *Coaseanism*, *supra* chap. 4, note 22, at 624 (emphasis added). *See also* Hager, *supra* chap. 4, note 13, at 18–19.

69. Steven Shavell, *Foundations of Economic Analysis of Law* 668 (2004).

70. *Id.* at 669.

71. *See, e.g., id.* at 3 ("if one assumes that the income tax and transfer system will be used to bring about desirable changes in the distribution of income, the distributional effect of the choice of legal rules should not matter."). Unfortunately, as Daniel Farber and Brett McDonnell observe, "lump-sum taxes and transfers are not achievable in the real world. Any actual system of taxing and transferring will affect the behavioral incentives of some persons, and hence lead to some degree of inefficiency." Daniel A. Farber & Brett H. McDonnell, *Why (and How) Fairness Matters at the IP/Antitrust Interface*, 87 *Minn. L. Rev.* 1817, 1824 (2003). *Cf.* Mark Kelman, *Strategy or Principle? The Choice Between Regulation and Taxation* (1999); Joseph E. Stiglitz, *The Invisible Hand and Modern Welfare Economics* 2–3 (NBER Working Paper No. 3641) (1991).

72. Shavell simplistically equates welfare economics with utilitarianism. He first defines morality as separate from utility, then conveniently states that only utility should matter: "I am defining a (nondistributional) notion of morality to be a principle for the evaluation of situations that (a) does not depend exclusively on the utilities of individuals, and (b) is associated with the distinctive psychological attributes leading, as described, to virtue and guilt, praise and disapproval." *Shavell, supra* chap. 4, note 69, at 601. The argument is plainly circular. In an earlier article, Shavell even admits the tautology. *See* Louis Kaplow & Steven Shavell, *Fairness v. Welfare*, 114 *Harv. L. Rev.* 961, 971 (2001) ("Our first argument, that advancing notions of fairness reduces individuals' well-being, is in fact tautological on a general level."). Critics have pounced. *See, e.g.,* Michael B. Dorff, *Why Welfare Depends on Fairness: A Reply to Kaplow and Shavell*, 75 *S. Cal. L. Rev.* 847, 857 (2002); David Dolinko, *The Perils of Welfare Economics*, 97 *Nw. U. L. Rev.* 351, 353 (2002). For an eloquent defense of the need for deontology in economics, see Etzioni, *Moral Dimension, supra* chap. 4, note 48.

73. For a detailed discussion of *Foundations of Economic Analysis of Law*, Shavell's monumental overview of the application of economics to law, see Reza Dibadj, *The Limits of Utilitarianism*, 6 *Nevada L.J.* 201 (2005).

74. Hovenkamp, *After Chicago, supra* chap. 2, note 19, at 248.

75. Alice Kaswan, *Distributive Justice and the Environment*, 81 *N.C. L. Rev.* 1031, 1146–47 (2003).

76. Coase, *Social Cost, supra* chap. 2, note 2, at 19.

77. An alternative approach to social choice theory proposes a social welfare function that takes both consequential and deontological perspectives into account by redefining "utility" with respect to how closely a set of individual

preferences maps to a set of welfare-enhancing preferences. *See* Reza Dibadj, *Weasel Numbers*, 27 *Cardozo L. Rev.* 1325 (2006).

78. Priest, *supra* chap. 4, note 14, at 1284–85.

79. Leff, *supra* chap. 4, note 50, at 482. *See also* Rizzo, *supra* chap. 4, note 50, at 658.

80. Leff, *supra* chap. 4, note 50, at 452.

81. Bruce A. Ackerman, *Law, Economics, and the Problem of Legal Culture*, 1986 *Duke L.J.* 929, 935 (1986).

82. Mark G. Kelman, *Misunderstanding Social Life: A Critique of the Core Premises of "Law and Economics,"* 33 *J. Legal Educ.* 274, 278 (1983).

83. Hager, *supra* chap. 4, note 13, at 61.

84. Jeanne L. Schroeder, *The End of the Market: A Psychoanalysis of Law and Economics*, 112 *Harv. L. Rev.* 483, 511 (1998). *See also* Jeanne Lorraine Schroeder, *The Triumph of Venus: The Erotics of the Market* (2004). For an excellent discussion of Professor Schroeder's thesis, see William H. Widen, *Spectres of Law & Economics*, 102 *Mich. L. Rev.* 1423 (2004). *Cf.* David A. Westbrook, *Three Meditations on How Law Rules After Globalization*, 12 *Minn. J. Global Trade* 337 (2003).

85. Pierre Schlag, *The Problem of Transaction Costs*, 62 *S. Cal. L. Rev.* 1661, 1699 (1989). *Cf.* Etzioni, *Moral Dimension, supra* chap. 4, note 48, at 84.

86. Baird, *supra* chap. 4, note 10, at 1131–32.

87. *See Lochner v. New York*, 198 U.S. 45 (1905).

88. Posner *quoted in* Baird, *supra* chap. 4, note 10, at 1144 (emphasis added).

89. Ackerman, *Legal Culture, supra* chap. 4, note 81, at 934.

90. Skitol, *Shifting Sands, supra* chap. 1, note 25, at 248.

91. Rudolph J.R. Peritz, *Competition Policy in America, 1888–1992* 7 (1996).

92. *See* Olson, *supra* chap. 2, note 50, at 126.

93. *Id.* at 116. *See also* Etzioni, *Moral Dimension, supra* chap. 4, note 48, at 215.

94. *See* chapter 2.

95. *See* Richard A. Posner, *Taxation by Regulation*, 2 *Bell J. Econ. & Mgmt. Sci.* 22, 23 (1971). For a discussion of the difference between tax and regulatory policy, see chapter 1.

96. *See id.* at 23–27. *See also* Richard A. Posner, *Theories of Economic Regulation*, 5 *Bell J. Econ. & Mgmt. Sci.* 335, 341 (1974).

97. Posner, *Theories, supra* chap. 4, note 96, at 342.

98. *See id.* For example, the FCC currently regulates wireless and wireline carriers, cable, and satellite companies.

99. *See id.,* at 351.

100. Posner, *Taxation by Regulation, supra* chap. 4, note 95, at 39.

101. The relevant exception is core theory, where competition may not be efficient if the interaction among market participants has an "empty core." *See* chapter 5.

102. *See, e.g.,* Stephen G. Breyer, *Antitrust, Deregulation, and the Newly Liberated Marketplace,* 75 *Cal. L. Rev.* 1005, 1006 (1987).

103. Indeed, in the theoretical case of *"long run competitive equilibrium, firms earn zero economic profits."* Hylton, *Antitrust Law, supra* chap. 2, note 21, at 9.

104. Alan Murray, *Exile on G Street, Wall St. J.,* May 13, 2003, at A4.

105. Federal Communications Commission, Transcript: Spectrum Rights and Responsibilities Protection Public Workshop, Spectrum Policy Task Force (Aug. 9, 2002), at 10 (statement of Michael Powell, FCC Chairman), *available at* http://www.fcc.gov/sptf/workshops.html.

106. *Powell Says Telecommunication Litigation Is to Be Expected, Loc. Competition Rep.,* July 1, 2002.

107. Ashutosh Bhagwat, *Unnatural Competition? Applying the New Antitrust Learning to Foster Competition in the Local Exchange,* 50 *Hastings L.J.* 1479, 1500 (1999).

108. *See, e.g.,* Thomas A. Piraino, *A Proposed Antitrust Approach to High Technology Competition,* 44 *Wm. & Mary L. Rev.* 65, 152–53 (2002).

109. *See, e.g.,* Farber & Frickey, *supra* chap. 2, note 44, at 29.

110. Breyer, *Regulation, supra* chap. 1, note 1, at 388 n.38. *See also* Steven P. Croley, *Theories of Regulation: Incorporating the Administrative Process,* 98 *Colum. L. Rev.* 1, 42 (1998).

111. Farber & Frickey, *Public Choice, supra* chap. 2, note 44, at 24.

112. *See, e.g.,* David E. Sanger, *Mr. Deregulation's Regulations: Stuff of Politics, Mad Cows, and Suspect Dietary Pills, N.Y. Times,* Dec. 31, 2003, at A15.

113. Richard B. Stewart, *The Reformation of American Administrative Law,* 88 *Harv. L. Rev.* 1669, 1684–85 (1975).

114. *See id.* at 1685–86.

115. *See, e.g.,* Yochi J. Dreazen & Deborah Solomon, *Paying for Regulation, Wall St. J.,* Feb. 4, 2003, at A4.

116. *See, e.g.,* Dibadj, *Cable Competition, supra* chap. 3, note 11, at 250–57.

117. Viscusi et al., *Economics of Regulation, supra* chap. 1, note 3, at 492.

118. *See, e.g.,* Breyer, *Regulation, supra* chap. 1, note 1, at 388 n.38.

119. For a discussion of problems with New Zealand's former common law approach, see Michel Kerf & Damien Geradin, *Controlling Market Power in Telecommunications: Antitrust vs. Sector-Specific Regulation: An Assessment of the United States, New Zealand and Australian Experiences,* 14 *Berkeley Tech. L.J.* 919, 1018 (1999). In late 2001, the government of New Zealand created the role of Telecommunications Commissioner. *See* New Zealand Ministry of Economic Development, Landmark Telecommunications Act Passed (Dec. 18, 2001), *available at* http://www.med.govt.nz/pbt/telecom/minister20011218a.html.

120. *See, e.g.,* Huber, *Cyberspace, supra* chap. 4, note 11.

121. Breyer, *Regulation, supra* chap. 1, note 1, at 388 n.38.

122. *See* Kahn, *Political Feasibility, supra* chap. 1, note 22, at 254.

123. Joseph D. Kearney & Thomas W. Merrill, *The Great Transformation of Regulated Industries Law,* 98 *Colum. L. Rev.* 1323, 1406 (1998). *See also* David B. Spence, *Getting Beyond Cynicism: New Theories of the Regulatory State; A Public Choice Progressivism, Continued,* 87 *Cornell L. Rev.* 397, 436 (2002); Posner, *Theories, supra* chap. 4, note 96, at 353.

124. David B. Spence & Frank Cross, *A Public Choice Case for the Administrative State,* 89 *Geo. L.J.* 97, 119 (2000).

125. *Id.* at 121–22.

126. *Id.* at 122.

127. Richard W. Parker, *Grading the Government,* 70 *U. Chi. L. Rev.* 1345, 1347 (2003).

128. Croley, *supra* chap. 4, note 110, at 7.

129. *See id.* at 142–43.

130. *See id.* at 162.

131. *Id.* at 12.

132. *Id.* at 50–51. *See also* Etzioni, *Moral Dimension, supra* chap. 4, note 48, at 234–35.

133. Peter H. Schuck, *Delegation and Democracy: Comments on David Schoenbrod,* 20 *Cardozo L. Rev.* 775, 781 (1999).

134. *Cf.* Viscusi, *Economics of Regulation, supra* chap. 1, note 3.

135. Cass R. Sunstein, *Television and the Public Interest*, 88 *Cal. L. Rev.* 499, 512 (1999) (emphasis added). *See also* Hovenkamp, *Federal Antitrust Policy, supra* chap. 1, note 9, at 680.

136. *See, e.g.*, Breyer, *Regulation, supra* chap. 1, note 1, at 174–77.

137. Orly Lobel, *The Renew Deal: The Fall of Regulation and the Rise of Governance in Contemporary Legal Thought*, 89 *Minn. L. Rev.* 342, 366 (2004).

138. For example, one commentator marvels at how "[i]n an analytical tour de force, contemporary legal thought is promoting a shift from the traditional New Deal regulatory era to a 'Renew Deal' governance paradigm." *Id.* at 343.

139. Jody Freeman, *Extending Public Law Norms Through Privatization*, 116 *Harv. L. Rev.* 1285, 1285 (2003). This approach can be self-contradictory. For instance, one opinion piece touting the approach advocates for "public leaders who understand that their job is to produce public value and not merely to manage activities[,]" then immediately proceeds to suggest that public officials behave like private "managers skilled in negotiation, contract management and risk analysis." Stephen Goldsmith & William D. Eggers, *Government for Hire*, *N.Y. Times*, Feb. 21, 2005, at A19.

140. Freeman, *supra* chap. 4, note 139, at 1325–26.

141. *See, e.g.*, Gillian E. Metzger, *Privatization as Delegation*, 103 *Colum. L. Rev.* 1367, 1373 (2003).

142. Lobel, *supra* chap. 4, note 137, at 466 (emphasis added).

143. *See, e.g.*, Moshe Adler, *Sometimes Government Is the Answer*, *L.A. Times*, Mar. 4, 2006, at B15; David Datz, *For Service, Try Public Servants*, *L.A. Times*, Apr. 2, 2005.

144. *Cf.* Omri Yadlin, *Comments on Mark West's "Private Ordering at the World's First Futures Exchange,"* 98 *Mich. L. Rev.* 2620, 2625–26 (2000).

145. Freeman, *supra* chap. 4, note 139, at 1288.

146. *Id.*

147. For a detailed discussion of this problem, see Dibadj, *Weasel Numbers*, *supra* chap. 4, note 77. *See also* Zvika Neeman, *The Freedom to Contract and the Free-Rider Problem*, 15 *J.L. Econ. & Org.* 685, 700 (1999).

148. Mark A. Lemley, *Intellectual Property Rights and Standard-Setting Organizations*, 90 *Cal. L. Rev.* 1889, 1971–72 (2002). *See also* Mark A. Lemley & Lawrence Lessig, *The End of End-to-End: Preserving the Architecture of the Internet in the Broadband Era*, 48 *UCLA L. Rev.* 925, 934 (2001).

149. Mark J. Roe, *Chaos and Evolution in Law and Economics*, 109 *Harv. L. Rev.* 641, 666 (1996). After broaching the issue, Roe states that government in-

tervention is unwise, but that "this belief, based on my observation on the limits of American government, is expressed here off-the-cuff; it is neither derived from a sense that evolution inevitably yields the most efficient results nor deduced from thinking about path dependence." *Id.*

150. Peritz, *supra* chap. 4, note 91, at 302 (emphasis added).

151. Cass Sunstein makes a similar point in his discussion of the need for broadcast regulation. *See* Sunstein, *Television, supra* chap. 4, note 135, at 520. *See also* Richard D. Cudahy, *The Coming Demise of Deregulation*, 10 *Yale J. on Reg.* 1, 14 (1993). *See generally* Steven Kelman, *Making Public Policy: A Hopeful View of American Government* (1987) (highlighting the importance of "public spirit" in policy making).

152. Ezra Suleiman, *Dismantling Democratic States* 10 (2003).

153. *Id.* at 2.

154. *Id.* at 309. For a thought-provoking discussion of the relationship between privatization and federalism, see Peter H. Schuck, *Some Reflections on the Federalism Debate*, 14 *Yale L. & Pol'y Rev.* 1, 6–7 (1996).

155. Suleiman, *supra* chap. 4, note 152, at 5.

156. *Quoted in* Schlesinger, *The Deregulators, supra* Preface, note 1, at A12.

157. Recent scholarship is even beginning to show that an overreliance on markets has exacerbated racial and ethnic tensions in both the developed and developing world. *See, e.g.*, Amy L. Chua, *Markets, Democracy, and Ethnicity: Toward a New Paradigm for Law and Development*, 108 *Yale L.J.* 1 (1998). *Cf.* Suleiman, *supra* chap. 4, note 152, at 316; Etzioni, *Moral Dimension, supra* chap. 4, note 48, at 201–02.

158. Kahn, *Deregulation, supra* chap. 3, note 6, at 353.

159. Duffy, *supra* chap. 4, note 13, at 1080. *Cf.* Gruenspecht & Lave, *Health, Safety, and Environmental Regulation, supra* chap. 1, note 20, at 1511.

CHAPTER 5. ... TOWARD NEW RESEARCH

1. Michael S. Jacobs, *An Essay on the Normative Foundations of Antitrust Economics*, 74 *N.C. L. Rev.* 219, 225 (1995).

2. Rowe, *supra* chap. 4, note 17, at 1562 (emphasis added).

3. Paul L. Joskow, *Firm Decision-making Processes and Oligopoly Theory*, 65 *Am. Econ. Rev.* 270, 273 (1975).

4. *See, e.g.*, Braeutigam, *Natural Monopolies, supra* chap. 1, note 37, at 1296 ("Let us assume entry and exit are costless, that entrants will provide exactly the

same service as the incumbent, and that all firms (the incumbent and potential entrants) operate with access to the same technology, and therefore with the same cost functions.").

5. Of course, there are other economic critiques of regulation, such as those based on the theory of second best which argue that the deregulatory argument "is only valid if one assumes that deregulation of the industry at hand will be followed in short order with deregulation of all others, and the introduction of all the other elements of a free market." Etzioni, *Moral Dimension, supra* chap. 4, note 48, at 201. For an argument that the theory of second best should not be taken too seriously, see Dibadj, *Weasel Numbers, supra* chap. 4, note 77.

6. For an overview of the post-Chicago school, see Jonathan B. Baker, *Recent Developments in Economics that Challenge the Chicago School Views*, 58 *Antitrust L.J.* 645 (1989). *See also* Edward L. Rubin, *The New Legal Process, the Synthesis of Discourse, and the Microanalysis of Institutions*, 109 *Harv. L. Rev.* 1393, 1404 (1996); Mark Tushnet, *"Everything Old Is New Again": Early Reflections on the "New Chicago School,"* 1998 *Wis. L. Rev.* 579, 579 (1998).

7. *See, e.g.,* Jacobs, *supra* chap. 5, note 1, at 225.

8. *See* Jean Tirole, *The Theory of Industrial Organization* 7 (1998). Indeed, many of the original critiques of the Chicago school appeared in the tradition of IO. *See, e.g.,* William G. Shepherd & Joanna M. Shepherd, *The Economics of Industrial Organization* (5th ed. 2003).

9. *See* Coase, *Firm Market Law, supra* chap. 4, note 31, at 61.

10. *See* William J. Baumol, *On the Theory of Oligopoly*, 25 *Economica* 187, 187 (1958). *Cf.* Robin Marris, *A Model of the "Managerial" Enterprise*, 77 *Q. J. Econ.* 185, 209 (1963).

11. *See, e.g.,* Hovenkamp, *After Chicago, supra* chap. 2, note 19, at 257.

12. Michael A. Carrier, *Antitrust After the Interception: Of a Heroic Returner and Myriad Paths*, 55 *Stan. L. Rev.* 283, 287 (2002) (book review). The well-known Prisoner's Dilemma, for instance, is the archetypal noncooperative game. For an overview of game-theoretic approaches, see Tirole, *supra* chap. 5, note 8, at 423–59.

13. Robert Gibbons, Trust in Social Structures: Hobbes and Coase Meet Repeated Games 3 (2000) (unpublished manuscript), *available at* http://web.mit.edu/rgibbons/www/trust_st.pdf.

14. Some sophisticated regulatory economists appreciate both approaches. *See, e.g.,* Alfred E. Kahn, Talk to the New York Society of Security Analysts 24 (Feb. 2, 1978) (noting how "each [airline carrier] will take into account the probable response of its rivals to its fare reductions").

15. Bhagwat, *supra* chap. 4, note 107, at 1486 (emphasis added).

16. Ian Ayres, *Playing Games with the Law*, 42 *Stan. L. Rev.* 1291, 1315 (1990) (book review).

17. For a discussion of contestability, see chapter 2. *See also* Etzioni, *Moral Dimension*, *supra* chap. 4, note 48, at 202. For a persuasive critique of contestability theory, see William G. Shepherd, *"Contestability" vs. Competition*, 74 *Am. Econ. Rev.* 572 (1984).

18. For a superb analysis of the importance of sunk costs in the context of natural monopoly, see Jim Chen, *The Nature of the Public Utility: Infrastructure, the Market, and the Law*, 98 *Nw. U. L. Rev.* 1617 (2004).

19. *See, e.g.*, Crandall & Hausman, *supra* chap. 1, note 56, at 87–88; Jerry A. Hausman, The Effect of Sunk Costs in Telecommunications Regulation 3 (Oct. 1998) (unpublished manuscript), *available at* http://econ-www.mit.edu/faculty/download_pdf.php?id=258; Organisation for Econ. Co-operation and Dev. (OECD), Spectrum Allocation: Auctions and Comparative Selection Procedures, Doc. No. DSTI/ICCP/TISP(2000) 16/FINAL (2001).

20. *See, e.g.*, Jerry Hausman & Stewart Myers, *Regulating the United States Railroads: The Effects of Sunk Costs and Asymmetric Risk*, 22 *J. Reg. Econ.* 287, 308 (2002). *See also* Kahn, *Whom the Gods*, *supra* chap. 2, note 23, at 11.

21. *See, e.g.*, Paul L. Joskow, *Deregulation and Regulatory Reform in the U.S. Electric Power Sector*, in *Deregulation of Network Industries* 131 (Sam Peltzman & Clifford Winston eds., 2000).

22. For a proposal to separate contestable from noncontestable portions of an industry, see chapter 6.

23. Bailey & Baumol, *supra* chap. 2, note 38, at 128. *See also* Willig, *Airline Industry*, *supra* chap. 3, note 7, at 699.

24. Willig, *Airline Industry*, *supra* chap. 3, note 7, at 699. *See also* Steven A. Morrison & Clifford Winston, *The Remaining Role for Government Policy in the Deregulated Airline Industry*, in *Deregulation of Network Industries*, *supra* chap. 5, note 21, at 24.

25. Kahn, *Deregulatory Schizophrenia*, *supra* chap. 3, note 8, 1062. *See also* Kahn, *Whom the Gods*, *supra* chap. 2, note 23, at 37 ("airline routes are not as contestable as most proponents of deregulation had claimed or hoped"). One is left wondering how much better airline regulation would have turned out if Kahn's recommendations had been followed in toto. *See, e.g.*, Alfred E. Kahn, *Applications of Economics to an Imperfect World*, 69 *Am. Econ. Rev.* 1, 9 (1979) (noting how each separately owned airport "charges landing fees based on its own embedded costs, and few if any follow peak pricing principles even modestly" and arguing for "a more efficient allocation of scarce take off and landing space.").

26. *See* Demsetz, *Why Regulate Utilities? supra* chap. 2, note 25. For recent expositions based at least in part on a Demsetzian point of view, see Jim Rossi, *Regulatory Bargaining and Public Law* (2005); José A. Gómez-Ibáñez, *Regulating Infrastructure: Monopoly, Contracts, and Discretion* (2003).

27. *See, e.g.*, Viscusi et al., *Economics of Regulation, supra* chap. 1, note 3.

28. *See* Hovenkamp, *After Chicago, supra* chap. 2, note 19, at 278.

29. *See* A. Michael Spence, *Entry, Capacity, Investment and Oligopolistic Pricing*, 8 *Bell J. Econ.* 534, 534 (1977). *See also* Avinash Dixit, *The Role of Investment in Entry Deterrence*, 90 *Econ. J.* 95 (1980); Steven C. Salop, *Strategic Entry Deterrence*, 69 *Am. Econ. Rev.* 335 (1979).

30. *See, e.g.*, Thomas G. Krattenmaker & Steven C. Salop, *Anticompetitive Exclusion: Raising Rivals' Costs to Achieve Power over Price*, 96 *Yale L.J.* 209, 214 (1986).

31. *See generally id.*

32. *See* Steven C. Salop & R. Craig Romaine, *Preserving Monopoly: Economic Analysis, Legal Standards, and Microsoft*, 7 *Geo. Mason L. Rev.* 617, 626 (1999) ("Input foreclosure refers to excluding rivals from high quality access to important inputs or raising rivals' costs of inputs supplied by the monopolist or others.").

33. Krattenmaker & Salop, *supra* chap. 5, note 30, at 223–24. *See also* Steven C. Salop & David T. Scheffman, *Raising Rivals' Costs*, 73 *Am. Econ. Rev.* 267 (1983).

34. As Steven Salop and Craig Romaine point out: "Customer foreclosure refers to using exclusive contracts and other strategies that exclude rivals from access to a sufficient customer base." Salop & Romaine, *supra* chap. 5, note 32, at 627.

35. *See* Philippe Aghion & Patrick Bolton, *Contracts as Barrier to Entry*, 77 *Am. Econ. Rev.* 388 (1987).

36. *See* Eric B. Rasmusen, et al., *Naked Exclusion*, 81 *Am. Econ. Rev.* 1137, 1144 (1991). *See also* Neeman, *supra* chap. 4, note 147, at 686.

37. Joseph F. Brodley & Ching-to Albert Ma, *Contract Penalties, Monopolizing Strategies, and Antitrust Policy*, 45 *Stan. L. Rev.* 1161, 1211 (1993). *See also* B. Douglas Bernheim & Michael D. Whinston, *Exclusive Dealing*, 106 *J. Pol. Econ.* 64, 90 (1998).

38. See chapter 2. For a discussion of the infirmities of the Chicago school approach in the context of exclusionary agreements, see Rasmusen et al., *supra* chap. 5, note 36, at 1144.

39. *See, e.g.*, Bittlingmayer, *Fixed Costs, supra* chap. 1, note 11, at 741.

40. Lester G. Telser, *Cooperation, Competition, and Efficiency*, 28 *J.L. & Econ.* 271, 274 (1985). *See also* John Shepard Wiley, *Antitrust and Core Theory*, 54 *U. Chi. L. Rev.* 556 (1987).

41. Stephen Craig Pirrong, *An Application of Core Theory to the Analysis of Ocean Shipping Markets*, 35 *J.L. & Econ.* 89, 89 (1992). *See also* George Bittlingmayer, *Decreasing Average Cost and Competition: A New Look at the Addyston Pipe Case*, 25 *J.L. & Econ.* 201, 202 (1982).

42. *See, e.g.,* Cudahy, *supra* chap. 4, note 151, at 10.

43. Bittlingmayer, *Fixed Costs, supra* chap. 1, note 11, at 755.

44. Telser, *supra* chap. 5, note 40, at 272.

45. *See* George Bittlingmayer, *Did Antitrust Policy Cause the Great Merger Wave?* 28 *J.L. & Econ.* 77, 84 (1985). *See also* Michael F. Sproul, *Antitrust and Prices*, 101 *J. Pol. Econ.* 741, 753 (1993).

46. *See, e.g.,* Joskow, *Electric Power Sector, supra* chap. 5, note 21, at 148. For a recent example, see Ken Belson, *Huge Phone Deal Seeks to Thwart Smaller Rivals*, *N.Y. Times*, Mar. 6, 2006, at A1.

47. *See, e.g.,* Pirrong, *supra* chap. 5, note 41, at 129; Bittlingmayer, *Fixed Costs, supra* chap. 1, note 11, at 752.

48. *See* Coase, *Nature of the Firm, supra* chap. 4, note 32, at 389.

49. Bittlingmayer, *Great Merger Wave, supra* chap. 5, note 45, at 84.

50. For example, in the context of organizations that set standards for intellectual property (IP), Mark Lemley argues that "antitrust law should show great deference to legitimate efforts to set collective rules for dealing with IP, even if those rules require competitors to discuss both the technical merits of their products and the price of an IP license." Lemley, *supra* chap. 4, note 148, at 1937. Similarly, Cass Sunstein proposes a code of broadcasting self-regulation, but realizes that this might pose a cartelization problem under the antitrust laws. *See* Sunstein, *Television, supra* chap. 4, note 135, at 549–59. *See also* Michael L. Katz & Carl Shapiro, *Network Externalities, Competition, and Compatibility*, 75 *Am. Econ. Rev.* 424 (1985).

51. Bittlingmayer, *Decreasing Average Cost, supra* chap. 5, note 41, at 203–04 (emphasis added).

52. Chapter 6 provides several examples, including components of transportation and telecommunications networks.

53. For an overview of behavioral law and economics, see *Choices, Values, and Frames* (Daniel Kahneman & Amos Tversky eds., 2000). A number of excellent academic articles also exist. *See, e.g.,* Matthew Rabin, *Psychology and Economics*, 36 *J. Econ. Lit.* 11 (1998); Donald C. Langevoort, *Behavioral Theories of Judgment*

and Decision Making in Legal Scholarship: A Literature Review, 51 *Vand. L. Rev.* 1499 (1998); Craig R. Fox & Amos Tversky, *Ambiguity Aversion and Comparative Ignorance*, 110 *Q. J. Econ.* 585 (1995). For an early example of behavioral analysis applied to economics, see George Katona, *On the Function of Behavioral Theory and Behavioral Research in Economics*, 58 *Am. Econ. Rev.* 146 (1968).

54. Roger G. Noll & James E. Krier, *Some Implications of Cognitive Psychology for Risk Regulation*, 19 *J. Legal Stud.* 747, 777 (1990).

55. Cass R. Sunstein, *Economics & Real People*, 3 *Green Bag* 2d 397, 404 (2000) (emphasis added).

56. The argument that regulators themselves suffer from behavioral biases is addressed in chapter 7.

57. Kahn, *Deregulation, supra* chap. 3, note 6, at 352. *See also* Alfred E. Kahn, *Reforming the FCC and Its Mission: Lessons from the Airline Experience*, 4 *J. Telecomm. & High Tech. L.* 43 (2005).

58. *See* Cass R. Sunstein & Richard H. Thaler, *Libertarian Paternalism Is Not an Oxymoron*, 70 *U. Chi. L. Rev.* 1159, 1159 (2003) ("Equipped with an understanding of behavioral findings of bounded rationality and bounded self-control, libertarian paternalists should attempt to steer people's choices in welfare-promoting directions without eliminating freedom of choice.").

59. *See* Colin Camerer et al., *Regulation for Conservatives: Behavioral Economics and the Case for "Asymmetric Paternalism,"* 151 *U. Pa. L. Rev.* 1211, 1212 (2003) ("A regulation is asymmetrically paternalistic if it creates large benefits for those who make errors, while imposing little or no harm on those who are fully rational.").

60. *See, e.g.,* Sunstein & Thaler, *supra* chap. 5, note 58, at 1186; Camerer et al., *supra* chap. 5, note 59, at 1224.

61. *See, e.g.,* Bernard S. Black & Richard J. Pierce, *The Choice Between Markets and Central Planning in Regulating the U.S. Electricity Industry*, 93 *Colum. L. Rev.* 1341, 1389–98 (1993).

62. John F. Nash, Jr., *The Bargaining Problem*, 18 *Econometrica* 155 (1950).

63. *Id.* at 155.

64. Colin F. Camerer, *Progress in Behavioral Game Theory*, 11 *J. Econ. Persp.* 167, 167 (1997).

65. *Id.* at 185.

66. *See, e.g.,* Matthew Rabin, *Incorporating Fairness into Game Theory and Economics*, 83 *Am. Econ. Rev.* 1281 (1993).

67. *See, e.g.,* Jon Elster, *Emotions and Economic Theory*, 36 *J. Econ. Lit.* 47 (1998).

68. *See, e.g.*, Joseph Henrich, *Does Culture Matter in Economic Behavior? Ultimatum Game Bargaining Among the Machiguenga of the Peruvian Amazon*, 90 *Am. Econ. Rev.* 973 (2000).

69. *See, e.g.*, Paul Milgrom & John Roberts, *Informational Asymmetries, Strategic Behavior, and Industrial Organization*, 77 *Am. Econ. Rev.* 184 (1987); Dallas Burtaw, *Bargaining with Noisy Delegation*, 24 *Rand J. Econ.* 40 (1993).

70. *See, e.g.*, Dale Griffin & Amos Tversky, *The Weighing of Evidence and the Determinants of Confidence*, 24 *Cognitive Psychol.* 411, 432 (1992) ("The significance of overconfidence to the conduct of human affairs can hardly be overstated.").

71. Donald C. Langevoort, *Organized Illusions: A Behavioral Theory of Why Corporations Mislead Stock Market Investors (and Cause Other Social Harms)*, 146 *U. Pa. L. Rev.* 101, 139 (1997).

72. Bratton, *Enron, supra* chap. 3, note 23, at 1283.

73. Russell B. Korobkin & Thomas S. Ulen, *Law and Behavioral Science: Removing the Rationalist Assumption from Law and Economics*, 88 *Cal. L. Rev.* 1051, 1093 (2000).

74. Robert A. Prentice, *The SEC and MDP: Implications of the Self-Serving Bias for Independent Auditing*, 61 *Ohio St. L.J.* 1597, 1669 (2000) (emphasis added).

75. Robert J. Shiller, *Conversation, Information, and Herd Behavior*, 85 *Am. Econ. Rev.* 181, 181 (1995).

76. Marleen A. O'Connor, *The Enron Board: The Perils of Groupthink*, 71 *U. Cin. L. Rev.* 1233, 1238–39 (2003).

77. *See, e.g.*, Cass R. Sunstein, *Deliberative Trouble? Why Groups Go to Extremes*, 110 *Yale L.J.* 71, 88 (2000).

78. *See, e.g.*, Robert Frank & Elena Cherney, *Paper Tigers: Lord Black's Board; A-List Played Acquiescent Role*, Wall St. J., Sept. 27, 2004, at A1; Monica Langley & Ian McDonald, *Marsh Directors Consider Having CEO Step Aside*, Wall St. J., Oct. 22, 2004, at A1.

79. *See, e.g.*, Herbert A. Simon, *New Developments in the Theory of the Firm*, 52 *Am. Econ. Rev.* 1 (1962); R.M. Cyert & James G. March, *Organizational Factors in the Theory of Oligopoly*, 70 *Q. J. Econ.* 44 (1956).

80. Etzioni, *Moral Dimension, supra* chap. 4, note 48, at 178.

81. *See* Reza Dibadj, *Reconceiving the Firm*, 26 *Cardozo L. Rev.* 1459 (2005).

82. Korobkin & Ulen, *supra* chap. 5, note 73, at 1058.

83. Linda Babcock & George Loewenstein, *Explaining Bargaining Impasse: The Role of Self-Serving Biases*, 11 *J. Econ. Persp.* 109, 124 (1997).

84. Viscusi et al., *Economics of Regulation*, *supra* chap. 1, note 3, at 2.

85. Korobkin & Ulen, *supra* chap. 5, note 73, at 1054. *See also* Lewis A. Kornhauser, *The Great Image of Authority*, 36 Stan. L. Rev. 349, 353 (1984).

86. *See, e.g.*, Leff, *supra* chap. 4, note 50, at 490; Ackerman, Foreword, *supra* chap. 4, note 67, at 900.

87. Leff, *supra* chap. 4, note 50, at 454. *See also* Ackerman, *Legal Culture*, *supra* chap. 4, note 81, at 939; Crespi, *supra* chap. 4, note 50, at 245–46.

88. Langevoort, *Behavioral Theories*, *supra* chap. 5, note 53, at 1499–1500.

89. Bork, *Antitrust Paradox*, *supra* chap. 2, note 22, at 117.

90. *See, e.g.*, Langevoort, *Behavioral Theories*, *supra* chap. 5, note 53, at 1500.

91. *See, e.g.*, Richard A. Posner, *Rational Choice, Behavioral Economics, and the Law*, 50 Stan. L. Rev. 1551, 1559 (1998); Posner, *Economic Analysis*, *supra* chap. 2, note 17, at 18. *Cf.* Leff, *supra* chap. 4, note 50, at 454.

92. Robert C. Ellickson, *Coaseanism*, *supra* chap. 4, note 22, at 613.

93. Jon D. Hanson & Douglas A. Kysar, *Taking Behavioralism Seriously: Some Evidence of Market Manipulation*, 112 Harv. L. Rev. 1420, 1572 (1999).

94. Jon Hanson & David Yosifon, *The Situation: An Introduction to Situational Character, Critical Realism, Power Economics, and Deep Capture*, 152 U. Pa. L. Rev. 129, 139 (2003).

95. *See* Warren & Warren Tyagi, *supra* chap. 3, note 39, at 144–49. Warren concludes that "America has had more than twenty years to observe the effects of a deregulated lending industry, and the evidence is overwhelming. It is time to call the experiment a failure." *Id.* at 149.

96. *Id.* at 145.

97. *See, e.g.*, Vernon L. Smith, *Bargaining and Market Behavior: Essays in Experimental Economics* (2000).

98. *See, e.g.*, Vernon Smith & Lynne Kiesling, *Socket to California*, Wall St. J., Nov. 10, 2003, at A16; Vernon Smith, *Power to the People*, Wall St. J., Oct. 16, 2002, at A20. *Cf.* Kahn, *Political Feasibility*, *supra* chap. 1, note 22, at 257.

99. *See* Peter H. Schuck & E. Donald Elliott, *To the Chevron Station: An Empirical Study of Federal Administrative Law*, 1990 Duke L.J. 984, 1029–35.

100. *See, e.g.*, Christine Jolls, *Behavioral Economic Analysis of Redistributive Legal Rules*, 51 Vand. L. Rev. 1653, 1677 (1998); Polinsky, *supra* chap. 4, note 22, at 119–27.

101. *See, e.g.*, Katz & Shapiro. *Network Externalities*, *supra* chap. 5, note 50, at 439; Michael D. Whinston, *Tying, Foreclosure, and Exclusion*, 80 Am. Econ. Rev.

837, 856 (1990); Howard P. Marvel & Stephen McCafferty, *The Welfare Effects of Resale Price Maintenance*, 28 *J.L. & Econ.* 363, 378 (1985).

102. Etzioni, *Moral Dimension, supra* chap. 4, note 48, at 16.

103. Coase, *Firm Market Law, supra* chap. 4, note 31, at 5. *See also* Etzioni, *Moral Dimension, supra* chap. 4, note 48, at 27.

104. *See, e.g.*, Peter Huber, *Antitrust's Real Legacy*, *Wall St. J.*, Dec. 26, 2002, at A14. For a different perspective, see Reza Dibadj, *Small Firms, Speak Up Loudly for Innovation*, *San Jose Mercury News*, Jan. 30, 2005, at 5P.

105. For example, competition in markets for wireless telephony was historically ensured via spectrum caps, which limited the amount of bandwidth an individual company could operate. *See, e.g.*, Jube Shiver, Jr., *FCC Gets Rid of Limits on Mobile Airwaves*, *L.A. Times*, Nov. 9, 2001, at C3. And the Internet, developed through federal government funds, is, as Jim Chen aptly points out, "a far cry from an object lesson in the virtues of laissez-faire economics." Jim Chen, *The Authority to Regulate Broadband Internet Access over Cable*, 16 *Berkeley Tech. L.J.* 677, 714 (2001).

106. *See, e.g.*, Janusz A. Ordover & Robert D. Willig, *Antitrust for High-Technology Industries: Assessing Research Joint Ventures and Mergers*, 28 *J.L. & Econ.* 311 (1985); Carl Shapiro, Antitrust in Network Industries, Address Before the American Law Institute and American Bar Association (Jan. 25, 1996), *available at* http://www.usdoj.gov/atr/public/speeches/0593.pdf.

107. Joseph A. Schumpeter, *Capitalism, Socialism and Democracy* 83 (3d ed. 1950).

108. *See, e.g.*, Robert Pitofsky, *Antitrust and Intellectual Property: Unresolved Issues at the Heart of the New Economy*, 16 *Berkeley Tech. L.J.* 535, 542–43 (2001); Carl Shapiro, *Exclusivity in Network Industries*, 7 *Geo. Mason L. Rev.* 673, 674 (1999).

109. *See, e.g.*, Pitofsky, *Antitrust and Intellectual Property, supra* chap. 5, note 108, at 537.

110. *See, e.g.*, Mark A. Lemley & David McGowan, *Legal Implications of Network Economic Effects*, 86 *Cal. L. Rev.* 479, 502 (1998).

111. Katz & Shapiro, *Network Externalities, supra* chap. 5, note 50, at 424. *See also* A. Douglas Melamed, *Network Industries and Antitrust*, 23 *Harv. J.L. & Pub. Pol'y* 147 (1999); Michael L. Katz & Carl Shapiro, *Systems Competition and Network Effects*, 8 *J. Econ. Persp.* 93 (1994).

112. *See, e.g.*, Piraino, *supra* chap. 4, note 108, at 88.

113. Indeed, the classic exposition of the demand-side phenomenon discusses the telephone network. *See* Jeffrey Rohlfs, *A Theory of Interdependent Demand for a Communications Service*, 5 *Bell J. Econ. & Mgmt. Sci.* 16 (1974).

114. *See, e.g.,* Kahn, *Talk to Security Analysts, supra* chap. 5, note 14, at 21.

115. Shapiro, *Exclusivity in Network Industries, supra* chap. 5, note 108, at 673.

116. *See, e.g.,* Joseph Farrell & Garth Saloner, *Installed Base and Compatibility: Innovation, Product Preannouncements, and Predation,* 76 *Am. Econ. Rev.* 940 (1986).

117. Katz & Shapiro, *Network Externalities, supra* chap. 5, note 50, at 425. One commentator has even studied the danger of network effects to suggest enhanced regulation of securities markets. *See* Robert B. Ahdieh, *Making Markets: Network Effects and the Role of Law in the Creation of Strong Securities Markets,* 76 *S. Cal. L. Rev.* 277 (2003).

118. *See, e.g.,* Katz & Shapiro, *Network Externalities, supra* chap. 5, note 50, at 425 ("We find that firms with good reputations or large existing networks will tend to be against compatibility, even when welfare is increased by the move to compatibility."). Often these tactics can backfire against the incumbents. *See* Dibadj, *Cable Competition, supra* chap. 3, note 11, at 282.

119. Pitofsky, *Antitrust and Intellectual Property, supra* chap. 5, note 108, at 538–39. *See also* Piraino, *supra* chap. 4, note 108, at 77; Shapiro, *Exclusivity in Network Industries, supra* chap. 5, note 108, at 674.

120. Robert Pitofsky, Competition Policy in Communications Industries: New Antitrust Approaches, Glasser LegalWorks Seminar on Competitive Policy in Communications Industries 6 (Mar. 10, 1997), *available at* http://www.ftc.gov/speeches/pitofsky/newcomm.htm.

121. *See* Dibadj, *Saving Antitrust, supra* chap. 1, note 21, at 780. A durable-goods monopolist faces the problem that already existing units serve as a potential substitute for every new unit of production that enters the stream of commerce, thereby reducing the monopolist's power. *See, e.g.,* Patrick Rey & Jean Tirole, A Primer on Foreclosure 13 (unpublished manuscript) (Jan. 2006), *available at* http://www.idei.fr/doc/by/tirole/primer.pdf; John Shepard Wiley et al., *The Leasing Monopolist,* 37 *UCLA L. Rev.* 693, 694 (1990); Dennis W. Carlton & Robert Gertner, *Market Power and Mergers in Durable-Good Industries,* 32 *J.L. & Econ.* S203 (1989); Jeremy I. Bulow, *Durable-Goods Monopolists,* 90 *J. Pol. Econ.* 314 (1982).

122. For a discussion of the interaction between network effects and path dependence, see Shelanski & Sidak, *supra* chap. 1, note 32, at 8.

123. *Cf.* Skitol, *Shifting Sands, supra* chap. 1, note 25, at 257; Daniel L. Rubinfeld, Competition, Innovation, and Antitrust Enforcement in Dynamic Network Industries, Address Before the Software Publishers Ass'n 13 (Mar. 24, 1998), *available at* http://www.apeccp.org.tw/doc/USA/Policy/speech/1611.htm.

124. Ellickson, *Rational Actors, supra* chap. 2, note 33, at 55.

125. *See* Reza Dibadj, *Beyond Facile Assumptions and Radical Assertions: A Case for "Critical Legal Economics,"* 2003 *Utah L. Rev.* 1155. The "critical legal economics" that I have proposed is neither progressive nor conservative. To the extent that it blends economics, traditionally associated with the "Right," with deconstruction, conventionally ascribed to the "Left," it has the ambition of blending the best of both.

126. 2 Alfred E. Kahn, *The Economics of Regulation* 327 (1970).

127. *See, e.g.,* Roberto Mangabeira Unger, *The Critical Legal Studies Movement,* 96 *Harv. L. Rev.* 561 (1983); Duncan Kennedy, *The Structure of Blackstone's Commentaries,* 28 *Buff. L. Rev.* 205 (1979); Duncan Kennedy, *Form and Substance in Private Law Adjudication,* 89 *Harv. L. Rev.* 1685 (1976).

128. Hovenkamp, *After Chicago, supra* chap. 2, note 19, at 223–24. *Cf.* Adams & Brock, *supra* chap. 3, note 12, at 284; Stewart, *supra* chap. 4, note 113, at 1703.

129. Kahn, *Political Feasibility, supra* chap. 1, note 22, at 258.

130. *Quoted in* Baird, *supra* chap. 4, note 10, at 1137. *See also* John Cassidy, *The Decline of Economics, New Yorker,* Dec. 2, 1996, at 50, 52 ("it is gradually becoming clear that the attempt to convert economics into an exact science has failed").

131. *Quoted in* Baird, *supra* chap. 4, note 10, at 1151. *See also* Tushnet, *supra* chap. 5, note 6, at 581 n.8.

CHAPTER 6. SUBSTANTIVE REFORM

1. *See also* Reza Dibadj, *Now Is the Time to Reshape America's Regulators, Fin. Times,* Sept. 26, 2003, at 15.

2. Pigou, *supra* chap. 4, note 39, at 131. Pigou goes on to define the marginal social net product as "the total net product of physical things or objective services due to the marginal increment of resources in any given use or place, no matter to whom any part of this product may accrue." *Id.* at 134. On the other hand, the marginal private net product is "that part of the total net product of physical things or objective services due to the marginal increment of resources in any given use or place which accrues in the first instance . . . to the person responsible for investing resources there." *Id.* at 134–35.

3. Breyer, *Regulation, supra* chap. 1, note 1, at 96.

4. *Id.* at 101. *Cf.* Gruenspecht & Lave, *Health, Safety, and Environmental Regulation, supra* chap. 1, note 20, at 1510.

5. Breyer, *Regulation, supra* chap. 1, note 1, at 101–02.

6. Parker, *supra* chap. 4, note 127, at 1421.

7. *Id.* at 1420–21.

8. *Id.* at 1353.

9. *Id.* at 1355. *See also* Frank Ackerman & Lisa Heinzerling, *Priceless: On Knowing the Price of Everything and the Value of Nothing* (2004).

10. *See also* Peter H. Schuck, *On the Chicken Little School of Regulation*, Wash. Post, Jan. 28, 1979, at C1.

11. Gruenspecht & Lave, *Health, Safety, and Environmental Regulation*, *supra* chap. 1, note 20, at 1534 (emphasis added).

12. *Id.* at 1520.

13. *Cf. id.* at 1534 ("Although the textbooks assume that economists get their quantification of effects from scientists and engineers, in fact economists play a leading role in estimating the effects of air pollution, water pollution, and in other areas.") (citations omitted).

14. *Cf.* Breyer, *Regulation*, *supra* chap. 1, note 1, at 272 ("putting a price tag on pollution would allow buyers to balance the competing environmental and industrial goods.").

15. Kahn, *Political Feasibility*, *supra* chap. 1, note 22, at 259.

16. Johansson, *Welfare Economics*, *supra* chap. 1, note 35, at 86.

17. Gruenspecht & Lave, *Health, Safety, and Environmental Regulation*, *supra* chap. 1, note 20, at 1544.

18. *Cf.* Parker, *supra* chap. 4, note 127, at 1355; Gruenspecht & Lave, *Health, Safety, and Environmental Regulation*, *supra* chap. 1, note 20, at 1537.

19. Gruenspecht & Lave, *Health, Safety, and Environmental Regulation*, *supra* chap. 1, note 20, at 1511.

20. *Id.* at 1544.

21. *Cf.* Parker, *supra* chap. 4, note 127, at 1421–22.

22. Posner, *Natural Monopoly*, *supra* chap. 1, note 38, at 549.

23. *See* chapter 2.

24. Breyer, *Regulation*, *supra* chap. 1, note 1, at 341.

25. *Id.* at 368.

26. Kearney & Merrill, *supra* chap. 4, note 123, at 1384.

27. Joskow & Noll, *supra* chap. 2, note 9, at 1251.

28. *See, e.g.*, Jerry A. Hausman & J. Gregory Sidak, *A Consumer-Welfare Approach to the Mandatory Unbundling of Telecommunications Networks*, 109 *Yale L.J.* 417 (1999).

29. Eli M. Noam, *Will Universal Service and Common Carriage Survive the Telecommunications Act of 1996?* 97 *Colum. L. Rev.* 955, 956 (1997).

30. *See, e.g.*, Joskow & Noll, *supra* chap. 2, note 9, at 1291–97.

31. Joskow, *Electric Power Sector*, *supra* chap. 5, note 21, at 177. For additional discussions of new possibilities in electricity restructuring, *see, e.g.*, Black & Pierce, *supra* chap. 5, note 61, at 1389–98; Paul L. Joskow, *Restructuring, Competition and Regulatory Reform in the U.S. Electricity Sector*, 11 *J. Econ. Persp.* 119, 120 (1997).

32. Curtis Grimm & Clifford Winston, *Competition in the Deregulated Railroad Industry: Sources, Effects, and Policy Issues*, in *Deregulation of Network Industries* 46 (Sam Peltzman & Clifford Winston eds., 2000). *Cf.* Kahn, *Deregulation*, *supra* chap. 3, note 6, at 327.

33. *See* Grimm & Winston, *supra* chap. 6, note 32, at 47.

34. William P. Rogerson, *The Regulation of Broadband Telecommunications, the Principle of Regulating Narrowly Defined Input Bottlenecks, and Incentives for Investment and Innovation*, 2000 *U. Chi. Legal F.* 119, 135.

35. *See* 47 U.S.C. § 251(c)(3) (2002) (imposing a "duty to provide, to any requesting telecommunications carrier for the provision of a telecommunications service, nondiscriminatory access to network elements on an unbundled basis at any technically feasible point. . . .").

36. *See* FERC Order No. 888, 61 Fed. Reg. 21,540 (1996) (codified at 18 C.F.R. pts. 35, 385).

37. Some sophisticated analysts such as Alfred Kahn understood this problem. *See, e.g.*, Kahn, *Deregulation*, *supra* chap. 3, note 6, at 346 ("During my tenure as Chairman of the Civil Aeronautics Board, I pointed out that it was the responsibility of government to respond to the increased demands generated by the competitive forces we were unleashing, by expanding airport and air traffic control capacity, and by pricing access to those scarce facilities rationally."). *See also* Alfred E. Kahn, *The Competitive Consequences of Hub Dominance: A Case Study*, 8 *Rev. Indus. Org.* 381 (1993); Scott McCartney, *Why Travelers Benefit When an Airline Hub Closes*, *Wall St. J.*, Nov. 1, 2005, at D1.

38. *See* Reza Dibadj, *Competitive Debacle in Local Telephony: Is the 1996 Telecommunications Act to Blame?* 81 *Wash. U. L.Q.* 1, 27–28 (2003). This pricing technique is known as "total element long-run incremental cost" (TELRIC). It is supported by a number of prominent scholars. *See, e.g.*, Chen, *Public Utility*, *supra* chap. 5, note 18; Ingo Vogelsang & Bridger M. Mitchell, *Telecommunications*

Competition (1997). For an incisive critique of TELRIC, see Kahn, *Whom the Gods, supra* chap. 2, note 23, at 5.

39. *See, e.g.,* William J. Baumol & J. Gregory Sidak, *The Pricing of Inputs Sold to Competitors,* 11 *Yale J. on Reg.* 171 (1994). The pricing technique is known as the "efficient component pricing rule" (ECPR). Its central idea is that an incumbent firm should be able to recoup the opportunity cost of not being able to sell or use the bottleneck input itself. Critics of ECPR maintain that it allows incumbents to maintain artificially high interconnection prices by maintaining an inefficient network. However, a modification to ECPR, M-ECPR, does address this issue by basing the interconnection price on that of the most efficient competitor in the market. For a detailed comparison of ECPR to TELRIC, see Dibadj, *Competitive Debacle, supra* chap. 6, note 38, at 27–39.

40. *See, e.g.,* Dibadj, *Competitive Debacle, supra* chap. 6, note 38, at 19–24.

41. *AT&T Corp. v. Iowa Utils. Bd.,* 525 U.S. 366, 429 (1999) (Breyer, J., concurring) (emphasis added).

42. Jerry Hausman, *Internet-Related Services: The Results of Asymmetric Regulation* in *Broadband* 129, 152 (Robert W. Crandall & James H. Alleman, eds., 2002). *See also* Dibadj, *Competitive Debacle, supra* chap. 6, note 38, at 33–34.

43. For an overview of the doctrine, see Robert Pitofsky, The Essential Facilities Doctrine Under United States Law (2002), *available at* http://www.ftc.gov/os/comments/intelpropertycomments/pitofskyrobert.pdf. For a history of the essential facilities in the telecommunications context, see John T. Soma et al., *The Essential Facilities Doctrine in the Deregulated Telecommunications Industry,* 13 *Berkeley Tech. L.J.* 565 (1998).

44. 708 F.2d 1081 (7th Cir. 1983).

45. *Id.* at 1132–33.

46. Robinson, *Refusing to Deal, supra* chap. 1, note 12, at 1207.

47. *See, e.g., United States v. Terminal Railroad Ass'n of St. Louis,* 224 U.S. 383 (1912); *Otter Tail Power v. United States,* 410 U.S. 366 (1973); *Aspen Skiing Co. v. Aspen Highlands Skiing Corp.,* 472 U.S. 585 (1985).

48. *Cf. AT&T Corp. v. Iowa Utils. Bd.,* 525 U.S. 366, 428 (1999) (Breyer, J., concurring).

49. Phillip Areeda, *Essential Facilities: An Epithet in Need of Limiting Principles,* 58 *Antitrust L.J.* 841, 841 (1990).

50. Hovenkamp, *Federal Antitrust Policy, supra* chap. 1, note 9, at 305.

51. Michael Boudin, *Antitrust Doctrine and the Sway of Metaphor,* 75 *Geo. L.J.* 395, 402 (1986).

52. Hylton, *Antitrust Law, supra* chap. 2, note 21, at 206.

53. *See* Michael K. Powell, Chairman, Federal Communications Commission, Remarks at the Goldman Sachs Communicopia XI Conference (Oct. 2, 2002), *available at* http://hraunfoss.fcc.gov/edocs_public/attachmatch/DOC-226929A1.pdf. *See also* Hovenkamp, *Federal Antitrust Policy, supra* chap. 1, note 9, at 311.

54. *See, e.g.,* Laffont & Tirole, *Telecommunications, supra* chap. 1, note 16, at 22.

55. *See, e.g.,* Huber, *Cyberspace, supra* chap. 4, note 11, at 4.

56. *See, e.g.,* Dibadj, *Cable Competition, supra* chap. 3, note 11, at 275–76; Dibadj, *Competitive Debacle, supra* chap. 6, note 38, at 7–10.

57. Joskow & Noll, *supra* chap. 2, note 9, at 1281.

58. Abbott B. Lipsky & J. Gregory Sidak, *Essential Facilities,* 51 *Stan. L. Rev.* 1187, 1195 (1999). *See also* Gregory J. Warden, *The Law and Economics of the Essential Facilities Doctrine,* 32 *St. Louis U. L.J.* 433, 479 (1987).

59. Lipsky & Sidak, *supra* chap. 6, note 58, at 1222–23 (emphasis added).

60. Joskow & Noll, *supra* chap. 2, note 9, at 1249–50 (emphasis added).

61. *See United States v. American Telephone & Telegraph Co.,* 552 F. Supp. 131 (D.C. Cir. 1982). *See also* Joseph D. Kearney, *From the Fall of the Bell System to the Telecommunications Act: Regulation of Telecommunications under Judge Greene,* 50 *Hastings L.J.* 1395, 1403 (1999).

62. The United States Court of Appeals for the District of Columbia Circuit was uncomfortable with the divestiture remedy. *See United States v. Microsoft Corp.,* 253 F.3d 34, 105 (D.C. Cir. 2001).

63. *See United States v. Microsoft Corp.,* No. 98-1232, 2002 U.S. Dist. LEXIS 22864, at *9-*10 (D.D.C. Nov. 12, 2002).

64. Rey & Tirole, *supra* chap. 5, note 121, at 1.

65. *See* chapter 5.

66. A similar conclusion may be reached through careful sociological analysis, without deploying the essential facilities doctrine or core theory. *See* Etzioni, *Moral Dimension, supra* chap. 4, note 48, at 202.

67. William J. Kolasky & Andrew R. Dick, The Merger Guidelines and the Integration of Efficiencies into Antitrust Review of Horizontal Mergers 2 (2002) (unpublished manuscript), *available at* http://www.usdoj.gov/atr/hmerger/11254.pdf.

68. Robinson, *Refusing to Deal, supra* chap. 1, note 12, at 1203.

69. *See also* Kahn, *Whom the Gods, supra* chap. 2, note 23, at 5–11.

70. Kearney & Merrill, *supra* chap. 4, note 123, at 1361–62. *See also* Crandall & Hausman, *supra* chap. 1, note 56, at 75–76.

71. *See, e.g.*, Hausman & Sidak, *supra* chap. 6, note 28, at 479–80. *Cf.* Pablo T. Spiller, *Value-Creating Interconnect Unbundling and the Promotion of Local Telephone Competition: Is Unbundling Necessary in Norway?* Foundation for Research in Economics and Business Administration (SNF), Breiviken, Norway (Mar. 1998).

72. Kearney & Merrill, *supra* chap. 4, note 123, at 1323.

73. 47 U.S.C. § 303 (2002).

74. *Before the Senate Committee on Commerce, Science, and Transportation,* United States Senate at 2 (Jan. 14, 2003) (statement of Michael J. Copps, Commissioner, Federal Communications Commission), *available at* http://www.fcc.gov/commissioners/copps/statements2003.html.

75. *See* Farber & Frickey, *supra* chap. 2, note 44, at 32.

76. Thomas W. Hazlett, *The Wireless Craze, the Unlimited Bandwidth Myth, the Spectrum Auction Faux Pas, and the Punchline to Ronald Coase's "Big Joke": An Essay on Airwave Allocation Policy,* 14 Harv. J. Law & Tech. 335, 401 (2001). *See also* George J. Alexander, *Antitrust and the Telephone Industry After the Telecommunications Act of 1996,* 12 Santa Clara Computer & High Tech. L.J. 227, 237 (1996).

77. *Cf.* Suleiman, *supra* chap. 4, note 152, at 313 ("Cynicism about politics does not result from routine government inefficiencies but from the fact that politics scarcely accords much importance to the public interest.").

78. Thomas W. Hazlett, *The Rationality of U.S. Regulation of the Broadcast Spectrum,* 33 J.L. & Econ. 133, 170 (1990).

79. *See* R.H. Coase, *The Federal Communications Commission,* 2 J.L. & Econ. 1, 32 (1959). *See also* White, *supra* chap. 4, note 29, at 27.

80. *See* Michael Calabrese, Battle Over the Airwaves: Principles for Spectrum Policy Reform 4 (New America Found., Spectrum Series Working Paper No. 1, 2001), *available at* http://www.newamerica.net/Download_Docs/pdfs/Pub_File_610_1.pdf.

81. Scott Woolley, *Dead Air, Forbes,* Nov. 25, 2002, at 138, 142.

82. *Poletown Neighborhood Council v. City of Detroit,* 304 N.W.2d 455, 459 (Mich. 1981) (emphasis added). A recent U.S. Supreme Court decision has reignited this debate. *See Kelo v. City of New London,* 125 S. Ct. 2655 (2005).

83. *See, e.g.*, Okediji, *supra* chap. 3, note 74, at 110–11.

84. Kathleen Q. Abernathy, My Vision of the Future of American Spectrum Policy, Remarks Before the Cato Institute's Sixth Annual Technology &

Society Conference (Nov. 14, 2002) (emphasis added), *available at* http://www.fcc.gov/Speeches/Abernathy/2002/spkqa228.html.

85. White, *supra* chap. 4, note 29, at 35. *See also* Leo Herzel, Comment, *"Public Interest" and the Market in Color Television Regulation*, 18 U. Chi. L. Rev. 802, 809 (1951).

86. Stewart, *supra* chap. 4, note 113, at 1682–83.

87. Charles A. Reich, *The New Property*, 73 Yale L.J. 733, 771 (1964).

88. Hazlett, *Wireless Craze*, *supra* chap. 6, note 76, at 452.

89. And, of course, thereby conflate "consumer" and "producer" surplus. Perhaps the best example of this misuse occurs in antitrust law. *See, e.g.*, Bork, *Antitrust Paradox*, *supra* chap. 2, note 22, at 91. *See also* Frank H. Easterbrook, *Does Antitrust Have a Comparative Advantage?* 23 Harv. J.L. & Pub. Pol'y 5, 6 (1999); Posner, *Antitrust Law*, *supra* chap. 2, note 22, at 2.

90. *See, e.g.*, Hausman & Sidak, *supra* chap. 6, note 28, at 450–51; Jerry Hausman & Howard Shelanski, *Economic Welfare and Telecommunications Regulation: The E-Rate Policy for Universal-Service Subsidies*, 16 Yale J. on Reg. 19, 28 (1999).

91. A monopsony is a market where there is a single buyer.

92. Ian Ayres & John Braithwaite, *Partial-Industry Regulation: A Monopsony Standard for Consumer Protection*, 80 Cal. L. Rev. 13, 30 (1992).

93. *Id.* at 52.

94. *Id.* at 34.

95. *Id.* at 32. *Cf.* Spencer Weber Waller, *Antitrust as Consumer Choice: Comments on the New Paradigm*, 62 U. Pitt. L. Rev. 535 (2001).

96. *See* Federal Communications Commission, Implementation of Section 3 of the Cable Television Consumer Protection and Competition Act of 1992, *Statistical Report on Average Rates for Basic Service, Cable Programming Service, and Equipment*, FCC Doc. No. 02-107, MM Docket No. 92-266, at ¶ 37 (Apr. 4, 2002) (report on cable industry prices).

97. *See, e.g.*, Reza Dibadj, *Monopoly v. Municipality*, Nat'l L. J., Feb. 14, 2005, at 26.

98. *See, e.g.*, Janet Wilson, *Potential Cost of Utility Sparks Dispute in Irvine*, L.A. Times, Jan. 14, 2003, at B3.

99. *See* Gerald E. Frug, *The City as Legal Concept*, 93 Harv. L. Rev. 1057, 1128 (1980).

100. *See, e.g.*, Gerald Torres, *Who Owns the Sky?* 19 *Pace Envtl. L. Rev.* 515, 529 (2002).

101. 6 N.J.L. 1 (1821).

102. 41 U.S. 367 (1842).

103. 146 U.S. 387 (1892).

104. *Id.* at 456.

105. *Nat'l Audubon Soc'y v. Superior Court of Alpine County*, 658 P.2d 709 (Cal. 1983).

106. Louis Kaplow, *An Economic Analysis of Legal Transitions*, 99 *Harv. L. Rev.* 509, 534–35 (1986) (emphasis added).

107. Joseph L. Sax, *Liberating the Public Trust Doctrine from Its Historical Shackles*, 14 *U.C. Davis L. Rev.* 185, 188 (1980) (footnote omitted).

108. *Cf.* Charles F. Wilkinson, *The Public Trust Doctrine in Public Land Law*, 14 *U.C. Davis L. Rev.* 269, 312 (1980) (arguing that the public trust doctrine is not merely a limitation on agency power, but a mechanism to force agencies to act proactively).

109. *See* Guido Calabresi & A. Douglas Melamed, *Property Rules, Liability Rules, and Inalienability: One View of the Cathedral*, 85 *Harv. L. Rev.* 1089 (1972).

110. *Id.* at 1092 (emphasis added).

111. *Id.* (emphasis added).

112. Ian Ayres & Eric Talley, *Solomonic Bargaining: Dividing a Legal Entitlement to Facilitate Coasean Trade*, 104 *Yale L.J.* 1027, 1101–02 (1995) (footnotes omitted).

113. *Id.* at 1082.

114. *See, e.g.*, James E. Krier & Stewart J. Schwab, *Property Rules and Liability Rules: The Cathedral in Another Light*, 70 *N.Y.U. L. Rev.* 440, 453 (1995).

115. Calabresi & Melamed, *supra* chap. 6, note 109, at 1092.

116. Louis Kaplow & Steven Shavell, *Property Rules Versus Liability Rules: An Economic Analysis*, 109 *Harv. L. Rev.* 713, 719 (1996).

117. *Cf.* Reich, *New Property*, *supra* chap. 6, note 87, at 786–87.

118. *See* Dibadj, *Reconceiving the Firm*, *supra* chap. 5, note 81.

119. Kent Greenfield, *Using Behavioral Economics to Show the Power and Efficiency of Corporate Law as a Regulatory Tool*, 35 *U.C. Davis L. Rev.* 581, 583–84 (2002).

120. *See, e.g.*, Peter C. Kostant, *Team Production and the Progressive Corporate Law Agenda*, 35 U.C. Davis L. Rev. 667, 679–80 (2002).

121. Langevoort, *Organized Illusions*, *supra* chap. 5, note 71, at 169.

122. Kostant, *Team Production*, *supra* chap. 6, note 120, at 677.

123. Lucian A. Bebchuk, *Making Directors Accountable*, Harv. Mag., Nov.–Dec. 2003, at 31.

124. Eric W. Orts, *Shirking and Sharking: A Legal Theory of the Firm*, 16 Yale L. & Pol'y Rev. 265, 282 (1998) (emphasis added).

125. *See, e.g.*, Bebchuk, *supra* chap. 6, note 123.

126. Thomas Lee Hazen, *The Corporate Persona, Contract (and Market) Failure, and Moral Values*, 69 N.C. L. Rev. 273, 318 (1991) (emphasis added). *See also* Reza Dibadj, *Delayering Corporate Law*, 34 Hofstra L. Rev. 469 (2005); Reza Dibadj, *The Misguided Transformation of Loyalty Into Contract*, 41 Tulsa L. Rev. __ (forthcoming 2006).

127. *Cf.* Arthur Levitt, Jr. *Money, Money, Money*, Wall St. J., Nov. 22, 2004, at A14.

128. *See, e.g.*, A. Mechele Dickerson, *A Behavioral Approach to Analyzing Corporate Failures*, 38 Wake Forest L. Rev. 1, 54 (2003).

129. *Cf.* Dibadj, *Reconceiving the Firm*, *supra* chap. 5, note 81.

130. For a discussion of how the law currently allows these conflicts of interest, see John R. Emshwiller, *Many Companies Report Transactions with Top Officers*, Wall St. J., Dec. 29, 2003, at A1.

131. *See, e.g.*, Langevoort, *Organized Illusions*, *supra* chap. 5, note 71, at 158.

132. Sunstein, *Deliberative Trouble*, *supra* chap. 5, note 77, at 109.

133. *See, e.g.*, Frank & Cherney, *supra* chap. 5, note 78.

134. *See, e.g.*, O'Connor, *supra* chap. 5, note 76, at 1304.

135. *See, e.g.*, *id.*

136. *See, e.g.*, Greenfield, *supra* chap. 6, note 119, at 643.

137. *See also* Edward L. Rubin, *Images of Organizations and Consequences of Regulation*, 6 Theoretical Inq. L. 347, 390 (2005).

138. Coase, *Firm Market Law*, *supra* chap. 4, note 31, at 9. *See also* Peter H. Schuck, *Concluding Thoughts* in *Creating Competitive Markets* (Marc K. Landy, et al. eds., forthcoming 2006).

139. Laurie P. Cohen & Kate Kelly, *NYSE Turmoil Poses Question: Can Wall Street Regulate Itself? Wall St. J.*, Dec. 31, 2003, at A1. *See also* Kate Kelly, *SEC Plans to Punish Exchanges, Wall St. J.*, Oct. 8, 2004, at C1; Deborah Solomon, *SEC Seeks to Overhaul Markets, Wall St. J.*, Feb. 25, 2004, at C1.

140. David Wessel, *A Lesson from the Blackout: Free Markets Also Need Rules, Wall St. J.*, Aug. 28, 2003, at A1. *See also* Deborah Solomon & Michael Schroeder, *How Refco Fell Through Regulatory Cracks, Wall St. J.*, Oct. 18, 2005, at A4.

141. Bratton, *Enron, supra* chap. 3, note 23, at 1283–84.

142. A measure of net income after taxes divided by number of shares outstanding. The numerator, of course, is the number most susceptible to manipulation.

143. Berenson, *supra* chap. 3, note 31, at 219.

144. Paul Krugman, *Enron and the System, N.Y. Times,* Jan. 9, 2004, at A19. Perhaps unsurprisingly, some companies are downplaying the new accounting rules by emphasizing pro forma results which typically do not include option expenses. *See, e.g.,* Joseph Nocera, *Stock Options: So Who's Counting? N.Y. Times,* Aug. 6, 2005, at C1.

145. Frank Partnoy, *Barbarians at the Gatekeepers? A Proposal for a Modified Strict Liability Regime,* 79 *Wash. U. L.Q.* 491, 540 (2001).

146. *See, e.g.,* Langevoort, *Organized Illusions, supra* chap. 5, note 71, at 160.

147. *See, e.g.,* Charles R.P. Pouncy, *The Rational Rogue: Neoclassical Economic Ideology in the Regulation of the Financial Professional,* 26 *Vt. L. Rev.* 263, 377 (2002).

148. *See, e.g.,* Alec Klein, *Borrowers Find System Open to Conflicts, Manipulation, Wash. Post,* Nov. 22, 2004, at A1.

149. Jill E. Fisch & Kenneth M. Rosen, *How Did Corporate and Securities Law Fail? Is There a Role for Lawyers in Preventing Future Enrons?* 48 *Vill. L. Rev.* 1097, 1131 (2003).

150. *Id.* at 1132.

151. *Id.*

152. *See id.* at 1133–36. On the importance of enforcing the antifraud provisions of the securities laws, see Reza Dibadj, *From Incongruity to Cooperative Federalism,* 40 *U.S.F. L. Rev.* __ (forthcoming 2006).

153. Bill George, *Wanted: Authentic Leaders, Wall St. J.*, Dec. 16, 2003, at B2 (emphasis added).

154. *Cf.* Berenson, *supra* chap. 3, note 31, at 85–87.

155. *See* chapter 5.

156. Kaplow, *Monopoly Power, supra* chap. 2, note 21, at 551. Kaplow's central argument is that monopoly leveraging must be examined within a class of "practices designed to affect market share and elasticity of market demand. . . . These practices do not increase short-run profits, and might even decrease them. The firm's motivation is to change the structural conditions it faces in the future in order that it may receive greater profits in the future." *Id.* at 524.

157. Harry S. Gerla, *A Micro-Microeconomic Approach to Antitrust Law: Games Managers Play*, 86 *Mich. L. Rev.* 892, 918–19 (1988).

158. *See, e.g.*, Avishalom Tor, *The Fable of Entry: Bounded Rationality, Market Discipline, and Legal Policy*, 101 *Mich. L. Rev.* 482, 555 (2002). *Cf.* Kahn, *Whom the Gods, supra* chap. 2, note 23, at 38.

159. *See* Dan M. Kahan, *Social Influence, Social Meaning, and Deterrence*, 83 *Va. L. Rev.* 349, 371 (1997).

160. *Id.* at 373.

161. *Id.* at 378.

162. *Id.* at 382. *Cf.* Weber Waller, *Thurman Arnold, supra* chap. 1, note 25, at 581 (noting how Thurman Arnold, a particularly effective head of the Department of Justice's Antitrust Division in the 1940s, "shrewdly observed how even the mere bringing of an indictment usually lowered prices and ended the alleged anticompetitive practices harming the public.").

163. Robert E. Lane, *Why Business Men Violate the Law*, 44 *J. Crim. L. Criminology & Police Sci.* 151, 154 (1953).

164. *See, e.g.*, Deborah Solomon & Michael Schroeder, *Back Off! Businesses Go Toe to Toe with SEC, Wall St. J.*, Oct. 27, 2004, at C1.

CHAPTER 7. INSTITUTIONAL CHANGES

1. Neoclassical economic theory has, by and large, ignored institutions. *See, e.g.*, Douglass C. North, *Institutions and Economic Growth: An Historical Introduction*, 17 *World Dev.* 1319 (1989). A notable exception is Alfred E. Kahn, who devotes volume 2 of his monumental *The Economics of Regulation* to blending institutional and theoretical analysis. *See* 2 Kahn, *Economics of Regulation, supra* chap. 5, note 126, at xii ("When we turn from the normative question of *what we want* to the institutional question of *how we get it*, we find ourselves launched into the baffling arena of social and political as well as economic behavior and organization, into the real world of ignorance, error and corruption, where all institutions are in varying degrees imperfect.").

2. Kahn, *Whom the Gods, supra* chap. 2, note 23, at 2. *See also* Kahn, *Deregulation, supra* chap. 3, note 6, at 340 ("if competition is to work well, it

requires a great variety of governmental interventions to remedy imperfections and market failures—interventions that, however validly they may be characterized as regulatory, differ fundamentally from the kind of direct economic regulation previously administered by such agencies as the CAB [Civil Aeronautics Board] and ICC [Interstate Commerce Commission], and still practiced by most of the state public utility commissions.").

3. Duffy, *supra* chap. 4, note 13, at 1140.

4. *Cf.* Bhagwat, *supra* chap. 4, note 107, at 1501.

5. Stewart, *supra* chap. 4, note 113, at 1672.

6. Stewart outlines the four characteristics of the traditional model:

> *(1) The imposition of administratively determined sanctions on private individuals must be authorized by the legislature through rules which control agency action.*

> *(2) The decisional procedures followed by the agency must be such as will tend to ensure the agency's compliance with requirement (1).*

> *(3) The decisional processes of the agency must facilitate judicial review to ensure agency compliance with requirements (1) and (2).*

> *(4) Judicial review must be available to ensure compliance with requirements (1) and (2).*

Id. at 1671–76.

7. Maremont & Solomon, *SEC's Failings, supra* chap. 3, note 27, at A1. *See also* Jesse Eisinger, *SEC Screwdriver Joins Spitzer Hammer as Hedge-Trimmer, Wall St. J.,* Oct. 27, 2004, at C1.

8. Duffy, *supra* chap. 4, note 13, at 1133–34.

9. *See id.*

10. Former SEC chairman Arthur Levitt had proposed a similar idea for the SEC. *See* Schlesinger, *The Deregulators, supra* Preface, note 1, at A12.

11. *See,* Dibadj, *Saving Antitrust, supra* chap. 1, note 21, at 840–60. *See also* Reza Dibadj, *At 90, Time to Reform, Nat'l L. J.,* Oct. 11, 2004, at 23.

12. Bartlett & Steele, *supra* chap. 3, note 38, at 11 (emphasis added).

13. *See, e.g.,* Phil B. Fontanarosa et al., *Postmarketing Surveillance—Lack of Vigilance, Lack of Trust,* 292 *J. Am. Med. Ass'n.* 2647 (2004); Merrill Goozner, *Overdosed and Oversold, N.Y. Times,* Dec. 21, 2004, at A29. There has at least been a small step in this direction. *See* Anna Wilde Mathews & Leila Abboud, *FDA Establishes Board to Review Approved Drugs, Wall St. J.,* Feb. 16, 2005, at A1.

14. Gary DeWaal, *America Must Create a Single Financial Regulator, Fin. Times,* May 19, 2005, at 13.

15. Parker, *supra* chap. 4, note 127, at 1356.

16. *Id.* at 1356. *See also* Breyer, *Regulation, supra* chap. 1, note 1, at 362.

17. Stewart, *supra* chap. 4, note 113, at 1810.

18. Duffy, *supra* chap. 4, note 13, at 1123.

19. *See, e.g.*, Jolls et al., *supra* chap. 4, note 52, at 1545.

20. Posner, *Rational Choice, supra* chap. 5, note 91, at 1572.

21. Stephen M. Bainbridge, *Mandatory Disclosure: A Behavioral Analysis*, 68 *U. Cin. L. Rev.* 1023, 1058 (2000).

22. Stephen J. Choi & A.C. Pritchard, *Behavioral Economics and the SEC*, 56 *Stan. L. Rev.* 1, 5 (2003).

23. Daryl J. Levinson, *Making Government Pay: Markets, Politics, and the Allocation of Constitutional Costs*, 67 *U. Chi. L. Rev.* 345, 415 (2000).

24. *Id.* at 416–17 (emphasis added).

25. Choi & Pritchard, *supra* chap. 7, note 22, at 44 (emphasis added).

26. *Id.* at 50 (emphasis added).

27. Levinson, *Making Government Pay, supra* chap. 7, note 23, at 415.

28. Wilson, *supra* chap. 1, note 50, at 348.

29. *See* Kahan, *Social Influence, supra* chap. 6, note 159, at 369.

30. *Id.* at 389.

31. Robert Prentice, *Whither Securities Regulation? Some Behavioral Observations Regarding Proposals for Its Future*, 51 *Duke L.J.* 1397, 1502–03 (2002).

32. Paul G. Mahoney & Chris William Sanchirico, *Norms, Repeated Games, and the Role of Law*, 91 *Cal. L. Rev.* 1281, 1288 (2003).

33. *Id.* at 1310.

34. Lawrence Lessig, *Commons and Code*, 9 *Fordham Intell. Prop. Media & Ent. L.J.* 405, 418 (1999). *See also* Kahn, *Liberalism, supra* chap. 1, note 27, at 6 ("the government has a creative role to play in promoting economic progress—in financing research and development, particularly of alternative energy technologies, for example. It is not clear at all that most conservatives fully recognize the insufficiency of an exclusive reliance on 'getting the government off our backs.' ").

35. A. D. Woozley, *What Is Wrong with Retrospective Law?* 18 *Phil. Q.* 40, 43 (1968). *See also* Donald Wittman, *Prior Regulation Versus Post Liability: The Choice Between Input and Output Monitoring*, 6 *J. Legal Stud.* 193 (1977).

36. Posner, *Antitrust Law, supra* chap. 2, note 22, at 1.

37. *See* Hazlett, *Telecommunications Act, supra* chap. 2, note 57, at 239.

38. *See, e.g.,* Haar, *supra* chap. 3, note 65, at 138; Posner, *Antitrust Law, supra* chap. 2, note 22, at 280.

39. Stewart, *supra* chap. 4, note 113, at 1763.

40. *See, e.g.,* Torres, *Who Owns the Sky? supra* chap. 6, note 100, at 559.

41. A classic example is *S. Burlington County NAACP v. Township of Mount Laurel,* 456 A.2d 390 (N.J. 1983) (Mt. Laurel II). During the course of a 216-page opinion, the court appointed a panel of three judges to manage housing cases.

42. Salop & Romaine, *supra* chap. 5, note 32, at 671. *Cf.* Peter H. Schuck, *Just the Verdict, Please, L.A. Times,* Aug. 29, 2005, at B11.

43. *See, e.g.,* Posner, *Natural Monopoly, supra* chap. 1, note 38, at 549.

44. *Cf.* Patrick Bolton et al., *Predatory Pricing: Strategic Theory and Legal Policy,* 88 Geo. L.J. 2239, 2241 (2000); Hylton, *Antitrust Law, supra* chap. 2, note 21, at 214.

45. *Verizon Comms. v. FCC,* 535 U.S. 467, 561–62 (2002) (Breyer, J., dissenting).

46. Haar, *supra* chap. 3, note 65, at 184.

47. *Seattle Audubon Society v. Evans,* 771 F. Supp. 1081, 1096 (W.D. Wash. 1991). *Cf. S. Burlington County NAACP v. Township of Mount Laurel,* 456 A.2d 390, 490 (N.J. 1983) (Mt. Laurel II) (judges "may not build houses, but we do enforce the Constitution").

48. Haar, *supra* chap. 3, note 65, at 179.

49. Farber & Frickey, *supra* chap. 2, note 44, at 61–62.

50. *Cf.* Schuck, *Delegation and Democracy, supra* chap. 4, note 133, at 787–90.

51. Gerald E. Frug, *The Ideology of Bureaucracy in American Law,* 97 Harv. L. Rev. 1276, 1382 (1984).

52. Stewart, *supra* chap. 4, note 113, at 1807.

53. William H. Widen, *Enron at the Margin,* 58 Bus. Law. 961, 962–63 (2003) (emphasis added).

54. *Id.* at 1002.

55. Frug, *Ideology of Bureaucracy, supra* chap. 7, note 51, at 1386.

56. Jürgen Habermas, *Between Facts and Norms* 442 (William Rehg trans., 1996) (emphasis added).

57. Amitai Etzioni, *Next* 22 (2001). Moral dialogues, in turn, "are composed of large numbers of hours spent over meals, at bars, in car pools, at work, and in the media (e.g., call-in shows) on one 'hot' moral issue." *Id.* at 33.

58. *Cf.* 1 Kahn, *Economics of Regulation, supra* chap. 1, note 22, at 14.

59. Etzioni, *Moral Dimension, supra* chap. 4, note 48, at 242.

60. Morton J. Horwitz, *The History of the Public/Private Distinction*, 130 U. Pa. L. Rev. 1423, 1424 (1982).

61. Hovenkamp, *Knowledge About* Welfare, *supra* chap. 1, note 23, at 809–10.

62. *See, e.g.*, Morris R. Cohen, *Property and Sovereignty*, 13 *Cornell L.Q.* 8, 21 (1927).

63. Some scholars argue that public values could infuse these new private entities. *See, e.g.*, Martha Minow, *Public and Private Partnerships: Accounting for the New Religion*, 116 *Harv. L. Rev.* 1229, 1229–37 (2003).

64. Duncan Kennedy, *The Stages of Decline of the Public/Private Distinction*, 130 U. Pa. L. Rev. 1349, 1357 (1982). *See also* Freeman & Mensch, *supra* chap. 3, note 84, at 248.

65. Frug, *City as Legal Concept, supra* chap. 6, note 99, at 1138–39.

66. Karl E. Klare, *The Public/Private Distinction in Labor Law*, 130 U. Pa. L. Rev. 1358, 1422 (1982).

67. Etzioni, *Moral Dimension, supra* chap. 4, note 48, at 217. For an illustration, see Brody Mullins, *Junket Bonds: More Lawmakers Take Trips Funded by Corporations*, *Wall St. J.*, Apr. 15, 2005, at A1.

68. *See, e.g.*, Levinson, *Making Government Pay, supra* chap. 7, note 23, at 419 (arguing that bad publicity will affect governments who react mainly to political, not financial, incentives).

69. *See, e.g.*, Harold J. Krent & Nicholas S. Zeppos, *Monitoring Governmental Disposition of Assets: Fashioning Regulatory Substitutes for Market Controls*, 52 *Vand. L. Rev.* 1703, 1771–72 (1999).

70. *See id.* at 1770.

71. *See, e.g.*, Stewart, *supra* chap. 4, note 113, at 1790.

72. *See id.* at 1801.

73. Habermas, *supra* chap. 7, note 56, at 119.

74. A. Michael Froomkin, *Habermas@Discourse.Net: Toward a Critical Theory of Cyberspace*, 116 *Harv. L. Rev.* 751, 775 (2003).

75. John Denvir, for instance, argues that the U.S. Constitution should be interpreted in a manner that gives citizens positive rights—such as the opportunity

to earn a living and education—to set the preconditions for true engagement in participatory democracy. *See* John Denvir, *Democracy's Constitution* (2001).

76. Olson, *supra* chap. 2, note 50, at 167. "Selective incentives" can be thought of as by-products of a group's main purpose, such as professional organizations offering insurance and technical publications to their members. *See id.* at 132–39.

77. *Id.* at 143 (emphasis added).

78. Ellickson, *Order Without Law*, *supra* chap. 4, note 30, at 284 (emphasis added).

79. *Id.* at 249.

80. *See* Walton, *supra* chap. 3, note 64, at 181; Dibadj, *Reconceiving the Firm*, *supra* chap. 5, note 81.

81. Suleiman, *supra* chap. 4, note 152, at 7. *See also* Kelman, *Public Policy*, *supra* chap. 4, note 151, at 88–113.

AFTERWORD

1. *Cf.* 1 Kahn, *Economics of Regulation*, *supra* chap. 1, note 22, at 13 ("This purpose must not be interpreted as reflecting a belief that any simple set of rules can answer all problems of regulatory policy. On the contrary, each regulated industry (in fact, each unregulated one, too) is in essential respects unique and must be so treated."). *See also* 2 Kahn, *Economics of Regulation*, *supra* chap. 5, note 126, at 325.

2. Etzioni, *Moral Dimension*, *supra* chap. 4, note 48, at 205.

3. 198 U.S. 45 (1905).

4. *Id.* at 75 (Holmes, J., dissenting).

5. For example, by equalizing information asymmetries and aggressively curbing monopolistic behavior.

6. *See, e.g.*, Kahn, Talk to Security Analysts, *supra* chap. 5, note 14, at 1–4.

7. *Cf.* Etzioni, *Moral Dimension*, *supra* chap. 4, note 48, at 250 ("*The more people accept the neoclassical paradigm as a guide for their behavior, the more the ability to sustain a market economy is undermined.*").

8. As Coase notes with elegant simplicity, "Economic theory has suffered in the past from a failure to state clearly its assumptions." Coase, *Nature of the Firm*, *supra* chap. 4, note 32, at 386. *See also* Fischel, *supra* chap. 4, note 25, at 122.

9. Laffont & Tirole, *Telecommunications*, *supra* chap. 1, note 16, at 2.

BIBLIOGRAPHY

BOOKS

Ackerman, Frank & Lisa Heinzerling. *Priceless: On Knowing the Price of Everything and the Value of Nothing* (2004).

Baumol, William J. & J. Gregory Sidak. *Toward Competition in Local Telephony* (1994).

Berenson, Alex. *The Number* (2003).

Bork, Robert H. *The Antitrust Paradox* (1978).

Breyer, Stephen. *Regulation and Its Reform* (1982).

Choices, Values, and Frames (Daniel Kahneman & Amos Tversky eds., 2000).

Coase, R. H. *The Firm the Market and the Law* (1988).

Denvir, John. *Democracy's Constitution* (2001).

Dirlam, Joel B. & Alfred E. Kahn. *Fair Competition: The Law and Economics of Antitrust Policy* (1954).

Ellickson, Robert C. *Order Without Law* (1991).

Etzioni, Amitai. *Next* (2001).

———. *The Moral Dimension* (1988).

Farber, Daniel A. & Philip P. Frickey. *Law and Public Choice: A Critical Introduction* (1991).

The Federalist No. 10 (James Madison) (Jacob E. Cooke ed., 1961).

Fischel, William A. *The Economics of Zoning Laws: A Property Rights Approach to American Land Use Controls* (1985).

Friedman, Milton. *Capitalism and Freedom* (1962).

Gómez-Ibáñez, José A. *Regulating Infrastructure: Monopoly, Contracts, and Discretion* (2003).

Haar, Charles M. *Suburbs Under Siege: Race, Space, and Audacious Judges* (1996).

Habermas, Jürgen. *Between Facts and Norms* (William Rehg, trans., 1996).

Handbook of Industrial Organization (Richard Schmalensee & Robert D. Willig, eds., 1989).

Hovenkamp, Herbert. *Federal Antitrust Policy* (2d ed. 1999).

Huber, Peter. *Law and Disorder in Cyberspace: Abolish the FCC and Let Common Law Rule the Telecosm* (1997).

Hume, David. *A Treatise of Human Nature* (L. A. Selby-Bigge ed., Oxford University Press 2d ed. 1978) (1740).

Hylton, Keith N. *Antitrust Law* (2003).

Jackson, Kenneth T. *Crabgrass Frontier* (1985).

Johansson, Per-Olov. *An Introduction to Modern Welfare Economics* (1991).

Kahn, Alfred E. *Lessons from Deregulation: Telecommunications and Airlines after the Crunch* (2004).

———. *Whom the Gods Would Destroy, or How Not to Deregulate* (2001).

———. *The Economics of Regulation. Vol. 1, Economic Principles* (1970). *Vol. 2, Institutional Issues* (1970).

Kalman, Laura. *The Strange Career of Legal Liberalism* (1996).

Kelman, Mark. *Strategy or Principle? The Choice Between Regulation and Taxation* (1999).

Kelman, Steven. *Making Public Policy: A Hopeful View of American Government* (1987).

Laffont, Jean-Jacques & Jean Tirole. *Competition in Telecommunications* (2000).

Olson, Mancur. *The Logic of Collective Action* (1971).

Peritz, Rudolph J. R. *Competition Policy in America, 1888–1992* (1996).

Pigou, A. C. *The Economics of Welfare* (4th ed. 1932).

Polinsky, A. Mitchell. *An Introduction to Law and Economics* (2d ed. 1989).

Posner, Richard A. *Antitrust Law* (2d ed. 2001).

———. *Economic Analysis of Law* (5th ed. 1998).

Rossi, Jim. *Regulatory Bargaining and Public Law* (2005).

Schroeder, Jeanne Lorraine. *The Triumph of Venus: The Erotics of the Market* (2004).

Schumpeter, Joseph A. *Capitalism, Socialism and Democracy* (3d ed. 1950).

Shavell, Steven. *Foundations of Economic Analysis of Law* (2004).

Shepherd, William G. & Joanna M. Shepherd. *The Economics of Industrial Organization* (5th ed. 2003).

Smith, Adam. *An Inquiry into the Nature and Causes of the Wealth of Nations* (1900).

Smith, Vernon L. *Bargaining and Market Behavior: Essays in Experimental Economics* (2000).

Suleiman, Ezra. *Dismantling Democratic States* (2003).

Tirole, Jean. *The Theory of Industrial Organization* (1997).

Viscusi, W. Kip et al. *Economics of Antitrust and Regulation* (3d ed. 2000).

Vogelsang, Ingo & Bridger M. Mitchell. *Telecommunications Competition* (1997).

Warren, Elizabeth & Amelia Warren Tyagi. *The Two-Income Trap: Why Middle-Class Mothers and Fathers Are Going Broke* (2003).

Wilson, James Q. *Bureaucracy* (1989).

The World Capital Shortage (Alan Heslop ed., 1977).

JOURNAL ARTICLES

Ackerman, Bruce A. *Law, Economics, and the Problem of Legal Culture*, 1986 *Duke L.J.* 929 (1986).

———. *Foreword: Talking and Trading*, 85 *Colum. L. Rev.* 899 (1985).

Adams, Walter & James W. Brock. *Antitrust, Ideology, and the Arabesques of Economic Theory*, 66 *U. Colo. L. Rev.* 257 (1995).

Aghion, Philippe & Patrick Bolton. *Contracts as Barrier to Entry*, 77 *Am. Econ. Rev.* 388 (1987).

Ahdieh, Robert B. *Making Markets: Network Effects and the Role of Law in the Creation of Strong Securities Markets*, 76 *S. Cal. L. Rev.* 277 (2003).

Alexander, George J. *Antitrust and the Telephone Industry After the Telecommunications Act of 1996*, 12 *Santa Clara Computer & High Tech. L.J.* 227 (1996).

Areeda, Phillip. *Essential Facilities: An Epithet in Need of Limiting Principles*, 58 *Antitrust L.J.* 841 (1990).

Arlen, Jennifer. Comment, *The Future of Behavioral Economic Analysis of Law*, 51 *Vand. L. Rev.* 1765 (1998).

Averch, Harvey & Leland L. Johnson. *Behavior of the Firm Under Regulatory Constraint*, 52 *Am. Econ. Rev.* 1052 (1962).

Ayres, Ian. *Playing Games with the Law*, 42 *Stan. L. Rev.* 1291 (1990) (book review).

Ayres, Ian & John Braithwaite. *Partial-Industry Regulation: A Monopsony Standard for Consumer Protection*, 80 *Cal. L. Rev.* 13 (1992).

Ayres, Ian & Eric Talley. *Solomonic Bargaining: Dividing a Legal Entitlement to Facilitate Coasean Trade*, 104 *Yale L.J.* 1027 (1995).

Babcock, Linda & George Loewenstein. *Explaining Bargaining Impasse: The Role of Self-Serving Biases*, 11 *J. Econ. Persp.* 109 (1997).

Bailey, Elizabeth E. *Contestability and the Design of Regulatory and Antitrust Policy*, 71 *Am. Econ. Rev.* 178 (1981).

Bailey, Elizabeth E. & William J. Baumol. *Deregulation and the Theory of Contestable Markets*, 1 *Yale J. on Reg.* 111 (1984).

Bainbridge, Stephen M. *Mandatory Disclosure: A Behavioral Analysis*, 68 *U. Cin. L. Rev.* 1023 (2000).

Baird, Douglas G. *The Future of Law and Economics: Looking Forward; Introduction*, 64 *U. Chi. L. Rev.* 1129 (1997).

Baker, Jonathan B. *Recent Developments in Economics that Challenge the Chicago School Views*, 58 *Antitrust L.J.* 645 (1989).

Baumol, William J. *Contestable Markets: An Uprising in the Theory of Industry Structure*, 72 *Am. Econ. Rev.* 1 (1982).

———. *On the Theory of Oligopoly*, 25 *Economica* 187 (1958).

Baumol, William J., et al. *Weak Invisible Hand Theorems on the Sustainability of Multiproduct Natural Monopoly*, 67 *Am. Econ. Rev.* 350 (1977).

Baumol, William J. & J. Gregory Sidak. *The Pricing of Inputs Sold to Competitors*, 11 *Yale J. on Reg.* 171 (1994).

Benkler, Yochai. *Overcoming Agoraphobia: Building the Commons of the Digitally Networked Environment*, 11 *Harv. J.L. & Tech.* 287 (1998).

Bernheim, B. Douglas & Michael D. Whinston, *Exclusive Dealing*, 106 *J. Pol. Econ.* 64 (1998).

Berresford, John W. *Mergers in Mobile Telecommunications Services: A Primer on the Analysis of Their Competitive Effects*, 48 *Fed. Comm. L.J.* 247 (1996).

Bhagwat, Ashutosh. *Unnatural Competition? Applying the New Antitrust Learning to Foster Competition in the Local Exchange*, 50 *Hastings L.J.* 1479 (1999).

Bittlingmayer, George. *The Economic Problem of Fixed Costs and What Legal Research Can Contribute*, 14 *Law & Soc. Inquiry* 739 (1989).

———. *Did Antitrust Policy Cause the Great Merger Wave?* 28 *J.L. & Econ.* 77 (1985).

————. *Decreasing Average Cost and Competition: A New Look at the Addyston Pipe Case*, 25 *J.L. & Econ.* 201 (1982).

Black, Bernard S. & Richard J. Pierce. *The Choice Between Markets and Central Planning in Regulating the U.S. Electricity Industry*, 93 *Colum. L. Rev.* 1341 (1993).

Bolton, Patrick, et al. *Predatory Pricing: Strategic Theory and Legal Policy*, 88 *Geo. L.J.* 2239 (2000).

Boudin, Michael. *Antitrust Doctrine and the Sway of Metaphor*, 75 *Geo. L.J.* 395 (1986).

Bowman, Ward S. *Tying Arrangements and the Leverage Problem*, 67 *Yale L.J.* 19 (1957).

Bratton, William W. *Enron and the Dark Side of Shareholder Value*, 76 *Tul. L. Rev.* 1275 (2002).

Breyer, Stephen G. *Antitrust, Deregulation, and the Newly Liberated Marketplace*, 75 *Cal. L. Rev.* 1005 (1987).

Brodley, Joseph F. & Ching-to Albert Ma. *Contract Penalties, Monopolizing Strategies, and Antitrust Policy*, 45 *Stan. L. Rev.* 1161 (1993).

Buchanan, James M. *Contractarian Political Economy and Constitutional Interpretation*, 78 *Am. Econ. Rev.* 135 (1988).

————. *A Contractarian Paradigm for Applying Economic Theory*, 65 *Am. Econ. Rev.* 225 (1975).

————. *Politics, Policy, and the Pigovian Margins*, 29 *Economica* 17 (1962).

Bulow, Jeremy I. *Durable-Goods Monopolists*, 90 *J. Pol. Econ.* 314 (1982).

Burtaw, Dallas. *Bargaining with Noisy Delegation*, 24 *Rand J. Econ.* 40 (1993).

Calabresi, Guido & A. Douglas Melamed. *Property Rules, Liability Rules, and Inalienability: One View of the Cathedral*, 85 *Harv. L. Rev.* 1089 (1972).

Camerer, Colin F. *Progress in Behavioral Game Theory*, 11 *J. Econ. Persp.* 167 (1997).

Camerer, Colin, et al. *Regulation for Conservatives: Behavioral Economics and the Case for "Asymmetric Paternalism,"* 151 *U. Pa. L. Rev.* 1211 (2003).

Carlton, Dennis W. & Robert Gertner. *Market Power and Mergers in Durable-Good Industries*, 32 *J.L. & Econ.* S203 (1989).

Carrier, Michael A. *Antitrust After the Interception: Of a Heroic Returner and Myriad Paths*, 55 *Stan. L. Rev.* 283 (2002) (book review).

Chen, Jim. *The Nature of the Public Utility: Infrastructure, the Market, and the Law*, 98 *Nw. U. L. Rev.* 1617 (2004).

———. *The Authority to Regulate Broadband Internet Access over Cable*, 16 *Berkeley Tech. L.J.* 677 (2001).

Choi, Stephen J. & A.C. Pritchard. *Behavioral Economics and the SEC*, 56 *Stan. L. Rev.* 1 (2003).

Chua, Amy L. *Markets, Democracy, and Ethnicity: Toward a New Paradigm for Law and Development*, 108 *Yale L.J.* 1 (1998).

Coase, R. H. *The Problem of Social Cost*, 3 *J.L. & Econ.* 1 (1960).

———. *The Federal Communications Commission*, 2 *J.L. & Econ.* 1 (1959).

———. *The Nature of the Firm*, 4 *Economica* 386 (1937).

Cohen, Morris R. *Property and Sovereignty*, 13 *Cornell L.Q.* 8 (1927).

Coleman, Jules L. *Afterword: The Rational Choice Approach to Legal Rules*, 65 *Chi.-Kent L. Rev.* 177 (1989).

Crespi, Gregory Scott. *The Mid-Life Crisis of the Law and Economics Movement: Confronting the Problems of Nonfalsifiability and Normative Bias*, 67 *Notre Dame L. Rev.* 231 (1991).

Croley, Steven P. *Theories of Regulation: Incorporating the Administrative Process*, 98 *Colum. L. Rev.* 1 (1998).

Cudahy, Richard D. *The Coming Demise of Deregulation*, 10 *Yale J. on Reg.* 1 (1993).

Cyert, R. M. & James G. March. *Organizational Factors in the Theory of Oligopoly*, 70 *Q. J. Econ.* 44 (1956).

Dahlman, Carl J. *The Problem of Externality*, 22 *J.L. & Econ.* 141 (1979).

D'Amato, Anthony. *Post-Revolutionary Law and Economics: A Foreword to the Symposium*, 20 *Hofstra L. Rev.* 757 (1992).

Demsetz, Harold. *Barriers to Entry*, 72 *Am. Econ. Rev.* 47 (1982).

———. *Why Regulate Utilities?* 11 *J.L. & Econ.* 55 (1968).

———. *Toward a Theory of Property Rights*, 57 *Am. Econ. Rev.* 347 (1967).

Dibadj, Reza. *Delayering Corporate Law*, 34 *Hofstra L. Rev.* 489 (2005).

———. *The Misguided Transformation of Loyalty Into Contract*, 41 *Tulsa L. Rev.* __ (forthcoming 2006).

———. *From Incongruity to Cooperative Federalism*, 40 *U.S.F. L. Rev.* 469 (2005).

———. *Weasel Numbers*, 27 *Cardozo L. Rev.* 1325 (2006).

———. *The Limits of Utilitarianism*, 6 *Nevada L.J.* 201 (2005) (book review).

————. *Reconceiving the Firm*, 26 Cardozo L. Rev. 1459 (2005).

————. *Saving Antitrust*, 75 Univ. Colo. L. Rev. 745 (2004).

————. *Beyond Facile Assumptions and Radical Assertions: A Case for "Critical Legal Economics,"* 2003 Utah L. Rev. 1155.

————. *Regulatory Givings and the Anticommons*, 64 Ohio St. L.J. 1041 (2003).

————. *Competitive Debacle in Local Telephony: Is the 1996 Telecommunications Act to Blame?* 81 Wash. U. L.Q. 1 (2003).

————. *Toward Meaningful Cable Competition: Getting Beyond the Monopoly Morass*, 6 N.Y.U. J. Legisl. & Pub. Pol'y 245 (2003).

Dickerson, A. Mechele. *A Behavioral Approach to Analyzing Corporate Failures*, 38 Wake Forest L. Rev. 1 (2003).

Dixit, Avinash. *The Role of Investment in Entry Deterrence*, 90 Econ. J. 95 (1980).

Dolinko, David. *The Perils of Welfare Economics*, 97 Nw. U. L. Rev. 351 (2002).

Dorff, Michael B. *Why Welfare Depends on Fairness: A Reply to Kaplow and Shavell*, 75 S. Cal. L. Rev. 847 (2002).

Duffy, John F. *The FCC and the Patent System: Progressive Ideals, Jacksonian Realism, and the Technology of Regulation*, 71 U. Colo. L. Rev. 1071 (2000).

Eccles, Robert G., et al. *Are You Paying Too Much for that Acquisition?* Harv. Bus. Rev., July–Aug. 1999 at 136.

Ellickson, Robert C. *Bringing Culture and Human Frailty to Rational Actors: A Critique of Classical Law and Economics*, 65 Chi.-Kent. L. Rev. 23 (1989).

————. *The Case for Coase and Against "Coaseanism,"* 99 Yale L.J. 611 (1989).

Elster, Jon. *Emotions and Economic Theory*, 36 J. Econ. Lit. 47 (1998).

Farber, Daniel A. & Brett H. McDonnell. *Why (and How) Fairness Matters at the IP/Antitrust Interface*, 87 Minn. L. Rev. 1817 (2003).

Farrell, Joseph & Garth Saloner. *Installed Base and Compatibility: Innovation, Product Preannouncements, and Predation*, 76 Am. Econ. Rev. 940 (1986).

Fisch, Jill E. & Kenneth M. Rosen. *How Did Corporate and Securities Law Fail? Is There a Role for Lawyers in Preventing Future Enrons?* 48 Vill. L. Rev. 1097 (2003).

Fontanarosa, Phil B., et al. *Postmarketing Surveillance—Lack of Vigilance, Lack of Trust*, 292 J. Am. Med. Ass'n. 2647 (2004).

Fox, Craig R. & Amos Tversky. *Ambiguity Aversion and Comparative Ignorance*, 110 Q. J. Econ. 585 (1995).

Freeman, Alan & Elizabeth Mensch. *The Public-Private Distinction in American Law and Life*, 36 *Buff. L. Rev.* 237 (1987).

Freeman, Jody. *Extending Public Law Norms Through Privatization*, 116 *Harv. L. Rev.* 1285 (2003).

Froomkin, A. Michael. *Habermas@Discourse.Net: Toward a Critical Theory of Cyberspace*, 116 *Harv. L. Rev.* 751 (2003).

Frug, Gerald E. *The Ideology of Bureaucracy in American Law*, 97 *Harv. L. Rev.* 1276 (1984).

———. *The City as Legal Concept*, 93 *Harv. L. Rev.* 1057 (1980).

Gerla, Harry S. *A Micro-Microeconomic Approach to Antitrust Law: Games Managers Play*, 86 *Mich. L. Rev.* 892 (1988).

Gilson, Ronald J. & Mark J. Roe. *Understanding the Japanese Keiretsu: Overlaps Between Corporate Governance and Industrial Organization*, 102 *Yale L.J.* 871 (1993).

Graham, David R., et al. *Efficiency and Competition in the Airline Industry*, 14 *Bell J. Econ.* 118 (1983).

Greenfield, Kent. *Using Behavioral Economics to Show the Power and Efficiency of Corporate Law as a Regulatory Tool*, 35 *U.C. Davis L. Rev.* 581 (2002).

Griffin, Dale & Amos Tversky. *The Weighing of Evidence and the Determinants of Confidence*, 24 *Cognitive Psychol.* 411 (1992).

Hager, Mark M. *The Emperor's Clothes Are Not Efficient: Posner's Jurisprudence of Class*, 41 *Am. U. L. Rev.* 7 (1991).

Hammer, Peter J. & William M. Sage. *Antitrust, Health Care Quality, and the Courts*, 102 *Colum. L. Rev.* 545 (2002).

Hanson, Jon D. & Douglas A. Kysar. *Taking Behavioralism Seriously: Some Evidence of Market Manipulation*, 112 *Harv. L. Rev.* 1420 (1999).

Hanson, Jon & David Yosifon. *The Situation: An Introduction to Situational Character, Critical Realism, Power Economics, and Deep Capture*, 152 *U. Pa. L. Rev.* 129 (2003).

Harris, Ron. *The Uses of History in Law and Economics*, 4 *Theoretical Inq. L.* 659 (2003).

Hausman, Jerry & Stewart Myers. *Regulating the United States Railroads: The Effects of Sunk Costs and Asymmetric Risk*, 22 *J. Reg. Econ.* 287 (2002).

Hausman, Jerry & Howard Shelanski. *Economic Welfare and Telecommunications Regulation: The E-Rate Policy for Universal-Service Subsidies*, 16 *Yale J. on Reg.* 19 (1999).

Hausman, Jerry A. & J. Gregory Sidak. *A Consumer-Welfare Approach to the Mandatory Unbundling of Telecommunications Networks*, 109 *Yale L.J.* 417 (1999).

Hazen, Thomas Lee. *The Corporate Persona, Contract (and Market) Failure, and Moral Values*, 69 *N.C. L. Rev.* 273 (1991).

Hazlett, Thomas W. *The Wireless Craze, the Unlimited Bandwidth Myth, the Spectrum Auction Faux Pas, and the Punchline to Ronald Coase's "Big Joke": An Essay on Airwave Allocation Policy*, 14 *Harv. J. Law & Tech.* 335 (2001).

―――. *Explaining the Telecommunications Act of 1996: Comment on Thomas G. Krattenmaker*, 29 *Conn. L. Rev.* 217 (1996).

―――. *The Rationality of U.S. Regulation of the Broadcast Spectrum*, 33 *J.L. & Econ.* 133 (1990).

Henrich, Joseph. *Does Culture Matter in Economic Behavior? Ultimatum Game Bargaining Among the Machiguenga of the Peruvian Amazon*, 90 *Am. Econ. Rev.* 973 (2000).

Herzel, Leo. Comment, *"Public Interest" and the Market in Color Television Regulation*, 18 *U. Chi. L. Rev.* 802 (1951).

Horwitz, Morton J. *The History of the Public/Private Distinction*, 130 *U. Pa. L. Rev.* 1423 (1982).

Hovenkamp, Herbert. *Knowledge About Welfare: Legal Realism and the Separation of Law and Economics*, 84 *Minn. L. Rev.* 805 (2000).

―――. *The Areeda-Turner Treatise in Antitrust Analysis*, 41 *Antitrust Bull.* 815 (1996).

―――. *Antitrust Policy After Chicago*, 84 *Mich. L. Rev.* 213 (1985).

Hughes, Justin. *The Philosophy of Intellectual Property*, 77 *Geo. L.J.* 287 (1988).

Jacobs, Michael S. *An Essay on the Normative Foundations of Antitrust Economics*, 74 *N.C. L. Rev.* 219 (1995).

Jacoby, Sanford M. *Are Career Jobs Headed for Extinction?* 42 *Cal. Mgmt. Rev.* 123, 140 (1999).

Jensen, Michael C. & William H. Meckling. *Can the Corporation Survive?* 78 *Fin. Analysts J.* 31 (1978).

Jolls, Christine. *Behavioral Economic Analysis of Redistributive Legal Rules*, 51 *Vand. L. Rev.* 1653 (1998).

Jolls, Christine, et al. *A Behavioral Approach to Law and Economics*, 50 *Stan. L. Rev.* 1471 (1998).

Joskow, Paul L. *Transaction Cost Economics, Antitrust Rules and Remedies*, 18 *J.L. Econ. & Org.* 95 (2002).

————. *Restructuring, Competition and Regulatory Reform in the U.S. Electricity Sector*, 11 *J. Econ. Persp.* 119 (1997).

————. *Firm Decision-making Processes and Oligopoly Theory*, 65 *Am. Econ. Rev.* 270 (1975).

Joskow, Paul L. & Roger G. Noll. *The Bell Doctrine: Applications in Telecommunications, Electricity, and Other Network Industries*, 51 *Stan. L. Rev.* 1249 (1999).

Kahan, Dan M. *Social Influence, Social Meaning, and Deterrence*, 83 *Va. L. Rev.* 349 (1997).

Kahn, Alfred E. *Reforming the FCC and Its Mission: Lessons from the Airline Experience*, 4 *J. Telecomm. & High Tech L.* 43 (2005).

————. *The Competitive Consequences of Hub Dominance: A Case Study*, 8 *Rev. Indus. Org.* 381 (1993).

————. *Deregulation: Looking Backward and Looking Forward*, 7 *Yale J. on Reg.* 325 (1990).

————. *Deregulatory Schizophrenia*, 75 *Cal. L. Rev.* 1059 (1987).

————. *Applications of Economics to an Imperfect World*, 69 *Am. Econ. Rev.* 1 (1979).

Kaplow, Louis. *An Economic Analysis of Legal Transitions*, 99 *Harv. L. Rev.* 509 (1986).

————. *Extension of Monopoly Power Through Leverage*, 85 *Colum. L. Rev.* 515 (1985).

Kaplow, Louis & Steven Shavell. *Fairness v. Welfare*, 114 *Harv. L. Rev.* 961 (2001).

————. *Property Rules Versus Liability Rules: An Economic Analysis*, 109 *Harv. L. Rev.* 713 (1996).

Kaswan, Alice. *Distributive Justice and the Environment*, 81 *N.C. L. Rev.* 1031 (2003).

Katona, George. *On the Function of Behavioral Theory and Behavioral Research in Economics*, 58 *Am. Econ. Rev.* 146 (1968).

Katz, Michael L. & Carl Shapiro. *Systems Competition and Network Effects*, 8 *J. Econ. Persp.* 93 (1994).

————. *Network Externalities, Competition, and Compatibility*, 75 *Am. Econ. Rev.* 424 (1985).

Kearney, Joseph D. *From the Fall of the Bell System to the Telecommunications Act: Regulation of Telecommunications under Judge Greene*, 50 *Hastings L.J.* 1395 (1999).

Kearney, Joseph D. & Thomas W. Merrill. *The Great Transformation of Regulated Industries Law*, 98 *Colum. L. Rev.* 1323 (1998).

Kelman, Mark G. *Misunderstanding Social Life: A Critique of the Core Premises of "Law and Economics,"* 33 *J. Legal Educ.* 274 (1983).

Kennedy, Duncan. *The Stages of Decline of the Public/Private Distinction*, 130 *U. Pa. L. Rev.* 1349 (1982).

————. *The Structure of Blackstone's Commentaries*, 28 *Buff. L. Rev.* 205 (1979).

————. *Form and Substance in Private Law Adjudication*, 89 *Harv. L. Rev.* 1685 (1976).

Kerf, Michel & Damien Geradin. *Controlling Market Power in Telecommunications: Antitrust vs. Sector-Specific Regulation: An Assessment of the United States, New Zealand and Australian Experiences*, 14 *Berkeley Tech. L.J.* 919 (1999).

Kibel, Paul Stanton. *Reconstructing the Marketplace: The International Timber Trade and Forest Protection*, 5 *N.Y.U. Envtl. L.J.* 735 (1996).

Kim, E. Han & Vijay Singal. *Mergers and Market Power: Evidence from the Airline Industry*, 83 *Am. Econ. Rev.* 549 (1993).

Klare, Karl E. *The Public/Private Distinction in Labor Law*, 130 *U. Pa. L. Rev.* 1358 (1982).

Kornhauser, Lewis A. *The Great Image of Authority*, 36 *Stan. L. Rev.* 349 (1984).

Korobkin, Russell B. & Thomas S. Ulen. *Law and Behavioral Science: Removing the Rationalist Assumption from Law and Economics*, 88 *Cal. L. Rev.* 1051 (2000).

Kostant, Peter C. *Team Production and the Progressive Corporate Law Agenda*, 35 *U.C. Davis L. Rev.* 667 (2002).

Krattenmaker, Thomas G. *The Telecommunications Act of 1996*, 29 *Conn. L. Rev.* 123 (1996).

Krattenmaker, Thomas G. & Steven C. Salop. *Anticompetitive Exclusion: Raising Rivals' Costs to Achieve Power over Price*, 96 *Yale L.J.* 209 (1986).

Krent, Harold J. & Nicholas S. Zeppos. *Monitoring Governmental Disposition of Assets: Fashioning Regulatory Substitutes for Market Controls*, 52 *Vand. L. Rev.* 1703 (1999).

Krier, James E. & Stewart J. Schwab. *Property Rules and Liability Rules: The Cathedral in Another Light*, 70 *N.Y.U. L. Rev.* 440 (1995).

Landes, William M. *An Economic Analysis of the Courts*, 14 *J.L. & Econ.* 61 (1971).

Lane, Robert E. *Why Business Men Violate the Law*, 44 *J. Crim. L. Criminology & Police Sci.* 151 (1953).

Langevoort, Donald C. *Behavioral Theories of Judgment and Decision Making in Legal Scholarship: A Literature Review*, 51 *Vand. L. Rev.* 1499 (1998).

————. *Organized Illusions: A Behavioral Theory of Why Corporations Mislead Stock Market Investors (and Cause Other Social Harms)*, 146 U. Pa. L. Rev. 101 (1997).

Leff, Arthur Allen. *Economic Analysis of Law: Some Realism About Nominalism*, 60 Va. L. Rev. 451 (1974).

Lemley, Mark A. *Intellectual Property Rights and Standard-Setting Organizations*, 90 Cal. L. Rev. 1889 (2002).

Lemley, Mark A. & Lawrence Lessig. *The End of End-to-End: Preserving the Architecture of the Internet in the Broadband Era*, 48 UCLA L. Rev. 925 (2001).

Lemley, Mark A. & David McGowan. *Legal Implications of Network Economic Effects*, 86 Cal. L. Rev. 479 (1998).

Lessig, Lawrence. *Commons and Code*, 9 Fordham Intell. Prop. Media & Ent. L.J. 405 (1999).

Levinson, Daryl J. *Making Government Pay: Markets, Politics, and the Allocation of Constitutional Costs*, 67 U. Chi. L. Rev. 345 (2000).

Lipsky, Abbott B. & J. Gregory Sidak. *Essential Facilities*, 51 Stan. L. Rev. 1187 (1999).

Lobel, Orly. *The Renew Deal: The Fall of Regulation and the Rise of Governance in Contemporary Legal Thought*, 89 Minn. L. Rev. 342 (2004).

Mahoney, Paul G. & Chris William Sanchirico. *Norms, Repeated Games, and the Role of Law*, 91 Cal. L. Rev. 1281 (2003).

Malloy, Timothy F. *Regulating by Incentives: Myths, Models, and Micromarkets*, 80 Tex. L. Rev. 531 (2002).

Marris, Robin. *A Model of the "Managerial" Enterprise*, 77 Q. J. Econ. 185 (1963).

Marvel, Howard P. & Stephen McCafferty. *The Welfare Effects of Resale Price Maintenance*, 28 J.L. & Econ. 363 (1985).

Melamed, A. Douglas. *Network Industries and Antitrust*, 23 Harv. J.L. & Pub. Pol'y 147 (1999).

Metzger, Gillian E. *Privatization as Delegation*, 103 Colum. L. Rev. 1367 (2003).

Milgrom, Paul & John Roberts. *Informational Asymmetries, Strategic Behavior, and Industrial Organization*, 77 Am. Econ. Rev. 184 (1987).

Minow, Martha. *Public and Private Partnerships: Accounting for the New Religion*, 116 Harv. L. Rev. 1229 (2003).

Mitchell, Gregory. *Taking Behavioralism Too Seriously? The Unwanted Pessimism of the New Behavioral Analysis of Law*, 43 Wm. & Mary L. Rev. 1907 (2002).

Moffitt, Robert A. & Peter Gottschalk. *Trends in the Transitory Variance of Earnings in the United States*, 112 Econ. J. C68 (2002).

Moore, Thomas Gale. *Introduction to Antitrust and Economic Efficiency: A Conference Sponsored by the Hoover Institution*, 28 J.L. & Econ. 245 (1985).

Nash, John F., Jr. *The Bargaining Problem*, 18 Econometrica 155 (1950).

Neeman, Zvika. *The Freedom to Contract and the Free-Rider Problem*, 15 J.L. Econ. & Org. 685 (1999).

Noam, Eli M. *Will Universal Service and Common Carriage Survive the Telecommunications Act of 1996?* 97 Colum. L. Rev. 955 (1997).

Noll, Roger G. & James E. Krier. *Some Implications of Cognitive Psychology for Risk Regulation*, 19 J. Legal Stud. 747 (1990).

O'Connor, Marleen A. *The Enron Board: The Perils of Groupthink*, 71 U. Cin. L. Rev. 1233 (2003).

Okediji, Ruth. *Givers, Takers, and Other Kinds of Users: A Fair Use Doctrine for Cyberspace*, 53 Fla. L. Rev. 107 (2001).

Ordover, Janusz A. & Robert D. Willig. *Antitrust for High-Technology Industries: Assessing Research Joint Ventures and Mergers*, 28 J.L. & Econ. 311 (1985).

O'Rourke, Maureen A. *Toward a Doctrine of Fair Use in Patent Law*, 100 Colum. L. Rev. 1177 (2000).

Orts, Eric W. *Shirking and Sharking: A Legal Theory of the Firm*, 16 Yale L. & Pol'y Rev. 265 (1998).

Page, William H. *The Chicago School and the Evolution of Antitrust: Characterization, Antitrust Injury, and Evidentiary Sufficiency*, 75 Va. L. Rev. 1221 (1989).

Parker, Richard W. *Grading the Government*, 70 U. Chi. L. Rev. 1345 (2003).

Partnoy, Frank. *Barbarians at the Gatekeepers? A Proposal for a Modified Strict Liability Regime*, 79 Wash. U. L.Q. 491 (2001).

Piraino, Thomas A. *A Proposed Antitrust Approach to High Technology Competition*, 44 Wm. & Mary L. Rev. 65 (2002).

Pirrong, Stephen Craig. *An Application of Core Theory to the Analysis of Ocean Shipping Markets*, 35 J.L. & Econ. 89 (1992).

Pitofsky, Robert. *Antitrust and Intellectual Property: Unresolved Issues at the Heart of the New Economy*, 16 Berkeley Tech. L.J. 535 (2001).

Posner, Richard A. *Rational Choice, Behavioral Economics, and the Law*, 50 Stan. L. Rev. 1551 (1998).

———. *The Social Costs of Monopoly and Regulation*, 83 *J. Pol. Econ.* 807 (1975).

———. *Theories of Economic Regulation*, 5 *Bell J. Econ. & Mgmt. Sci.* 335 (1974).

———. *An Economic Approach to Legal Procedure and Judicial Administration*, 2 *J. Legal Stud.* 399 (1973).

———. *Taxation by Regulation*, 2 *Bell J. Econ. & Mgmt. Sci.* 22 (1971).

———. *Natural Monopoly and Its Regulation*, 21 *Stan. L. Rev.* 548 (1969).

Pouncy, Charles R.P. *The Rational Rogue: Neoclassical Economic Ideology in the Regulation of the Financial Professional*, 26 *Vt. L. Rev.* 263 (2002).

Prentice, Robert. *Whither Securities Regulation? Some Behavioral Observations Regarding Proposals for Its Future*, 51 *Duke L.J.* 1397 (2002).

———. *The SEC and MDP: Implications of the Self-Serving Bias for Independent Auditing*, 61 *Ohio St. L.J.* 1597 (2000).

Priest, George L. *The New Scientism in Legal Scholarship: A Comment on Clark and Posner*, 90 *Yale L.J.* 1284 (1981).

Rabin, Matthew. *Psychology and Economics*, 36 *J. Econ. Lit.* 11 (1998).

———. *Incorporating Fairness into Game Theory and Economics*, 83 *Am. Econ. Rev.* 1281 (1993).

Rasmusen, Eric B., et al. *Naked Exclusion*, 81 *Am. Econ. Rev.* 1137 (1991).

Reich, Charles A. *The New Property*, 73 *Yale L.J.* 733 (1964).

Rizzo, Mario J. *The Mirage of Efficiency*, 8 *Hofstra L. Rev.* 641 (1980).

Robinson, Glen O. *On Refusing to Deal with Rivals*, 87 *Cornell L. Rev.* 1177 (2002).

Roe, Mark J. *Chaos and Evolution in Law and Economics*, 109 *Harv. L. Rev.* 641 (1996).

Rogerson, William P. *The Regulation of Broadband Telecommunications, the Principle of Regulating Narrowly Defined Input Bottlenecks, and Incentives for Investment and Innovation*, 2000 *U. Chi. Legal F.* 119.

Rohlfs, Jeffrey. *A Theory of Interdependent Demand for a Communications Service*, 5 *Bell J. Econ. & Mgmt. Sci.* 16 (1974).

Rose-Ackerman, Susan. *Progressive Law and Economics—and the New Administrative Law*, 98 *Yale L.J.* 341 (1988).

Rossi, Jim. *The Common Law "Duty to Serve" and Protection of Consumers in an Age of Competitive Retail Public Utility Restructuring*, 51 *Vand. L. Rev.* 1233 (1998).

Rostow, Eugene V. *The New Sherman Act: A Positive Instrument of Progress*, 14 *U. Chi. L. Rev.* 567 (1947).

Rowe, Frederick M. *The Decline of Antitrust and the Delusions of Models: The Faustian Pact of Law and Economics*, 72 Geo. L.J. 1511 (1984).

Rubenfeld, Jed. *The Freedom of Imagination: Copyright's Constitutionality*, 112 Yale L.J. 1 (2002).

Rubin, Edward L. *Images of Organizations and Consequences of Regulation*, 6 Theoretical Inq. L. 357 (2005).

———. *New Directions: Law and the Methodology of Law*, 1997 Wis. L. Rev. 521.

———. *The New Legal Process, the Synthesis of Discourse, and the Microanalysis of Institutions*, 109 Harv. L. Rev. 1393 (1996).

Salop, Steven C. *Strategic Entry Deterrence*, 69 Am. Econ. Rev. 335 (1979).

Salop, Steven C. & R. Craig Romaine. *Preserving Monopoly: Economic Analysis, Legal Standards, and Microsoft*, 7 Geo. Mason L. Rev. 617 (1999).

Salop, Steven C. & David T. Scheffman. *Raising Rivals' Costs*, 73 Am. Econ. Rev. 267 (1983).

Sax, Joseph L. *Liberating the Public Trust Doctrine from Its Historical Shackles*, 14 U.C. Davis L. Rev. 185 (1980).

Schlag, Pierre. *The Problem of Transaction Costs*, 62 S. Cal. L. Rev. 1661 (1989).

Schroeder, Jeanne L. *The End of the Market: A Psychoanalysis of Law and Economics*, 112 Harv. L. Rev. 483 (1998).

Schuck, Peter H. *Delegation and Democracy: Comments on David Schoenbrod*, 20 Cardozo L. Rev. 775 (1999).

———. *Some Reflections on the Federalism Debate*, 14 Yale L. & Pol'y Rev. 1 (1996).

Schuck, Peter H. & E. Donald Elliott. *To the Chevron Station: An Empirical Study of Federal Administrative Law*, 1990 Duke L.J. 984.

Sen, Amartya. *The Impossibility of a Paretian Liberal*, 78 J. Pol. Econ. 152 (1970).

Shapiro, Carl. *Exclusivity in Network Industries*, 7 Geo. Mason L. Rev. 673 (1999).

Shelanski, Howard A. & Peter G. Klein. *Empirical Research in Transaction Cost Economics: A Review and Assessment*, 11 J.L. Econ. & Org. 335 (1995).

Shelanski, Howard A. & J. Gregory Sidak. *Antitrust Divestiture in Network Industries*, 68 U. Chi. L. Rev. 1 (2001).

Shepherd, William G. *"Contestability" vs. Competition*, 74 Am. Econ. Rev. 572 (1984).

Shiller, Robert J. *Conversation, Information, and Herd Behavior*, 85 Am. Econ. Rev. 181 (1995).

Sidak, J. Gregory & Daniel F. Spulber. *Deregulation and Managed Competition in Network Industries*, 15 Yale J. on Reg. 117 (1998).

———. *Deregulatory Takings and Breach of the Regulatory Contract*, 71 *N.Y.U. L. Rev.* 851 (1996).

Simon, Herbert A. *New Developments in the Theory of the Firm*, 52 *Am. Econ. Rev.* 1 (1962).

Singer, Joseph William. *Legal Realism Now*, 76 *Cal. L. Rev.* 467 (1988) (book review).

Skitol, Robert A. *The Shifting Sands of Antitrust Policy: Where It Has Been, Where It Is Now, Where It Will Be in Its Third Century*, 9 *Cornell J.L. & Pub. Pol'y* 239 (1999).

Soma, John T., et al. *The Essential Facilities Doctrine in the Deregulated Telecommunications Industry*, 13 *Berkeley Tech. L.J.* 565 (1998).

Spence, A. Michael. *Entry, Capacity, Investment and Oligopolistic Pricing*, 8 *Bell J. Econ.* 534 (1977).

Spence, David B. *Getting Beyond Cynicism: New Theories of the Regulatory State; A Public Choice Progressivism, Continued*, 87 *Cornell L. Rev.* 397 (2002).

Spence, David B. & Frank Cross. *A Public Choice Case for the Administrative State*, 89 *Geo. L.J.* 97 (2000).

Sproul, Michael F. *Antitrust and Prices*, 101 *J. Pol. Econ.* 741 (1993).

Stewart, Richard B. *The Reformation of American Administrative Law*, 88 *Harv. L. Rev.* 1669 (1975).

Stigler, George J. *The Theory of Economic Regulation*, 2 *Bell J. Econ. & Mgmt. Sci.* 3 (1971).

Stroup, Richard & John Baden. *Externality, Property Rights, and the Management of Our National Forests*, 16 *J.L. & Econ.* 303 (1973).

Sullivan, Lawrence A. *An Inquiry Into Antitrust, Intellectual Property, and Broadband Regulation as Applied to the "New Economy,"* 52 *Case W. Res. L. Rev.* 41 (2001).

Sunstein, Cass R. *Deliberative Trouble? Why Groups Go to Extremes*, 110 *Yale L.J.* 71 (2000).

———. *Economics & Real People*, 3 *Green Bag* 2d 397 (2000).

———. *Television and the Public Interest*, 88 *Cal. L. Rev.* 499 (1999).

Sunstein, Cass R. & Richard H. Thaler. *Libertarian Paternalism Is Not an Oxymoron*, 70 *U. Chi. L. Rev.* 1159 (2003).

Telser, Lester G. *Cooperation, Competition, and Efficiency*, 28 *J.L. & Econ.* 271 (1985).

Tor, Avishalom. *The Fable of Entry: Bounded Rationality, Market Discipline, and Legal Policy*, 101 *Mich. L. Rev.* 482 (2002).

Torres, Gerald. *Who Owns the Sky?* 19 *Pace Envtl. L. Rev.* 515 (2002).

Tushnet, Mark. *"Everything Old Is New Again": Early Reflections on the "New Chicago School,"* 1998 *Wis. L. Rev.* 579.

Tversky, Amos & Daniel Kahneman. *Judgment under Uncertainty: Heuristics and Biases,* 185 *Sci.* 1124 (1974).

Unger, Roberto Mangabeira. *The Critical Legal Studies Movement,* 96 *Harv. L. Rev.* 561 (1983).

Waller, Spencer Weber. *The Antitrust Legacy of Thurman Arnold,* 78 *St. John's L. Rev.* 569 (2004).

————. *Antitrust as Consumer Choice: Comments on the New Paradigm,* 62 *U. Pitt. L. Rev.* 535 (2001).

Walton, R. Brent. *Ellickson's Paradox: It's Suicide to Maximize Welfare,* 7 *N.Y.U. Envtl. L.J.* 153 (1999).

Warden, Gregory J. *The Law and Economics of the Essential Facilities Doctrine,* 32 *St. Louis U. L.J.* 433 (1987).

Westbrook, David A. *Three Meditations on How Law Rules After Globalization,* 12 *Minn. J. Global Trade* 337 (2003).

Whinston, Michael D. *Tying, Foreclosure, and Exclusion,* 80 *Am. Econ. Rev.* 837 (1990).

White, Lawrence J. *"Propertyzing" the Electromagnetic Spectrum: Why It's Important, and How to Begin,* 9 *Media L. & Pol'y* 19 (2000).

Widen, William H. *Spectres of Law & Economics,* 102 *Mich. L. Rev.* 1423 (2004).

————. *Enron at the Margin,* 58 *Bus. Law.* 961 (2003).

Wiley, John Shepard. *Antitrust and Core Theory,* 54 *U. Chi. L. Rev.* 556 (1987).

Wiley, John Shepard, et al. *The Leasing Monopolist,* 37 *UCLA L. Rev.* 693 (1990).

Wilkinson, Charles F. *The Public Trust Doctrine in Public Land Law,* 14 *U.C. Davis L. Rev.* 269 (1980).

Williamson, Oliver E. *Transaction-Cost Economics: The Governance of Contractual Relations,* 22 *J.L. & Econ.* 233 (1979).

————. *Franchise Bidding for Natural Monopolies—In General and with Respect to CATV,* 7 *Bell J. Econ.* 73 (1976).

Willig, Robert D. *Antitrust Lessons from the Airline Industry: The DOJ Experience,* 60 *Antitrust L.J.* 695 (1992).

Winston, Clifford, et al. *Explaining Regulatory Policy,* 1994 *Brookings Papers on Econ. Activity: Microeconomics* 1.

Wittman, Donald. *Prior Regulation versus Post Liability: The Choice Between Input and Output Monitoring,* 6 *J. Legal Stud.* 193 (1977).

Woozley, A.D. *What Is Wrong with Retrospective Law?* 18 *Phil. Q.* 40 (1968).

Yadlin, Omri. *Comments on Mark West's "Private Ordering at the World's First Futures Exchange,"* 98 *Mich. L. Rev.* 2620 (2000).

BOOK CHAPTERS

Baron, David P. *Design of Regulatory Mechanisms and Institutions,* in *Handbook of Industrial Organization* (Richard Schmalensee & Robert D. Willig eds., 1989).

Braeutigam, Ronald R. *Optimal Policies for Natural Monopolies,* in *Handbook of Industrial Organization* (Richard Schmalensee & Robert D. Willig eds., 1989).

Crandall, Robert W. & Jerry A. Hausman. *Competition in U.S. Telecommunications Services: Effects of the 1996 Legislation,* in *Deregulation of Network Industries* (Sam Peltzman & Clifford Winston eds., 2000).

Grimm, Curtis & Clifford Winston. *Competition in the Deregulated Railroad Industry: Sources, Effects, and Policy Issues,* in *Deregulation of Network Industries* (Sam Peltzman & Clifford Winston eds., 2000).

Gruenspecht, Howard K. & Lester B. Lave. *The Economics of Health, Safety, and Environmental Regulation,* in *Handbook of Industrial Organization* (Richard Schmalensee & Robert D. Willig eds., 1989).

Hausman, Jerry. *Internet-Related Services: The Results of Asymmetric Regulation* in *Broadband* (Robert W. Crandall & James H. Alleman, eds., 2002).

Jensen, Michael C. *The Debasement of Contracts and the Decline of Capital Markets,* in *The World Capital Shortage* (Alan Heslop ed., 1977).

Joskow, Paul L. *Deregulation and Regulatory Reform in the U.S. Electric Power Sector,* in *Deregulation of Network Industries* (Sam Peltzman & Clifford Winston eds., 2000).

———. *Mixing Regulatory and Antitrust Policies in the Electric Power Industry: The Price Squeeze and Retail Market Competition,* in *Antitrust and Regulation* (Franklin M. Fisher ed., 1985).

Joskow, Paul L. & Nancy L. Rose. *The Effects of Economic Regulation,* in *Handbook of Industrial Organization* (Richard Schmalensee & Robert D. Willig eds., 1989).

Kahn, Alfred E. *The Political Feasibility of Regulatory Reform,* in *Reforming Social Regulation: Alternative Public Policy Strategies* (Le Roy Graymer & Frederick Thompson eds., 1982).

McChesney, Fred S. *Be True to Your School: Chicago's Contradictory Views of Antitrust and Regulation*, in *The Causes and Consequences of Antitrust: The Public-Choice Perspective* (Fred S. McChesney & William F. Shughart II eds., 1995).

McChesney, Fred S. & William F. Shughart II. *Preface to The Causes and Consequences of Antitrust: The Public Choice Perspective* (Fred S. McChesney & William F. Shughart II eds., 1995).

———. *The Unjoined Debate*, in *The Causes and Consequences of Antitrust: The Public-Choice Perspective* (Fred S. McChesney & William F. Shughart II eds., 1995).

Morrison, Steven A. & Clifford Winston. *The Remaining Role for Government Policy in the Deregulated Airline Industry*, in *Deregulation of Network Industries* (Sam Peltzman & Clifford Winston eds., 2000).

Noll, Roger. *Economic Perspectives on the Politics of Regulation*, in *Handbook of Industrial Organization* (Richard Schmalensee & Robert D. Willig eds., 1989).

Schuck, Peter H. *Concluding Thoughts*, in *Creating Competitive Markets* (Marc K. Landy, et al. eds., forthcoming 2006).

NEWSPAPER AND MAGAZINE ARTICLES

Adler, Moshe. *Sometimes, Government Is the Answer*, L.A. Times, Mar. 4, 2006, at B15.

Aeppel, Timothy. *U.S. Waterway System Shows Its Age*, Wall St. J., Feb. 8, 2005, at A2.

Anderson, Curt. *Timber Sales Lost Millions in 1997*, Chattanooga Times, June 11, 1998, at C6.

Arndt, Michael. *Let's Talk Turkeys*, Bus. Wk., Dec. 11, 2000, at 44.

Balkin, Jack M. *Don't Use Those Words: Fox News Owns Them*, L.A. Times, Aug. 14, 2003, at B15.

Banks, Howard. *A Talk with the Nobel Laureate*, Forbes, Nov. 17, 1986, at 108.

Bartlett, Donald L. & James B. Steele. *The Health of Nations*, N.Y. Times, Oct. 24, 2004, at § 4 (The Week in Review), 11.

Bebchuk, Lucian A. *Making Directors Accountable*, Harv. Mag., Nov.–Dec. 2003, at 31.

Belson, Ken. *Huge Phone Deal Seeks to Thwart Smaller Rivals*, N.Y. Times, Mar. 6, 2006, at A1.

Benson, Dan. *Petri Targets "Rogue Movers,"* Milwaukee J.-Sentinel, Mar. 4, 2003, at 4B.

Berman, Dennis K. *Mergers Horror II: The Rhetoric*, Wall St. J., May 24, 2005, at C1.

Borgatta, Tina. *After Energy Jolt, Cities Think Small*, L.A. Times, May 26, 2002, at B1.

Cassidy, John. *Striking it Rich: The Rise and Fall of Popular Capitalism*, New Yorker, Jan. 14, 2002, at 63.

———. *The Decline of Economics*, New Yorker, Dec. 2, 1996, at 50.

Cohen, Laurie P. & Kate Kelly. *NYSE Turmoil Poses Question: Can Wall Street Regulate Itself?* Wall St. J., Dec. 31, 2003 at A1.

Cole, Michelle & Brent Walsh. *Mad Cow Case Reveals Food Safety System Flaws*, Sunday Oregonian, Feb. 1, 2004, at A1.

Costello, Daniel. *At What Cost? To Keep Health Coverage, More Workers Are Cutting Back on Food, Heat and Other Necessities*, L.A. Times, Apr. 4, 2005, at F1.

Coy, Peter. *How the Game Was Played—and Why Long-Term Lost*, Bus. Wk., Oct. 12, 1998, at 40.

Datz, David. *For Service, Try Public Servants*, L.A. Times, Apr. 2, 2005.

DeParle, Jason. *Goals Reached, Donor on Right Closes Up Shop*, N.Y. Times, May 29, 2005, § 1, at 1.

Deregulated, Consumer Rep., July 2002, at 30.

DeWaal, Gary. *America Must Create a Single Financial Regulator*, Fin. Times, May 19, 2005, at 13.

Dibadj, Reza. *Government Is Bad, Isn't It?* S.F. Chron., Sept. 8, 2005, at B9.

———. *Monopoly v. Municipality*, Nat'l L. J., Feb. 14, 2005, at 26.

———. *Small Firms, Speak Up Loudly for Innovation*, San Jose Mercury News, Jan. 30, 2005, at 5P.

———. *At 90, Time to Reform*, Nat'l. L. J., Oct. 11, 2004, at 23.

———. *Rescuing Broadband in America Requires a New Path*, L.A. Daily J., Sept. 30, 2004, at 6.

———. *Now Is the Time to Reshape America's Regulators*, Fin. Times, Sept. 26, 2003, at 15.

———. *Excesses of Burst Economic Bubble Persist in Aftermath*, L.A. Daily J., Sept. 23, 2003, at 6.

———. *Deregulation: A Tragedy in Three Acts*, Wash. Post, Sept. 13, 2003, at A21.

Dietrich, William. *From American Ethic to Global Imperative, the World of Work Turns*, Seattle Times, July 25, 2004, at 14.

Dreazen, Yochi J. & Deborah Solomon. *Paying for Regulation*, Wall St. J., Feb. 4, 2003, at A4.

Edmonson, R.G. *Stuck in the Doldrums: Cargo-Liability Reform Bogs Down at New York Meeting*, J. of Com., May 31, 2004, at 21.

Eichenwald, Kurt. *Could Capitalists Actually Bring Down Capitalism?* N.Y. Times, June 30, 2002, § 4 (The Week in Review), at 1.

Eisinger, Jesse. *SEC Screwdriver Joins Spitzer Hammer as Hedge-Trimmer*, Wall St. J., Oct. 27, 2004, at C1.

Emshwiller, John R. *Many Companies Report Transactions with Top Officers*, Wall St. J., Dec. 29, 2003, at A1.

Epstein, Richard A. *Classical, Liberal, Rational*, Wall St. J., Sept. 5, 2003, at A8.

Fleishman, Sandra. *From Foreclosure to the Cleaners*, Wash. Post, Dec. 25, 2004, at A1.

Frank, Robert & Elena Cherney. *Paper Tigers: Lord Black's Board; A-List Played Acquiescent Role*, Wall St. J., Sept. 27, 2004, at A1.

Geewax, Marilyn. *The Theory of Deregulation Proves Deadly in Practice*, Atlanta J. & Const., July 5, 1991, at A15.

George, Bill. *Wanted: Authentic Leaders*, Wall St. J., Dec. 16, 2003, at B2.

Goldsmith, Stephen & William D. Eggers. *Government for Hire*, N.Y. Times, Feb. 21, 2005, at A19.

Goozner, Merrill. *Overdosed and Oversold*, N.Y. Times, Dec. 21, 2004, at A29.

Gosselin, Peter G. *Corporate America Pulling Back Pension Safety Net*, L.A. Times, May 15, 2005, at A1.

———. *The New Deal: The Poor Have More Things Today—Including Wild Income Swings*, L.A. Times, Dec. 12, 2004, at A1.

———. *If America Is Richer, Why Are Its Families So Much Less Secure?* L.A. Times, Oct. 10, 2004, at A1.

———. *Private Prosperities, Public Breakdowns: Amid Nationwide Prosperity, ERs See a Growing Emergency*, L.A. Times, Aug. 6, 2001, at A1.

———. *Private Prosperities, Public Breakdowns: The '90s Private Boom Stingy on Public Good*, L.A. Times, Aug. 5, 2001, at A1.

Hacker, Jacob S. *Call It the Family Risk Factor*, N.Y. Times, Jan. 11, 2004, § 4, at 15.

Hansen, James. *Deregulation: Nothing Short of Disastrous*, Rocky Mountain News, Feb. 23, 2002, at 4W.

Harris, Gardiner. *At F.D.A, Strong Drug Ties and Less Monitoring*, N.Y. Times, Dec. 6, 2004, at A2.

Herbert, Bob. *We're More Productive. Who Gets the Money?* N.Y. Times, Apr. 5, 2004, at A21.

Huber, Peter. *Antitrust's Real Legacy*, Wall St. J., Dec. 26, 2002, at A14.

The Innovator That Quit Innovating, U.S. News & World Rep., Aug. 31–Sept. 7, 1992, at 23.

Ip, Greg. *The Deregulator: A Less-Visible Role for the Fed Chief; Freeing Up Markets*, Wall St. J., Nov. 19, 2004, at A1.

Johnson, Edward R. *The Law Against Sharing Knowledge*, Chron. Higher Educ., Feb. 14, 2003, at B14.

Johnston, David Cay. *Richest Are Leaving the Rich Far Behind*, N.Y. Times, June 5, 2005, § 1, at 1.

Jordan, Miriam. *Wealth Gap Widens in U.S. Between Minorities, Whites*, Wall St. J., Oct. 18, 2004, at A2.

Kahn, Alfred E. *Air Travel's Free Market Works*, L.A. Times, Sept. 16, 2004, at B11.

———. *Can Liberalism Survive Inflation?* Economist, Mar. 7, 1981, at 3.

Keefe, Bob. *Some Not Ready to Toss Lifelines to All Those Ailing*, Atlanta J. & Const., Oct. 5, 2001, at A8.

Kelly, Kate. *SEC Plans to Punish Exchanges*, Wall St. J., Oct. 8, 2004, at C1.

Klein, Alec. *Borrowers Find System Open to Conflicts, Manipulation*, Wash. Post, Nov. 22, 2004, at A1.

Knize, Perri. *The Mismanagement of the National Forests*, Atlantic Monthly, Oct. 1991, at 98.

Kranhold, Kathryn. *Short-Term Debt for Energy Industry Is Long-Term Problem*, Wall St. J., Nov. 6, 2002, at C1.

Krim, Jonathan & Griff Witte. *Average-Wage Earners Fall Behind*, Wash. Post, Dec. 31, 2004, at A1.

Krugman, Paul. *The Debt-Peonage Society*, N.Y. Times, Mar. 8, 2005, at A23.

———. *Enron and the System*, N.Y. Times, Jan. 9, 2004 at A19.

Kuttner, Robert. *AT&T and Comcast: A Bad Deal for Almost Everybody*, Bus. Wk., May 20, 2002, at 26.

———. *The Road to Enron*, Am. Prospect, Mar. 25, 2002, at 2.

Langley, Monica & Theo Francis. *Insurers Reel from Spitzer's Strike*, Wall St. J., Oct. 18, 2004, at A1.

Langley, Monica & Ian McDonald. *Marsh Directors Consider Having CEO Step Aside*, Wall St. J., Oct. 22, 2004, at A1.

Lent, Ron. *Ship Reform Act Leaves Underwriters at Sea, J. of Com.*, Sept. 1, 1999, at 8.

Levitt, Jr., Arthur. *Money, Money, Money, Wall St. J.*, Nov. 22, 2004, at A14.

MacFarquhar, Larissa. *The Bench Burner, New Yorker*, Dec. 10, 2001, at 78.

Manning, Anita & Elizabeth Wise. *Who is Minding the USA's Food Store, USA Today*, Jan. 27, 2004, at 1D.

Maremont, Mark & Deborah Solomon. *Behind SEC's Failings: Caution, Tight Budget, '90s Exuberance, Wall St. J.*, Dec. 24, 2003, at A1.

Mathews, Anna Wilde & Abboud, Leila. *FDA Establishes Board to Review Approved Drugs, Wall St. J.*, Feb. 16, 2005, at A1.

McCartney, Scott. *Why Travelers Benefit When an Airline Hub Closes, Wall St. J.*, Nov. 1, 2005, at D1.

McGeehan, Patrick, et al. *Soaring Interest Is Compounding Credit Card Woes for Millions, N.Y. Times*, Nov. 21, 2004, § 1, at 1.

Mirabella, Lorraine & Dan Thanh Dang. *Utilities Add Blackout to Woes, Baltimore Sun*, Aug. 24, 2003, at 1D.

Mullins, Brody. *Junket Bonds: More Lawmakers Take Trips Funded by Corporations, Wall St. J.*, Apr. 15, 2005, at A1.

Murray, Alan. *Exile on G Street, Wall St. J.*, May 13, 2003, at A4.

Nocera, Joseph. *Stock Options: So Who's Counting? N.Y. Times*, Aug. 6, 2005, at C1.

North, Douglass C. *Institutions and Economic Growth: An Historical Introduction*, 17 *World Dev.* 1319 (1989).

Osborn, Torie. *Nonprofits Can't Take the Place of Government, L.A. Times*, Dec. 13, 2003, at B27.

Oster, Christopher, et al. *After Storms, Florida Wakes Up to New Insurance Reality, Wall St. J.*, Sept. 7, 2004, at A1.

Paltrow, Scott J. & Ianthe Jeanne Dugan. *State-Based Regulation Gets Scrutiny, Wall St. J.*, Oct. 18, 2004, at A15.

Pearlstein, Steven. *Regulation vs. Competition: No Winner Yet, Wash. Post*, Nov. 2, 2002, at A14.

Powell Says Telecommunication Litigation Is to Be Expected, Loc. Competition Rep., July 1, 2002.

Rice, William. *Safe to Eat? Consumers Stand Last in Line on the Safe-food Battlefront, Chi. Trib.*, May 16, 1991, at C1.

Roberts, Dan & Christopher Swann. *America's Dilemma: As Business Retreats from its Welfare Role, Who Will Take Up the Burden? Fin. Times*, Jan. 13, 2006, at 17.

Roberts, Paul. *The Federal Chain-Saw Massacre, Harper's Mag.*, June 1997, at 37.

Rohatyn, Felix. *Free, Wealthy and Fair, Wall St. J.*, Nov. 11, 2003, at A18.

Rosen, Jeffrey. *The Unregulated Offensive, N.Y. Times Mag.*, Apr. 17, 2005, at 42.

Russakoff, Dale. *Retirement's Unraveling Safety Net, Wash. Post*, May 15, 2005, at A1.

Safire, William. *Regulate the F.C.C., N.Y. Times*, June 16, 2003, at A19.

———. *On Media Giantism, N.Y. Times*, Jan. 20, 2003, at A19.

Sanger, David E. *Mr. Deregulation's Regulations: Stuff of Politics, Mad Cows, and Suspect Dietary Pills, N.Y. Times*, Dec. 31, 2003, at A15.

Schlesinger, Jacob M. *What's Wrong? The Deregulators: Did Washington Help Set Stage for Current Business Turmoil? Wall St. J.*, Oct. 17, 2002 at A1.

Schlosser, Eric. *The Cow Jumped Over the U.S.D.A., N.Y. Times*, Jan. 2, 2004, at A17.

Schuck, Peter H. *Just the Verdict, Please, L.A. Times*, Aug. 29, 2005, at B11.

———. *On the Chicken Little School of Regulation, Wash. Post*, Jan. 28, 1979, at C1.

Scott, Janny. *Life at the Top in America Isn't Just Better, It's Longer, N.Y. Times*, May 16, 2005, at A1.

Scott, Janny & David Leonhardt. *Class in America: Shadowy Lines that Still Divide, N.Y. Times*, May 15, 2005, § 1, at 1.

Sculley Placed All Bets on the Proprietary Mac Way, InfoWorld, Feb. 17, 1997, at 53.

Shiver, Jube, Jr., *FCC Gets Rid of Limits on Mobile Airwaves, L.A. Times*, Nov. 9, 2001, at C3.

Smith, Patrick. *Travel Plans, N.Y. Times*, Dec. 22, 2004, at A31.

Smith, Rebecca. *States Seek Ways to Curb Surging Electricity Bills. Wall St. J.*, Feb. 28, 2006, at A1.

———. *Texas Electricity Deregulation Hasn't Aided Small Power Users, Wall St. J.*, May 5, 2005, at A2.

———. *Hard Line: How a Texas Power Company Got Tough with Consumers, Wall St. J.*, Mar. 22, 2005, at A1.

Smith, Vernon. *Power to the People, Wall St. J.*, Oct. 16, 2002, at A20.

Smith, Vernon & Lynne Kiesling. *Socket to California, Wall St. J.*, Nov. 10, 2003, at A16.

Solomon, Deborah. *SEC Seeks to Overhaul Markets, Wall St. J.*, Feb. 25, 2004, at C1.

Solomon, Deborah & Ian McDonald. *Spitzer Decries Lax Regulation over Insurance,* Wall St. J., Nov. 17, 2004, at C1.

Solomon, Deborah & Michael Schroeder. *How Refco Fell Through Regulatory Cracks,* Wall St. J., Oct. 18, 2005, at A4.

———. *Back Off! Businesses Go Toe to Toe with SEC,* Wall St. J., Oct. 27, 2004, at C1.

Stelzer, Irwin. *Deregulation: It's Their Loss and Your Gain,* Sunday Times, Aug. 25, 2002, at 4.

Stern, Gary H. & Ron Feldman. *Big Banks, Big Bailouts,* Wall St. J., Jan. 27, 2004, at A14.

Uchitelle, Louis. *Looking for Ways to Make Deregulation Keep Its Promises,* N.Y. Times, July 28, 2002, at C12.

Vrana, Debora. *Health Insurance Costs Jump 11.2%,* L.A. Times, Sept. 10, 2004, at A1.

Wessel, David. *As Rich-Poor Gap Widens in the U.S., Class Mobility Stalls,* Wall St. J., May 13, 2005, at A1.

———. *A Lesson from the Blackout: Free Markets Also Need Rules,* Wall St. J., Aug. 28, 2003, at A1.

Where's The Stick? Economist, Oct. 11, 2003, at 13.

Willman, David. *The National Institutes of Health: Public Servant or Private Marketer?* L.A. Times, Dec. 22, 2004, at A1.

Wilson, Janet. *Potential Cost of Utility Sparks Dispute in Irvine,* L.A. Times, Jan. 14, 2003, at B3.

Wingfield, Nick. *Apple's Products Continue to Pay Off,* Wall St. J., July 14, 2005, at A3.

Woolley, Scott. *Dead Air,* Forbes, Nov. 25, 2002, at 138.

Zuckerman, Laurence. *How the Antitrust Wars Wax and Wane,* N.Y. Times, Apr. 11, 1998, at B7.

CASES, STATUTES, AND REGULATIONS

Air Commerce Act of 1926, Pub. L. No. 69-254, 44 Stat. 568 (1926).

Arnold v. Mundy, 6 N.J.L. 1 (1821).

Aspen Skiing Co. v. Aspen Highlands Skiing Corp., 472 U.S. 585 (1985).

AT&T Corp. v. Iowa Utils. Bd., 525 U.S. 366 (1999).

Communications Act of 1934, Pub. L. No. 73-416, ch. 652, 48 Stat. 1064 (1934) (codified as amended at 47 U.S.C. §§ 151614 (1934)).

Digital Millennium Copyright Act (DMCA), Pub. L. No. 105-304, § 103(a), 112 Stat. 2863 (1998) (codified at 17 U.S.C. § 1201(a)–(b) (2000)).

FERC Order No. 888, 61 Fed. Reg. 21,540 (1996) (codified at 18 C.F.R. pts. 35, 385).

Illinois Central Railroad Co. v. Illinois, 146 U.S. 387 (1892).

Kelo v. City of New London, 125 S. Ct. 2655 (2005).

Lochner v. New York, 198 U.S. 45 (1905).

Martin v. Wadell's Lessee, 41 U.S. 367 (1842).

MCI Communications v. AT&T, 708 F.2d 1081 (7th Cir. 1983).

Nat'l Audubon Soc'y v. Superior Court of Alpine County, 658 P.2d 709 (Cal. 1983).

Northern Pacific Railway Co. v. United States, 356 U.S. 1 (1958).

Otter Tail Power v. United States, 410 U.S. 366 (1973).

Poletown Neighborhood Council v. City of Detroit, 304 N.W.2d 455 (Mich. 1981).

Seattle Audubon Society v. Evans, 771 F. Supp. 1081 (W.D. Wash. 1991).

Sonny Bono Copyright Term Extension Act of 1998, Pub. L. No. 105-298, § 120(a), 112 Stat. 2827 (1998) (codified at 17 U.S.C. §§ 301–304 (2000)).

S. Burlington County NAACP v. Township of Mount Laurel, 336 A.2d 713 (N.J. 1975) (Mt. Laurel I).

S. Burlington County NAACP v. Township of Mount Laurel, 456 A.2d 390 (N.J. 1983) (Mt. Laurel II).

State St. Bank & Trust Co. v. Signature Fin. Group, 149 F.3d 1368 (Fed. Cir. 1998).

Telecommunications Act of 1996, Pub. L. No. 104-104, 110 Stat. 56 (1996) (codified in scattered sections of 47 U.S.C.).

United States v. American Telephone & Telegraph Co., 552 F. Supp. 131 (D.C. Cir. 1982).

United States v. Microsoft Corp., 253 F.3d 34 (D.C. Cir. 2001).

United States v. Microsoft Corp., No. 98-1232, 2002 U.S. Dist. LEXIS 22864, at *9-*10 (D.D.C. Nov. 12, 2002).

United States v. Terminal Railroad Ass'n of St. Louis, 224 U.S. 383 (1912).

Verizon Comms. v. FCC, 535 U.S. 467 (2002)

OTHER SOURCES

Abernathy, Kathleen Q. My Vision of the Future of American Spectrum Policy, Remarks Before the Cato Institute's Sixth Annual Technology & Society Conference (Nov. 14, 2002), *available at* http://www.fcc.gov/Speeches/Abernathy/2002/spkqa228.html.

American Society of Civil Engineers. Report Card for America's Infrastructure: 2003 Progress Report 1, *available at* www.asce.org/reportcard/.

Calabrese, Michael. Battle over the Airwaves: Principles for Spectrum Policy Reform 4 (New America Found., Spectrum Series Working Paper No. 1, 2001), *available at* http://www.newamerica.net/Download_Docs/pdfs/Pub_File_610_1.pdf.

Copps, Michael J. Statement Before the Senate Committee on Commerce, Science, and Transportation, United States Senate at 2 (Jan. 14, 2003), *available at* http://www.fcc.gov/commissioners/copps/statements2003.html.

Federal Communications Commission. Implementation of Section 3 of the Cable Television Consumer Protection and Competition Act of 1992, Statistical Report on Average Rates for Basic Service, Cable Programming Service, and Equipment, FCC Doc. No. 02-107, MM Docket No. 92-266 (Apr. 4, 2002) (report on cable industry prices).

Federal Communications Commission. News Release, FCC Sets Limits on Media Concentration (June 2, 2003), *available at* http://hraunfoss.fcc.gov/edocs_public/attachmatch/DOC-235047A1.pdf.

Federal Communications Commission. Ninth Annual Assessment, of the Status of Competition in the Market for the Delivery of Video Programming (2002), *available at* http://hraunfoss.fcc.gov/edocs/public/attachmatch/FCC-02-338A1.pdf.

Federal Energy Regulatory Commission. Inquiry Concerning the Commission's Merger Policy under the Federal Power Act: Policy Statement, Order 592, Issued Dec. 18, 1996, 77 FERC ¶¶ 61, 263.

Gibbons, Robert. Trust in Social Structures: Hobbes and Coase Meet Repeated Games (2000) (unpublished manuscript), *available at* http://web.mit.edu/rgibbons/www/trust_st.pdf.

Hausman, Jerry A. The Effect of Sunk Costs in Telecommunications Regulation (Oct. 1998) (unpublished manuscript), *available at* http://econ-www.mit.edu/faculty/download_pdf.php?id=258.

Kahn, Alfred E. Talk to the New York Society of Security Analysts (Feb. 2, 1978).

Kolasky, William J. & Andrew R. Dick. The Merger Guidelines and the Integration of Efficiencies into Antitrust Review of Horizontal Mergers (2002) (unpublished manuscript), *available at* http://www.usdoj.gov/atr/hmerger/11254.pdf.

New Zealand Ministry of Economic Development. Landmark Telecommunications Act Passed (Dec. 18, 2001), *available at* http://www.med.govt.nz/pbt/telecom/minister20011218a.html.

Noam, Eli M. *Before the U.S. Senate Committee on Commerce on Radio Spectrum Allocations and Valuation*, 104th Cong. (July 25, 1995) (prepared testimony of Eli M. Noam), *available at* http://www.citi.columbia.edu/elinoam/articles/spectrum_allocation_testimony.htm.

Organisation for Econ. Co-operation and Dev. (OECD). Spectrum Allocation: Auctions and Comparative Selection Procedures, Doc. No. DSTI/ICCP/TISP(2000)/FINAL (2001).

Pitofsky, Robert. The Essential Facilities Doctrine Under United States Law (2002), *available at* http://www.ftc.gov/os/comments/intelpropertycomments/pitofskyrobert.pdf.

———. Competition Policy in Communications Industries: New Antitrust Approaches, Glasser LegalWorks Seminar on Competitive Policy in Communications Industries 6 (Mar. 10, 1997), *available at* http://www.ftc.gov/speeches/pitofsky/newcomm.htm.

Powell, Michael K. Remarks at the Goldman Sachs Communicopia XI Conference (Oct. 2, 2002), *available at* http://hraunfoss.fcc.gov/edocs_public/attachmatch/DOC-226929A1.pdf.

———. Transcript: Spectrum Rights and Responsibilities Protection Public Workshop, Federal Communications Commissions Spectrum Policy Task Force (Aug. 9, 2002) *available at* http://www.fcc.gov/sptf/workshops.html.

Rey, Patrick & Jean Tirole. *A Primer on Foreclosure* (Jan. 2006), *available at* http://idei.fr/doc/by/tirole/primer.pdf.

Rubinfeld, Daniel L. Competition, Innovation, and Antitrust Enforcement in Dynamic Network Industries, Address Before the Software Publishers Ass'n (Mar. 24, 1998), *available at* http://www.apeccp.org.tw/doc/USA/Policy/speech/1611.htm.

Shapiro, Carl. Antitrust in Network Industries, Address Before the American Law Institute and American Bar Association (Jan. 25, 1996), *available at* http://www.usdoj.gov/atr/public/speeches/0593.pdf.

Spiller, Pablo T. *Value-Creating Interconnect Unbundling and the Promotion of Local Telephone Competition: Is Unbundling Necessary in Norway?* Foundation for Research in Economics and Business Administration (SNF), Breiviken, Norway (Mar. 1998).

Stiglitz, Joseph E. *The Invisible Hand and Modern Welfare Economics* (NBER Working Paper No. 3641) (1991).

U.S. Census Bureau. *Income, Poverty and Health Insurance Coverage in the United States: 2004* (Aug. 2005), *available at* http://www.census.gov/prod/2005pubs/p60-229.pdf.

U.S. Dep't of Justice. Overview: Antitrust Division (2002), *available at* http://www.usdoj.gov/atr/overview.html.

INDEX